MISSUSES AND MOUL

1240??
4107

MISSUSES AND MOULDRUNNERS

An Oral History of Women Pottery–Workers
at Work and at Home

JACQUELINE SARSBY

OPEN UNIVERSITY PRESS
Milton Keynes · Philadelphia

Open University Press
Open University Educational Enterprises Limited
12 Cofferidge Close
Stony Stratford
Milton Keynes MK11 1BY

and 242 Cherry Street
Philadelphia, PA 19106, USA

First Published 1988

British Library Cataloguing in Publication Data

Sarsby, Jacqueline, *1943–*
Missuses & mouldrunners : an oral history
of women pottery-workers at work and at home.
1. Staffordshire. Potteries, The. Pottery —
Pottery & porcelain industries. Women
personnel. Social life, 1900–1980
I. Title
331.4′8663942463

ISBN 0-335-15865-X
ISBN 0-335-15864-1 Pbk

Library of Congress Cataloging-in-Publication Data

Sarsby, Jacquie.
Missuses & mouldrunners : an oral history of women pottery-workers
at work and at home / by Jacqueline Sarsby.
p.   cm.
Bibliography: p.
Includes index.
1. Women potters——Great Britain——History. 2. Work and family——
Great Britain——History. I. Title. II. Title: Missuses and
mouldrunners.
HD6073.P82G77   1988   331.4′8663941——dc19   88-2866

ISBN 0-335-15865-X
ISBN 0-335-15864-1 (pbk.)

Printed in Great Britain at the Alden Press, Oxford

For the women of the Potteries,
past and present, and to their future

Contents

PREFACE

When I first went to the Potteries, a raw Southerner who had been living in London for over a decade, I thought I was going to a foreign land. I looked at it on the map, miles of roads, thousands of acres of farmland, cities away from anything I knew, but offering me my first academic job. To the people of the Potteries, of course, Keele University was also a foreign land, 'that place on the hill'. But by chance, I was uniquely privileged to come down from that hill, and to meet people who were some of the most open, the kindliest, and indeed the most interesting that I had ever come across.

I was brought up in Devon, and knew nothing of factories, nothing of mines and slag heaps, nothing of pottery and porcelain, nothing of the excitement and the ugliness of the industrial revolution. But when I went to Stoke-on-Trent, I discovered them all: at first my heart sank, my appendix grumbled (they did not take it out for ten years) and I was a mean and difficult member of University departmental meetings, but gradually the fascination of pots and potters overcame me, and much later, when I had another university lectureship at the opposite end of the country, I came back to do the research on which this book is based.

My greatest debt, of course, is to the people I interviewed, potters, casters, handlers, handlemakers, paintresses, dippers, dippers' assistants, warehousewomen, fettlers, towers, placers, even the proverbial saggarmaker's bottom knocker: I am unashamedly devoted to these skilful, unassuming people, who were not suspicious of an awkward, rather too shy woman with a tape recorder. My great sorrow is that I cannot thank them here individually, nor use their real names in this book; they would prefer it, but they were so frank in their descriptions of people and working-conditions that the laws of libel would not allow it. I cannot risk it for their sake, or for the sake of my publishers, but I am most grateful to those who have talked to me, and I hope they will read this book and recognize themselves. I hope too that other pottery-workers will recognize their own experience in the experience described here.

The School of Continuing Education at the University of Kent gave me leave to go to Stoke and do this research, and the Nuffield Foundation gave me a grant, which helped me with my research expenses, and for which I am most grateful. Many typists helped me with the transcripts of my tapes, rather too many to mention, so I must thank them collectively, and just single out for special thanks June Matcham; a wonderful word processor enabled me to type the book myself. John Skelton, my publisher, had faith in the eventual arrival of this manuscript, in spite of its rather lengthy gestation, and greeted it kindly; I am grateful to him for encouragement and understanding in the various stages of its production.

I am particularly grateful to the women of the women's advisory committee of the Ceramic and Allied Trades Union, who both helped me in my research and read a large part of the finished manuscript, as did Ursula Sharma and Clementine and Violet Brough: my thanks to all of them. I also wish to thank Marguerite Dupree, the Feminist Review editorial collective which originally published much of the material on which Chapter 2 was based, Alf Clowes, General Secretary of C.A.T.U, those members of the National Executive who are quoted here and so not named in the text, these and other Union officials and members who also helped me, Pat Halfpenny and Kathy Niblett of the City Museum and Art Gallery, Stoke-on-Trent, the Gladstone Museum, Gaye Blake-Roberts of the Wedgwood Museum, and Martin Phillips, librarian of the local collection in Keele University library. Finally, I must pay tribute to Reg Haggar and Paul Atterbury, who fostered my love of pots at evening classes many years ago, and to Paul Thompson, who has encouraged oral historians and promoted oral history vigorously, so that it now has a sure and valued place in social history.

CHAPTER 1

Remember the Potters, Remember the Miners

The Potteries are six towns in North Staffordshire famous since the eighteenth century for making fine pottery and porcelain.[1] Their success was and is based on three local assets: coal, clay and human skill. In England, a country suffering from a shortage of timber since Tudor times, coal was needed in huge quantities to harden the pots by firing them in kilns. The Potteries were a soot-covered landscape resting on a coalfield, with hundreds of bottle ovens poking smokily from factories and lines of terrace houses. Local clay, the second asset, was dug out of deep marl-holes, and left often in great piles or banks outside the factories; the factories came to be called potbanks. But the third asset was perhaps the most important and is perhaps the least understood: this landscape of dusty, grey-red potbanks, tilebanks and brickworks has depended on three centuries of people who knew how to mix clay, mould and cast teapots, make plates, stick handles on jugs, smooth saucers, turn foot-rims on cups, fire ware of all kinds in kilns, dip it in glaze, decorate it, gild it, select it for quality, carry it about on long boards, pack it so it would not break and sell it. Potters, the working people of these little towns, are the living chain, the learners and the teachers of the hundreds of processes of potting which any manufacturer must have, to start up a factory.

Even now when a company wants to open a factory in another area – a depressed area, perhaps, where wages are low – it must take with it a nucleus of this undervalued but vital capital, skilled people who can teach others to cast and dip, to stick on a handle and smooth away the roughness of a piece that is to be fired.

But skill in potting is only part of the story. The pottery industry has always been international and subject to the vicissitudes of international trade. War and peace at home and abroad, recession, the career of the dollar or the pound, a royal wedding – anything may cause the pottery trade to surge or to falter, to flick its tail and devour work like a beast suddenly famished for human and mechanical energy, so that it can swell into an altogether bigger enterprise, or to grow sluggish without the attention of buyers and slough off its superfluous workers like an ill-fitting skin.

For most of the twentieth century, women have provided the heart and the skin. They have made up the bulk of the workforce; at different times they have learned to do almost all the tasks that pottery requires. They have started as young women and finished as old ladies. Since the Second World War they have been able to stay at home with their young children until the order books were full; then the factories have written to them, or people have been sent knocking on their doors, begging them to return, just for a few hours, and then a few more (and couldn't they possibly manage a few more?). With the recession, young mothers doing the twilight shift have been trimmed away. Most of the old ladies have also had to go, following trade union policy. The upturn of the dollar in the mid-1980s made another reversal of fortunes, but the pottery industry is still a lean beast. The memories of some women working in the industry today show how they have had to indulge the whims of international trade, allowing themselves to be wooed and spurned like eternal Cinderellas, alternately called up to the pottery palace or home to the mop and pail.

But again, the elasticity of women's labour is only part of the story. Work and family life are enmeshed in a way that is revealed even in bare statistics. In 1981 almost 64 per cent of married women aged 16 to 59 were economically active in the Potteries, as opposed to not quite 57 per cent in Great Britain as a whole, and only 43 per cent of those who were employed worked part-time – as opposed to over 50 per cent nationally.[2] Between the ages of 40 and 50, about 74 per cent of all women were economically active, the peak decade in the life cycle for women to be at work in the Potteries. This is in line with national trends for women, as described in the Department of Employment/Office of Population Censuses and Surveys Women and Employment survey, but this survey also found that the crucial factor affecting whether women worked or not, nationally, was the age of the youngest child.[3] In the Potteries, 19.5 per cent of children have mothers working full-time; the percentage nationally is lower, 13.4 per cent.[4] But there are more households with only one child (15.8 per cent as opposed to 14 per cent in Britain) and fewer households with two, three or more children. We can summarize these statistics as indicating that the women of the Potteries tend to have smaller families and to work longer hours than is the experience of the average British married woman. To find out how they dealt with the demands of their work and their families was one of the starting-points for this book.

The research was based on life histories, recorded interviews conducted in the early 1980s with women of all ages who worked or had worked in the potteries of Stoke-on-Trent.[5] The research enabled me to flesh out the statistics with the details of everyday life at work and at home in the first eight decades of the twentieth century. Initially, I had been very struck by the way women helped one another across the generations – the old helping the young to get jobs, the young 'turning up' their wages to their mothers, who later looked after their daughters' young children, so that they could go out to work at the time when wages were most needed. This was the old pattern of life in Stoke, but it was more than that. Gradually I became aware that help between the generations – letting young couples start their married life in a portion of the house, or putting up grandchildren or nephews and nieces at night, or child-minding by day – these and other 'accommodations' and kindnesses were as predictable and necessary as other cultural forms in other contexts. It was the culture of the potters, and particularly the mutual help between women, which allowed them to survive in spite of overcrowding and their erratic and inadequate wages. It was the culture of the potters which allowed the manufacturers and the jobs to continue as they were. It was the culture of the potters which could deal with such important crises as serious illness and early death in the family – the accompaniment to industries based on lungs full of dust. Indeed, having touched on this, one may note that statistics hint not only at the way women's work and family size are interrelated, but also at the heavy burdens which await women when they finally leave employment.

In 1971, there were 13,920 men in North Staffordshire aged 60 to 64; and of these, 4,190 men, that is 30 per cent, were permanently sick. In the same age group there were 15,820 women, and only 195 were permanently sick.[6] In the 1981 Census for Stoke-on-Trent it was noticeable that the numbers of men and women in the 55 to 59 age group were roughly equal (8,626 men and 8,441 women); but as men got into their sixties and above, their numbers dropped sharply, so that there were only 1,062 men aged 80 to 84, but double that number of women, 2,539. In case one should think that these figures are just an indication of the unfairness of the human condition and women's superior constitutions, let us turn again to the permanently sick. If we were to compare the men of Stoke with those in the much more middle-class areas of Berkshire and Oxfordshire, where men more rarely sit in breathless corners, fighting for air in their dust-filled lungs, we would find 12,740 of them in the 60 to 64 age group, and only 470 men, that is 3.68 per cent permanently sick.

I cannot but remember these statistics when Potteries women speak of long years spent with an invalid in the house, of nervous breakdowns when the caring is over. I remember them when women describe violent, bad-tempered fathers, miners who kept their wages to themselves, or hid pound notes under the floorboards. I remember them when I hear of the wives of miners having to go back to work in spite of their big families, and of couples who argued and fought throughout their working lives and who now live quietly together in retirement. There was no history of pots without pits: the gilders and paintresses might sit quietly at their benches, and walk home clean and fresh after a day's work, but the bottle ovens blazed, and cups and plates had to be returned again and again to the fire as they went through the various stages of potting, glazing and decorating. The soot of bottle ovens, clinging to brick walls and window-glass, griming the washing lines and the aprons of women cleaning their doorsteps, was the soot of coal, the life-blood of the potbanks and the death, the lingering death, of the men of the six towns. Even though the kilns changed over to gas and electricity, the pits remain, and the lives of women pottery-workers were and still are intimately bound up with this fact.

This book is a study of an occupation and a community as seen through women's eyes. It attempts to provide a self-portrait of the women of the

Potteries through oral history – that is, through what they have said about themselves – focusing on women of all ages and from various trades in the industry, to try to show how their work and home lives are interlinked, and how their experience has changed in the last eighty years. In particular, it aims to show how wartime and boom and slump affect the relationships between women and men, between parents and children, in a particular industrial area, and how family life in its particular local forms has enabled the industry to flourish. I have focused on women in the industry partly because it seems to me that the power, adaptability and kindliness of their relationships with kin provide pivotal relationships enabling family members to adapt to working in the industry. But above all, as a portrait of women, the book also tries to add something useful to the growing body of research on women's employment, family life and leisure during the present century.[7] It is particularly preoccupied with questions relating to women's whole life cycle, from childhood, through adolescence, marriage, motherhood and grandmotherhood, to old age and often widowhood. The life-history method tends to produce material leading naturally to an emphasis on the continuities and discontinuities in the lives of individuals, but it is also able to discern the relationship between family events and national events, the personal and the public and social. It does not have to ignore the way lives are marked by and have their place in historical moments, episodes, social movements and structures.

The book will begin with a historical background to women's work before people's recollections begin, that is before the twentieth century, comparing it with what women do in the industry today, and looking at the way history has been twisted and forgotten, to justify the overall inequality between men's and women's wages. In Chapter 3 we begin the accounts which women gave me of their lives. Chapters 3, 4, 5 and 6 deal with life at home and at work before the Second World War, Chapters 7, 8 and 9 with life after the war, to sharpen our picture of changes in living conditions, in employment and unemployment, in work and leisure, and to explain further the attitudes and priorities of working women in the Potteries today. Some aspects of their stories are similar to those of women who worked in other towns, or in other industries, but life in working-class areas of Britain is diverse. Generalizations about women textile workers, for example, cannot necessarily be transplanted to the Potteries. Elizabeth Roberts's illuminating study of Barrow, Lancaster and Preston in Lancashire between 1890 and 1940 is rich in its analysis and detail of family life, but the overall emphasis on working-class respectability and conformity which pervades her descriptions does not find such a strong echo in my pages.[8] Life in the Potteries, it seems to me, demanded more adaptations than rules, at least in the areas of sexuality, housing and money management.

I cannot pretend to have covered all the areas of these women's lives, but the questions which have particularly absorbed me relate to the whole life cycle. I wanted to know what it was like for the little girl whose childhood was spent with a mother in full-time employment. How was she cared for or minded in 1900 or 1930 or 1950? How much was she involved in keeping the family going? How did living conditions affect her freedom and her opportunities?

What was expected of her and allowed her in terms both of work and of social activities as a young girl? Were her obligations more arduous, was her freedom more constrained, than her brother's? What did school mean to her, and how did it prepare her in turn for work on the pots?

When she left school, how free was she to choose a job, and how much were older people involved in getting her her first job? Did earning a wage change her position at home? What were the conditions like at work, the opportunities, the difficulties of factory life? Did families really work together, and did this involve fathers in a patriarchal role, instilling factory discipline? How did young women feel about management, about supervisors and about the trade union? What were their options: could a girl move from job to job, when she tired of a particular supervisor, or set of tasks, or her department altogether? Were her wages her own, or part of a long-term set of reciprocal obligations?

If we turn to the question of how new families were formed: how did she meet young men, and eventually her husband? What was the family's attitude to her getting married? Was a girl who married young perceived as not paying her debt to her family? Where did the couple live, and how much did her natal family continue to be involved both in easing her living conditions and in looking after her children? How long did she spend at home with her children, and what did she feel about going back to work, leaving them with her mother or a nursewoman? Did her own experience make her more reluctant to leave them to others? How did she view child-rearing itself? What was her view of herself? Did she see herself as a housewife or mother temporarily at work, or as a skilled working woman with responsibilities at home as well?

In another section I shall ask about the relationship between husbands and wives, and in particular about money management. How much has the pattern of looking after and using wages changed in the period under study? How much have men been involved in decision-making at home? How much do husbands matter in a community where mothers and daughters retain lifelong relationships of mutual help and affection? How much does the fact of a woman's wages, or the fact that she goes out to work all or most of the day, affect the relationship between wife and husband? How much support does he give her in those areas which are traditionally thought of as women's work at home? Research on women in other parts of Britain has also led me to question how important routines of housework or cleanliness were to the women of the Potteries, and how much a woman felt she needed to conform to middle-class notions of respectability and pride in household management.[9]

Two other aspects of marriage will be touched on: sexuality and violence, though here my findings are not so full as in some other aspects of this inquiry. It is easier to get information on violence in the parental generation than in people's own marriages, so I must warn the reader against an impression that it is all in the past. People are naturally reluctant to talk to strangers about the problems and failures in their own marriages, unless they have overcome them. Secondly, I did not collect systematic information on contraception, although where people discussed this with me, a trend and a change in attitudes seemed clearly indicated. A less faint-hearted interviewer could have collected a fuller account of this. Some attitudes to pre-marital sexuality were easier to discover, since many of my informants either had been conceived before marriage or themselves had had a child who had hurried their wedding along.

Ideas about love will also be touched on in the context of women's expectations in marriage. Does love ideology create false expectations in marriage? Do people marry for love, or for something much more calculating? How different are the confidence and personality of the married woman, as compared with the unmarried girl? How much accounting goes on of services received and rendered among husbands and wives, brothers and sisters, parents and children, aunts and nieces, grandparents and their descendants? What becomes of the spinster and the widow?

In all these questions there will be an attempt to chart both continuity and where changes have occurred during the course of this century. The continuity also present is, in part, the persistence of the industry itself, a mixture of comfort and cruelty which has absorbed men's and women's working lives for generations. But within these often Victorian buildings are people with plans and projects, with houses to be modernized or to be bought from the council, people with notions of what it is to be a happy couple, a comfortable family, successful parents, of what it is to be deprived or 'rough', or violent, or 'relations that you didn't want to know'. It is the interface between the factory and the home, the history and experience of work, poverty and these projects in the minds of working women, which I hope to throw some light on in these chapters.

Notes

1 The Potteries are generally held to consist of Hanley, Burslem, Tunstall, Stoke, Fenton and Longton. Stoke is a town within the city of Stoke-on-Trent.

2 Office of Population Censuses and Surveys (OPCS), *Census 1981*, 'Key statistics for urban areas: the Midlands cities and towns', p. 60, table 3, 'Economic activity and unemployment of usual residents'.

3 Of married women in the 45 to 49 age group in the Potteries, 73.29 per cent were economically active. These statistics can be derived from OPCS, *Census 1981*, 'County Report Staffordshire', part 1, p. 47, table 12, 'Usually resident population aged 16 and over: economic position by age by marital status by sex'. The DE/OPCS survey is by Jean Martin and Ceridwen Roberts, *Women and Employment: A Lifetime Perspective*, 1984, pp. 13–17.

4 OPCS, *Census 1981*, 'Key statistics for urban areas: the Midlands cities and towns', p. 88, table 5, 'Household characteristics, size and type, pensioners and children and travel to work'.

5 I interviewed just under seventy women in the Potteries in 1981, coming again to interview some of them again in 1985. I am very grateful to the Nuffield Foundation, which gave me a grant towards the expenses of my fieldwork and the subsequent analysis. I also interviewed some of the husbands, sons and fathers of women pottery-workers, and men who were managers, fellow-workers, owners and otherwise involved in the industry, not least some of the full-time officials in the Ceramic and Allied Trades' Union. I had already done intensive anthropological fieldwork at one time in the area, and wanted to combine the advantages of that method with the broader scope of interviewing a relatively large number of people of different ages and with an emphasis on time-depth. I was unwise to interview so many people with

the ambition of very close and detailed analysis based on transcripts from tape-recordings. The work was very laborious for someone in full-time employment, and I sometimes despaired of ever bringing it to fruition. The problem was not that of producing transcripts, but of synthesising, comparing and generalizing honestly from such an abundance of material. The advantage of this method has been that I have been given not only the intimacy and immediacy of the women's individual conversations, but some grasp of how usual or how rare were the individual's perceptions of her situation.

6 OPCS, *Census 1971*, 'Great Britain. Economic activity', part 1, 1973, p. 51, table 1, 'Economic activity: males by age, females by age'.

7 This is of course a growth industry, but two books form a useful starting-point to the range of research now being published: Jane Lewis (ed.), *Labour and Love: Women's Experience of Home and Family, 1850–1940*, 1986; and Angela John (ed.), *Unequal Opportunities: Women's Employment in England, 1900–1918*, 1986.

8 Elizabeth Roberts, *A Woman's Place: An Oral History of Working-Class Women, 1890–1940*, 1984.

9 See the previously mentioned books on the subject.

CHAPTER 2

The Forgotten Missuses: Myth-Making in the Pottery Industry

Until recently, the history of pots was written as the history of great names, in particular of pottery-owners – Josiah Wedgwood, the Wood family, Josiah Spode, Herbert Minton – or of innovations in types of ware like salt-glazed stoneware, creamware, jasper and later *pâte sur pâte* or fairy lustre. The names of the people at the top are so much easier to remember than the dozens of processes and scores of crafts-people who actually produced a teapot or a bowl.[1] Museums reflected the same attitude to history: pots were placed like jewels in their museum cases, admired but unexplained; conceived by the great, it was as if they had been fashioned by elves.

Potteries people have a sense of their own history and of the terrible debt which the pottery industry owes to the bodies of their parents and grandparents; it was always an unhealthy, even a killer, industry to work in. But they are also subject to myths about the past which help to explain and justify present-day inequalities in the wages of men and women. This chapter will try to sketch in a picture of the history and myths of work in the potbanks as they relate to this inequality.[2]

Although men and women have been employed together in the Potteries for more than two centuries, the proportion of males to females has changed over time, and has masked a considerable reorganization of work into men's and women's work at different periods. In the nineteenth century there were twice as many males as females, but in 1851 more than half the workforce were aged 18 or younger, and only just under a quarter were children.[3] For most of the twentieth century there have been more women working in the industry than men, but by 1981 women formed only 48 per cent of the workforce.[4]

In spite of the 1970 Equal Pay Act, women's earnings are still on average markedly lower than men's. The *Employment Gazette* shows that in April 1983, women pottery workers' (along with those in bricks, glass, cement etc.) average hourly earnings were 240.9p, under 70 per cent of men's average hourly earnings.[5] More recent figures from the British Ceramic Manufacturers' Federation show that the inequalities are even more marked when those branches of the industry in which women predominate – like general earthenware and china – are compared with a branch of the industry like sanitary-ware, where there are far more men working than women. In October 1986, 3,328 men in general earthenware were earning on average £3.34 per hour; 3,646 women in the same field were earning £2.81. In china (excluding fine china), 1,299 men and 1,814 women were earning on average £3.48 and £2.90 respectively; in sanitary-ware factories, where women were under 10 per cent of the labour-force, 1,946 men and 111 women were earning £4.35 and £3.09 respectively.[6] Thus in all branches of the trade, men are better paid than women, but where men have almost a monopoly of jobs the workforce is considerably better paid.

Why should this be? Surely the Equal Pay Act was intended to make sure that men and women doing work of the same or similar value should be equally rewarded? Is the work that men and women do in the industry so different and are the tasks that women do so inherently less valuable that their wages must be smaller? Two factors are important in answering this question: the first is the notion that there is a natural division of labour between men and women, and the second is that men's work is heavier and thus more valuable. The important word is 'thus'. History is apparently brought in to justify these beliefs, but in actuality history is forgotten and myths are substituted to make the inequality more comfortable.

Veronica Beechey, in a review of studies of women's employment, drew attention to the importance of sexual segregation as 'a major reason why the Equal Pay Act has proved virtually useless in rectifying inequalities between men and women'.[7] Where men and women are doing different jobs, the problems of comparing or evaluating their skills are obvious, as are the difficulties of making a case for changing traditional inequalities. The idea of a natural division of labour and of 'fit work for women' can in this way be a powerfully conservative force, and a means whereby certain jobs can be kept as male preserves with male wages attached to them. In the pottery industry, wages are further complicated by piece-work, so that, for example, although a man and a woman may both be casters, they will be given different pieces of work to do, each with its own separately negotiated price. But the price will be set so that the workers are able to earn their normal wages. A man will be expected to earn more because his work is 'harder', and the price will be set accordingly.

Undoubtedly, in some of the factories catering for the cheap end of the market – mugs for supermarkets, for example – the idea of a gender division of labour does not seem to be strongly developed. There may be no departments as such, and all the processes of potting, glazing and decorating may take place in one noisy hangar-like building, in which there is no place, physically or ideologically, for men's or women's domains. But even there, in 1981 protective legislation formally excluded women from doing certain jobs which involved night shift-work or carrying heavy weights. In many factories, however, where the labour force was involved in producing fine china, the traditional product of the city of Stoke, many of the processes were divided into men's and women's work, and men were rarely to be found doing the same work as women; women, too, worked in groups together, rather than sharing the same type of task with men. Protective legislation cannot account for this kind of gender division of labour.

Before going any further, it might be useful to explain how the clay becomes a cup or plate as it passes through the potbank. (The Glossary at the end of the book may also be helpful.) First, the clay and other materials (for example, china stone from Cornwall and bone in bone china) are prepared in the 'slip-house', where the mixture is passed through sieves, over electro-magnets, through a filter press (which extracts water), emerging from the pug-mill as a tube of clay without air bubbles or unwanted particles. The next processes take place in the 'clay end' or potting shop. Plates, saucers, etc., called 'flatware', are 'made', that is shaped, in the making department, most often nowadays by automated machines. After drying, articles are smoothed by sponging and fettling. Ware which has not been fired (that is, it has not been in the oven) is described as being in the clay state; after firing it is 'biscuit-ware'. Cups and bowls are made on a 'jolly', a machine-tool whose profile makes the inside profile of the pot; a tool which makes the outside profile is called a 'jigger', and this is used for flatware. The foot-rim of a cup may be turned by hand on a lathe or, more usually nowadays, on a semi-automated machine. Handles are made in moulds and put on by handlers.

Teapots, jugs, sugar-boxes, etc. are cast or 'casted' as the casters themselves say, that is, made out of liquid clay or 'slip', which is poured into moulds, left for a few minutes and then, once hardened, taken out, fitted together, sponged and dried. After firing, biscuit-ware is cleaned in a vibrating machine and brushed, and is then taken to the dippers and dipped in a tub of glaze, which gives the ware its shiny surface. Nowadays this can also be done by machine. Dipped ware is fired again in the 'glost oven' (the kiln for firing newly glazed ware), then sorted and applied with on-glaze decoration, before being fired again. Pottery can of course be decorated under the glaze, as was the case with much of the blue-and-white printed wares which are very popular with collectors, but if water-slide transfers or enamel painting are used, then they are glazed, fired, enamelled or printed and fired again, this time in the enamelling kiln. Lithographers have, since the mid-1950s, used water-slide transfers, which make for a very easy form of decoration; a gold band may also be painted on, or a background of colour laid on, or aerographed; there are many decorating processes, some of which will be described later. Finally, the ware is selected into different qualities and packed in the warehouse.

When I visited factories in 1981, women tended to be concentrated into certain jobs, and the same was true of men. Men worked in the sliphouse where the clay bodies were mixed. They were mostly involved in the making of the china or earthenware, turning (where it was a skilled operation), making moulds, casting large items of ware, dipping, placing the ware in the kilns, polishing faulty pieces, labouring and working in the finished warehouse. Women did dipping and casting of smaller ware, flower-making, machine-minding in the automated making and turning departments, fettling, sponging, towing, handling and warehouse work. Large numbers of women were involved in decorating, mostly applying water-slide transfers, but they also burnished gold on china and did gold-banding and stamping. Women acted as dippers' attendants and also casted handles. (Some factories said categorically that handle-casting was a man's job, others, equally categorically, that it was a woman's.) Generalizing more broadly, women were typically lithographers, machine-minders and assistants, and finishers (fettling, sponging and towing), although they also casted, aerographed, dipped and selected ware – jobs also performed by men. There were also women supervisors and occasionally managers.

Talking to members of the workforce gave some insight into the ideological underpinnings of this gender division of labour. At one factory of about 750 workers, men did the skilled turning, using a lathe, while women performed the semi-automatic process using a machine. I asked a male turner whether he would consider working on a machine, and he replied, no, that it was fit work for women, that your mind had to be able to go on a cheap day's excursion to do that kind of work. In the recession, young men will of course work on the automated making machines, but essentially it is women who are thought able to put up with boring, monotonous jobs, and to put up with agonizing monotony is not considered a valuable skill in the industry.

The idea that skilled work is appropriate for men, and that women can do repetitive, monotonous work during which the mind must wander away, is realized even in the decorating shops, which are considered *par excellence* the preserve of women. The area in which women would seem to have a monopoly is in the lithographing shops, where they do the monotonous but very deft 'slide-off' work, putting transfers on china. When it comes to the more highly paid enamelling or painting, women have entirely lost the monopoly. In spite of this, the belief is widely expressed by workers in the industry that women are especially suited to decorating work and that it is an essentially 'feminine' occupation; men are seemingly invisible in these jobs.

In 1980, 307 fine china lithographers received an average of £65.22 on piece-work for a $34\frac{1}{2}$ hour week. Had they done 40 hours, their wages would have been approximately £76.00 per week (information gathered at the headquarters of the Ceramic and Allied Trades' Union in November 1981). It was interesting to compare this with the wages of the all-male figure-ornamenters, who stuck the relief figures on to the jasper-wares: they received, on average, £112 for a 36 hour week. People do not think of them as decorators, but the male figure-ornamenters are essentially decorating the ware, and they are part of the phenomenon of the invisibility of men in decorating. The actual presence of men seems in no way to detract from the overall idea that decorating is fit work for women.

When I visited a Longton factory in 1981, much of the workforce was involved in work on souvenirs of the Royal Wedding. Women in rubber gloves were burnishing monograms in best gold on a Royal dinner service, while in another shop women lithographers, sitting in long lines facing one another's backs, were sticking pattern transfers on to the ware with nimble fingers. Meanwhile, in a cosy little studio, a group of men were painting free-hand landscapes on to commemorative chalices. They sat facing one another with their paints and brushes (always called 'pencils', eighteenth-century fashion, in the industry), doing probably the most creative free-hand decorating in the factory.

At another factory, famous for its figures, the prestigious figures were being painted by both men and women. Some of the finest work – face-painting – was being done exclusively by men, who had earned the right to this through length of service. Child-bearing is an obstacle to women gaining jobs given to the most experienced, with unbroken service.

The idea that women are suited to the decorating end of the pottery industry has as its corollary the idea that they are somehow less suited to the mucky, clay end, the preserve of men. This segregation is further sanctioned by the belief that women in the clay end are coarser and use bad language (also the preserve of men). Not all the decorators whom I spoke to made these assertions, saying only that they would not like to work anywhere other than in the decorating shops. People in the clay end tend to say that the decorators are 'toffee-nosed' and think they are better than anybody else. This is not just based on wage differences; for the most part, people seem to know little about one another's wages, particularly in different workshops.

Working in the clay end can be noisy and very messy. A handle-caster, for instance, told me how she would get her legs covered in slip (the liquid clay) in the course of her work. It is not convenient to eat one's sandwiches in the midst of all this clay (not legal either, of course), and the canteen will be full of casters, spongers, fettlers and dippers, whereas the lithographers may be found in some factories sitting at their benches, drinking a cup of tea, or chatting over a sandwich, away from the rest.

Several factors are involved in the idea of the superiority of the decorators. In the nineteenth century it was the paintresses who had this reputation. Simeon Shaw, whose *History of the Staffordshire Potteries* was published in 1829, mentions that 'many young women, of good families' were taught the art of painting in blue and white or colour.[8] Artists were ladies, and not to be confused with other factory workers. By the 1840s, when Samuel Scriven was reporting to the Royal Commission on the Employment of Children and Young Persons in the District of the Staffordshire Potteries, the idea of the superiority of the paintresses was maintained on the basis of the separation of the sexes among the young factory workers.[9] There were separate painting-rooms for girls and boys, whereas in other departments, such as throwing, turning and printing, the sexes were mixed.

Scriven's respondents in 1841 show this clearly. Eliza Beech, aged 28, from a girls' painting-room, said of the girls:

> They do not associate with the boys, but are kept exclusively to themselves. We have no men in the same department. . . . From the experience of many years I can form an opinion as to the general moral and religious character of potters' children in *my department*; compared with others, I think them superior. I never hear anything like vulgar or improper language from any of them; they are respectful, clean and well-conducted.[10]

The printing-room, by contrast, attracted criticism from Sarah Proctor, aged 30, for the association of men and girls:

My opinion of the general character of paper-cutters and transferrers is that they are not so good as they should be as it regards their spiritual welfare; their conduct does not correspond with what they are taught at Sunday-schools; their language is often indecent and profane; this is I think attributable to their associations with young and vulgar men. The printing-room is indeed a bad school for children.[11]

The same class distinctions based on the presence or absence of men were certainly still strong in the first half of this century. A paintress, Mrs Bede (her name, like all others here, is a pseudonym), born in 1907, made this clear to me:

[Would you ever have thought of working in the clay end?]
[Mrs Bede:] No, it's horrible in them places.
[What's horrible about it?]
I don't know. The people are different, shouting and gawping at each other – where we have got to be nice and quiet, it's the posher part, you know what I mean? You are quiet and painting. Because I used to have to go through one part to fetch some ware, when we were on B — s. I used to hate going through, and they're gawping and swearing at the men, and they think they sound big, but they don't, do they?

Mrs Farrier, who was born in 1902 and made bowls in the clay end, said: 'Like decorating – you were posh if you were allowed to go in the warehouse for about three and sixpence a week, or you went learning enamelling, or painting, or something like that – you'd got a posh job, see.'

Mrs Flowers, a lithographer, born in 1927, whose mother had been a cup-handler, suggested that there had been almost a spirit of apartheid: 'I've heard my mother say as if clay-end people were in toilets when the decorators were in, it never was right; they shouldn't have been in the same place.'

Some people were inclined to describe the distinction between the decorating end and the clay end as being all in the past. Mrs Adams, a caster-sponger:

On a small firm, you don't get this now, but years ago, if you worked in the clay end, the making end, you were nobody; but if you worked the decorating end, you know, paintress or something like that, you were a bit above them, you know what I mean?

Ed Gaskell, a male trade union representative for the clay end in his factory, asserted, on the contrary, that the distinctions continued:

Women and men who work in the decorating end treat people who work in the clay end as second-class citizens, and always have done, you know. Women at the clay end tend to swear, or whatever; women in the decorating end don't. Women in the clay end, I think, are more – they are not as pretentious, that's perhaps the best way of putting it.

Mrs Rugeley, a caster-sponger born in 1939, emphasized the same difference between women in potting or decorating:

Decorators go to work all make-up and best clothes and high heels, and totter up and down. Clay end don't: they go tidy, but change – trashers [old shoes] and something as is comfortable, because we have to stand all day, you see, whereas they sit all day.

Present-day lithographers are, to be truthful, the occupational descendants of the transferrers who worked with printers, rather than of the paintresses. But their image has fused into that of the historical paintresses. They have the superior status attached to a clean job without the presence of male manual workers (the only men are the labourers who serve them and the managers whom they serve) and without excessive noise. Women decorators complained to me on several occasions about the introduction of any machinery near them.

In some factories there are more women than men in the clay end even today, but the women are ideologically intruders, for heavy and dirty work is thought of as men's work, and the heaviness of men's work has come to justify, in many cases, men's higher wages. As will I hope become clear, women competed with men for the skilled and well-paid jobs in the clay end from the 1870s until the end of the Second World War. This intrusion into the male stronghold has been resisted by maintaining the Victorian middle-class ideal of the segregation of the sexes; women who worked alongside men were sullied by the idea of men's baseness, both verbal and sexual. We find just this character-ization of women who worked in the clay end before 1939.

Arthur Meeke, a retired warehouseman, for instance, alluded as usual to women's bad language, but also to his belief that the women in the clay end had been morally loose: ' Well, they were ladies of easy virtue, and they used bad language and things like that, you see. They were rough. . . . The language was absolutely filthy.' He also asserted that the noisy environment affected women's voices: 'You see, they tended – a lot of them worked in noise – and they tended therefore to have very loud, coarse voices.'

The image of these 'scruffy women walking around, covered in clay' (Ruth Evans, lithographer), with their bad language, coarse voices and loose morals, was a deterrent. If they worked like men, they were to be denied the attributes of 'nice' women: they were 'common', the wrong side of that basic distinction, enshrined in the English language, between women approved of by men and transgressors, 'sluts'.

The fact that so many women still work in the clay end, in spite of the ideal of women's work in the decorating end, could be seen as an argument against the influence of these informal sanctions. But two things have happened: men have won back certain jobs; and where women remain in the clay end, their presence has been rendered more 'comfortable' by a segregation of the sexes, visible in the division of labour in the clay end. Even where both sexes are doing the same job (casting, for instance) the men will work together in one place, and the women in another. Groups of women work together in the biscuit-warehouse, or are occupied with sticking handles on cups, fettling or sponging. Sometimes you will find a male dipper attended by women, but close proximity is the exception, and work is for the most part divided along gender lines, so that it is unusual for a man and a woman to be working as partners in a process in a factory. The great exception to this is in the most prestigious areas of free-hand painting on figures, where men and women work side by side but indepen-dently as 'artists'.

The idea that women are best suited to decorating is only one of the ideas about women's work which are important in maintaining lower wages for women. Separation of tasks is one method, but so also is the idea that women have traditionally been attendants on men. This idea is given as a reason or at least a stereotype (even at trade union headquarters) which accounts for entrenched resistance to improvements in women's wages. The woman as attendant, or subordinate, could scarcely hope to equal the wages of the craftsman himself. The stereotype is archetypically patriarchal; women were subordinate because they were attendants and because they were attendant on their husbands. The historical reality is a lot more complex, and may help to account for the hostility to women in the clay end which I have described above. It also suggests a kind of collective amnesia about women's former skills and responsibilities which has accompanied the extension of male categories of work since the war. It might be helpful at this point to take a brief look at what we know about pottery-workers at the dawn of the industry in this area.

For centuries, the factories of the Potteries have drawn in the population of the surrounding countryside. John Wesley described this in his journal for 28 March 1781: 'I returned to Burslem. How is the whole face of this country changed in about twenty years! Since the potteries were introduced [*sic*] inhabitants have constantly flowed in from every side. Hence the wilderness has literally become a fruitful field.'[12]

Lorna Weatherill has shown how the population of Burslem – the first of the six towns to flourish in the industry – grew between 1660 and 1760, as the numbers and sizes of pottery-works increased.[13] At this time, work was mainly for men and boys, although it must be said that our information about the workforce in the eighteenth century is scanty. A few young men, usually of 'influential families' and higher status than most workmen, were bound as apprentices.[14] We find a less formal apprenticeship for a girl in the pages of Thomas Whieldon's Notebook on 24 August 1752: 'hired little Bet Blour to learn to flower, 1st year p. week 1s., 2nd year 1s. 3d., 3rd year 1s. 6d.'[15]

Craftsmen at John Baddeley's pottery in the 1760s earned about 9s (shillings) a week, labourers between 5s and 6s a week, and two regular women workers between 2s 6d and 3s per week. Sometimes relatives did casual work, wives earning about 1s to 2s, young people ('lads' and 'wenches') about 1s.[16] At this stage, however, from the evidence that we have, fewer women were involved in the pottery industry. Earlier in the eighteenth century it was probably even more a male occupation. Simeon Shaw, in his *History of the Staffordshire Potteries* (1970, p. 166), says that

> Up to 1740, in each manufactory, all the persons employed were the slip-maker, thrower, two turners, handler (stouker), fireman, warehouseman, and a few children, and, to be really useful to the master, and secure sufficient employment, a good workman could *throw, turn* and *stouk*.

Josiah Wedgwood's letters, however, indicate that there were skilled women and all-women departments in the industry. Wedgwood refers, for example, to women who burnished gold at the Chelsea Pottery: 'I believe it is neither a secret or very curious art, for Women only are employed in it at Chelsea.'[17]

This suggests a certain disregard either for women's skill or for their ability to keep a secret, which was an important quality at a time when new processes were being invented and patents taken out, and competition among pottery factories was very keen. Nevertheless, Wedgwood could recognize women as good paintresses, and he discussed taking on a husband-and-wife team in which the wife was perhaps the superior in talent:

> This Willcox has a wife who paints and is very ingenious; she is at present finishing some work at Worcester. Willcox says that she is an excellent coppier [*sic*] of figures and other subjects, and a much better hand than himself. He showed me two heads of her doing in indian ink which are very well done.[18]

Bet Blour probably worked with her family – there are many other Blours at the Whieldon factory – and Mrs Willcox later worked with her husband at Wedgwood's works. But these were skilled workers, attendant on no one. The burnishers were not attendants either, but doing a separate process in an all-female department.

Simeon Shaw described the first woman transferrer in the district dying 'at a truly patriarchal age' in November 1828. This was a highly skilled job, working with the printer, and involved transferring the prints from the paper to the ware in the printing shop. This is the sort of woman who by 1841, in Scriven's evidence, would be sullied by her working with men. There is no evidence of this in Shaw's account of skilled women in the eighteenth century. Shaw also mentions a Sarah Elkin, who worked for Wedgwood at Etruria, as the first person to employ gold leaf successfully as ornament.[19] To sum up, some of the earliest references to women's work show that there were skilled occupations for women in the expanding pottery industry, and that women were not at this stage only or necessarily attendant on their husbands.

The Wedgwood Papers, owned by the Wedgwood Museum Trust and lodged at Keele University Library, contain valuable material which can throw light on employees in the last decade of the eighteenth century and the first two decades of the nineteenth.[20] The list of work-people at the Etruria Works on 13 April 1791 (ref. 29119–46) includes the names of two women as gilders; throwers, turners, pressers and claybeaters were men. In 1810 (ref. 17499–95) there were both men and women enamellers; in the list of people employed at the printing works on 5 December 1810 (ref. 29126–46) women are included in the warehouse and as painter, gilder, burnisher and brusher of ware. In another document of December 1810 (ref. 29127–46) there are both males and females as attendants 'at wheel' and 'at lathe', though they are probably all either young boys or women. In 1811 (ref. 29131–46) the list of workmen includes women as gilder, grinder (of colours) and scourer; males did the attendant work such as turning the lathe for the turner or the wheel for the thrower, or making sprigs for the ornamenter, or 'balling' (making balls of clay ready for the thrower). Noticeably, for the question of the extent of patriarchy and family discipline, the 'attendants' do not share the same surname as the person for whom they work, for example: (ref. 29134–46) 'James Edge turns lathe for Charles Bourne', 'Samuel Jones turns lathe for R. Nickinson', 'John

Nickinson spoutmaker for John Moreton', 'Absolam Nickinson spoutmaker for Isaac Hollinshead'. Members of the same family worked in the same factory, but it is clear that they often worked quite separately.

At the China Works in December 1812, females did work as attendants (ref. 29135–46). There is Ellen Fieldhouse as 'baller', Dina Kellshall as 'turner of lathe' and Hannah Kellshall also, while Susan Shenton is 'turner of wheel' and Elizabeth Shenton a 'blocker'. There are four Kellshalls, but the males are 'looker to ware' and 'slipmaker'; they work elsewhere. Another document, of 17 March 1815, listing employees and signed Richard Rhead, shows large numbers of paintresses and female burnishers, males and females in the warehouses, and males and females at the wheel, the lathe and working as mould-runners (ref. 29141–46).

In 1827 Ambrose Cuddon of 35 Bury Street, St James's, published *A Representation of the Manufacturing of Earthenware with twenty-one highly finished Copper Plate Engravings, and a short explanation of each, shewing the whole process of the Pottery.* Here we find women in their stereotypical nineteenth-century roles. The fourth picture is the first to show women, two women in fact, working with the 'thrower'; one girl is employed to turn the large potter's wheel, an item of equipment which required someone to turn it all day long and which had become standard from the 1720s.[21] The other woman is making clay into balls of a convenient size for the thrower to use. There is no doubt that they are attendants on the thrower. The fifth picture shows a turner, whose lathe is driven by the woman-power of a girl on a treadle. In the printing-room we again see a man and his assistants, two girls, one of whom is cutting up the prints, but the female transferrer sits independently and with her back to the printer, rubbing the print on to the ware. Another picture shows a woman preparing clay for a man who is 'pressing' or 'squeezing', which is making jugs, tureens and so on out of the clay. In the twelfth picture, women are preparing colours for the enameller or painter.

In all these pictures, except that of the print-room, the women have been standing to their work, whereas the male modeller, the thrower, the handler, the engraver, the painter and the men in the counting-house are shown sitting. Under 'Painting and Gilding China or Earthenware', two men are shown at one bench with their backs to a woman at the other bench. The woman does not wear a bonnet like the women in the clay end and the printing-shop; the male painters wear tailcoats and no caps; here, as in the engraving-room and the counting-house, there are pictures on the walls; in the engraving-room, the gentlemen artists even have a fire in their cosy little ducks-nest grate. It is obvious that in 1827 the class distinctions are already clear-cut, and that the stereotype of women as either attendants on male craftsmen or as lady artists or decorators is apparent. It is important to point out, though, that this visual evidence omits the all-female departments like those of the women scourers, who cleaned off all the flint particles which adhered to the ware during firing – thoroughly unhealthy, but attendant on no one – and the burnishers and warehousewomen, who had been employed since the time of the first Josiah Wedgwood, as well as the female enamellers and paintresses.

Scriven's account of 1841, based on testimony given to him by pottery-workers and others involved in the industry, makes it clear that men, women and children who went into the industry had more to worry about than the size of their wages. In particular, the men and boys who did dipping and the young women who did scouring were most at risk from the health hazards of their work. The dangers of using lead glaze were known, and so also were safe alternatives, from the time of Wedgwood; but to the eternal shame of the manufacturers, dippers were allowed to suffer from the lethal effects of the lead glazes throughout the nineteenth century. Celoria states that 'the danger was not fully eliminated until after 1900', but I have talked to women who worked as dippers in the 1940s and who at that time still had to line their stomachs at the start of the day with a glass of milk, and dose themselves with Epsom salts.[22]

In 1841 Scriven described the effects of the work on the dippers and their young assistants: 'I have been able to trace in their dull and cadaverous countenances its *insidious* workings.'[23] Noting that they had their hands and clothes almost always saturated with the glaze, and seldom changed or ate elsewhere, he blamed their own lack of care, although admitting that he had

> never seen rooms provided for cleansing, although it will appear in some of the returned schedules that there is plenty of water and vessels at their command. From their disregard of prophylactic measures, you will not be surprised that paralysis, colica pictonum, epilepsy, and a host of other nervous diseases, are to be met with in all their aggravated forms. The most constant, however, is that of partial paralysis of the extensors of the hands in men, and of epilepsy in children, accompanied at all times with obstinate constipation of the bowels and derangement of the alimentary canal.[24]

Scriven found that fathers, not unnaturally, were unwilling for their boys to go into this work. But very high wages acted as an inducement – an average of 30s a week for the men and 5s for boys as 'an equivalent for "the risk they run" '.

Scriven explained what scouring, the killer occupation for women, was like:

> When china ware is to be fired it is first placed in coarse earthen vessels called *saggers* – these contain a quantity of finely pulverized flint; this, during the firing, attaches itself strongly to the china; some two, three, or more young women, are employed to scour it off with sandpaper and brushes; the particles float abundantly in the atmosphere of the room, and cover their persons just as plentifully as flour does the miller; in every act of respiration a considerable quantity is deposited on the mucous surfaces of the fauces, trachaea, and bronchial tubes, and being acutely angular and irritating soon occasions thickening of these membranes, as evidenced by their small weak voices: asthma, chronic cough, tubercular development, consumption, soon follows, and death.[25]

In spite of the risk which these young women so obviously ran, their wages were only 10s for a 72 hour week, only 1s more than 'throwers' women', and 14s less than a gilder.[26] At this time, as at every period since, men were paid more as men, rather than because they were craftsmen or were doing heavy or dangerous work. Women were paid less, essentially because they were women. No other explanation can account for the fact that skilled women transferrers, for instance, were paid 10s, while warehousemen were paid 24s per week. Skilled men, of course, like turners, throwers, pressers, plate-, dish- and saucer-makers, moulders and modellers, were all earning upwards of 30s.[27]

Pottery factories made abundant use of children until prevented by legislation later in the century. The 1810 list of people employed in the Wedgwood Papers (ref. 29123–46) totals 205 men, 100 women and 145 children, making a combined workforce of 450. The report of the Commission on Children's Employment lists a total of 12,407 workers in the industry in 1842, of whom 978 boys and 522 girls were under the age of 13; in 1851 there were 19,000 adults, including 6,500 young people and 4,500 children.[28] In 1842 these young assistants were averaging about 2s $\frac{1}{2}$d when in full work, doing a 72 hour week.[29]

Scriven describes in detail the 'jiggers' and mouldrunners, who, he says, 'by the very nature of their work, are rendered pale, weak, diminutive, and unhealthy'.[30] The problem was partly one of overwork, but also of working in an atmosphere of 100 to 120 degrees Fahrenheit. The jigger turned the horizontal wheel for the plate-maker, from morning till night, while the mould-runner had to run backwards and forwards to the 'hothouse', a room with a stove, where the ware was put to dry, and from which fresh moulds were collected. Scriven remarks that 'It is admitted on all hands that their work is the most arduous and fatiguing of all others', and speaks of them 'labouring like little slaves'. This heavy, exhausting work of carrying moulds, wedging clay and constantly running to and fro in extremes of heat and cold was never considered worthy for that reason of a higher wage. When children could no longer do it, later in the century, mouldrunning became a young woman's job; we shall return to it later.

Although women and children worked in these nineteenth-century factories, the idea of a workforce of families working together with the father in charge, and mother and children as assistants, seems to contain an element of wishful thinking. Richard Whipp, who has produced so much interesting material on the potteries, nevertheless says: 'Family work groups upholding the authority of the male head were a strong feature of the industry throughout the nineteenth century.'[31] But were they? I have pointed out that in Scriven's account of 1841 the separation of the sexes is an important dimension of work in the pottery factories. Where it is not adhered to, as in the throwing- and turning-rooms, he describes them as 'emporiums of profligacy', adding that

> from the oral testimony of the magistrates and clergy, and from some of the manufacturers themselves, I find that sexual intercourse is of very common occurrence, and that bastardy, the natural result, is thought *very* lightly of. The excellent rector of Longton (Dr Vale) observes: 'the young girls consorting with males in the works have no sense of sin or whoredom, or of the bestiality of uncleanness.[32]

Plainly, this account is criticizing the mixing of men with unmarried girls, which is a very different typification from the stereotype of whole families working together under the father's supervision.

Figure 1. Mouldmakers (from Rev. Malcolm Graham M.A., Cup and Saucer Land, c.1908)

Marguerite Dupree's work also casts doubt on this picture of the nineteenth-century potbank. She points out that in 1861 pottery work was essentially a girl's or young woman's job, and that women tended to leave the industry on marriage.[33] Married women in the industry, it is true, tended to be the wives of potters, but the child or co-residing daughter of a miner would have been more likely to work in a potbank than the child or daughter of a potter. Fifty years on from the lists of employees we have described above, the sexual division of labour seems to have remained unchanged. Dupree tells us that lathe-treading and wheel-turning were done by women and girls as well as boys; but otherwise, 'specific tasks were age and sex graded. There were, for example, no female slipmakers, throwers, turners, flatpressers, hollow-ware pressers; instead, women were transferrers, paintresses, gilders, burnishers, scourers and warehousewomen.'[34]

In case one should think that all these people might have worked together physically in one place, even though they were doing separate jobs, one has to remember that potbanks were often and traditionally designed so that the various workshops should be separate, and so that people in one department would not know the secrets of another; they were often reached by an outside staircase, and did not communicate easily one with another. Perhaps only where a woman trod the lathe, or turned the wheel for her husband, would the patriarchal image have been correct, and although this stereotype of the wife attendant on the husband is not typical of women's work either in 1841 (as described by Scriven) or in 1861 (described by Dupree), it does find its examples, as one would expect for so prevailing an ideology. John Finney, aged 12, gave this account of his father to Scriven: 'He is a turner by trade, and mother, when he has work to do, treads lathe for him.'[35]

Later in the century may be the moment for the flowering of the stereotype. Dupree gives evidence to show that the increase in the proportion of the labour force made up of women and girls in the 1870s (from 31 per cent in 1861 to 35 per cent in 1871 and 38 per cent in 1881) was related to the Factory Acts, which reduced the availability of child labour. The proportion of child labour aged between 5 and 14 decreased from 17 per cent in 1861 to 12 per cent in 1871. Girls started to do the work that formerly young boys had done. Dupree quotes the Factory Inspector's report which testifies to 'girls being employed in those occupations which properly belong to boys.'[36] She also quotes the mayor of Hanley who, speaking before the Royal Commission on the Working of the Factory and Workshop Acts in 1875, said: 'The sexes have been brought more together in the workplaces . . . owing to the fact that because of the requirements of the Factory Act the supply of boys had been narrowed, and workmen had been obliged to get female labour.'[37]

At the same time, the introduction of the pug-mill enabled men to get more work done, and in 1877 the stereotype husband and wife-attendant emerged in a submission to the Board of Arbitration (13 January 1877) that: 'A good many men had their wives working with them, and it actually paid them to hire a nurse for their families.'[38]

Thus, in the last quarter of the century, more women were brought into the workforce to aid the expansion of production and to alleviate the shortage of child labour.

But at the same time as this, women were also taking over work which had traditionally belonged to men. Richard Whipp gives evidence to show the resistance by men to women who took on independent jobs as flat-pressers (plate-makers) using new machinery. They were accused of stealing men's jobs and of bringing wages down.[39] Whipp shows that arguments about how unwomanly these women were, were already being used. *The Potteries Examiner*, quoted by Whipp, speaks of 'these vigorous ladies, who devote themselves to these toilsome tasks for which the male sex were originally deemed . . . alone qualified' (23 March 1878 and 8 November 1879). Whipp points out, importantly, that male potters did not object to women doing very heavy work; what they objected to was their being hired independently in the clay end, instead of being sub-employed by male potters.[40] The last quarter of the century plainly does not fit neatly into the stereotype of women's labour any better than the previous three.

Where does it come from then, this picture that I had been given at trade union headquarters, of the whole family working together in the industry, the

Figure 2. Some women on a potbank (from Rev. Malcolm Graham M.A., Cup and Saucer Land, c.1908)

father as thrower, assisted by his wife and children? This picture of the domestic workforce, the 'natural' proto-industrial division of labour, transported intact from the farm pottery to the factory in the course of the eighteenth century, has a certain charm, denying as it does the idea of families rudely cast asunder by the factory bell. The inevitability of the potting-patriarchy arrangement – that the father should be the craftsman, the potter, his wife and children the assistants, carrying the ware, turning the wheel, etc. – has been shown not to be based on family work patterns in the mid-nineteenth century. It is further called into question in the twentieth century, when one talks to women who worked in the industry before and between the two world wars. Their evidence suggests that, on the contrary, at that time, the skilled operations of making, casting and dipping ware of all kinds were frequently performed by women assisted by less skilled women or young girls.

Mrs Barnes, born at the end of 1911, described how she had started as a 'carrier-in', carrying piles of plates and saucers: 'You carried them from the warehouse where they were brushed and sorted, into the dippers to dip. And then I got promoted before I was 16: I went dipping, and I had somebody to carry ware to me. I showed initiative, and they made me a dipper.'

Mrs Farrier, who was born in 1902, started on a potbank at the age of 13, and later worked as her mother's assistant on the jollying machine, which was used to make bowls:

> I worked for her, see, she was a bowl-jollier, pudding bowls, and I was what they call the sponger. And then me mother was going to have a baby, so I went apprentice in her place, and that's how I learned me job the *hard* way . . . You were on your feet all day on the jollying machine.

Mrs Gregory described how the skilled woman, the 'missus', had the responsibility for paying her assistants:

> We didn't get a pay-packet: our missuses were paid. They used to go down to the office on Thursday, what they call settling day, and settle for the prior week's wages, you see. And then she'd come into the making shop where we were, and she would pay us out of her wages, you see.

Born in 1915 and at work on the pots at the age of 14, Mrs Gregory started as a mouldrunner, carrying moulds for a woman who worked a 'double jolly', a machine that made two cups at a time. In this work, as in the experience of the other older women workers, women were in charge of other women. The older woman was the 'missus' for whom one worked when starting to learn the trade; she had responsibility and authority. Mrs Farrier, also a mouldrunner and later a bowl-jollier, gave up work when her machine was automated; she refused to become, as she put it, 'a slave to that machine'.

Mrs Box made teapot spouts from solid clay from about 1917, but later she learned to cast spouts, using liquid instead of solid clay, by watching the casters. As she described her skill: 'I casted enough spouts to keep three handlers going, fifty times twenty-four every day.' The different parts of a teapot were made by a team of people, all skilled, but she had not been formally trained as a caster, and after working for over forty years she was sacked with a fortnight's notice at the age of 53, 'owing to the general trend of trade and circumstances beyond our control'. This was later elaborated by the factory management as: 'Her trade from a girl has been as a spout-maker, and as we are no longer producing this type of product, we have unfortunately had to dispense with her services.' The firm no longer made teapots with solid clay, but Mrs Box had learned the new technique of casting. She said: 'Well, I learned all casting: I casted tea-pots, I casted all that were in there. But you see, he wanted to get rid of us old hands.'

Having been given notice by a young manager, Mrs Box appealed to the head of her firm, who had known her and her mother for years. He reinstated her, but by then she had decided to go. He wrote and told her she must come to him if she were ever in any need. That was the humanity of a good boss in an old family firm; his manager was one of the new breed of managers of which we shall hear more. Mrs Box went on to another firm as a caster, until stopped by ill health. Mrs Farrier and Mrs Box both show how changes in the processes of potting effectively eased them out of their jobs, making them give way to younger people.

It is now widely believed (or often asserted) that women cannot cast large items such as teapots and coffee-pots, and that this has always been men's work; women may cast cream-jugs and sugar-boxes, which require smaller moulds. Mrs Adams (born in 1923), however, who had been a caster before the Second World War, told me that she had known only women casters between the wars:

> [Were there men casters as well as women?]
> Not at that time, no.
> [No? When did they come in?]
> I think it was soon after the war. After the Second World War, I should think. Because I used to be a caster, and of course during the war I went into the forces, and when I came back, there weren't any women casters. Not a lot of women casters at all.
> [Before the war, did the women do the heavy casting, you know, like the teapots and the big, heavy dishes?]
> Oh yes, yes. There weren't any men, men casters.

I have quoted these examples at length because all these women are living proof of the falsity of two assertions: first, that women have always been atten-dants on men, and have not done the highly skilled work; and secondly, that women have not done the heavy work, which is frequently given now as a reason for men's higher wages. In many factories nowadays, casting is a much lighter job than it was in the days when women were making big teapots and coffee-pots: the slip or liquid clay is piped to the casters, whereas formerly the caster had to pour it into the moulds from a big jug. The relationship between heavy work and higher wages was never felt to be self-evident, least of all in the nineteenth century, when children did some of the most arduous work. Wedging has been mentioned, and this involved raising, dropping and pounding large slabs of clay, to prepare it and get rid of air bubbles. Children and later women did this until the introduction of the pug-mill, which produces a smooth consistency of clay and exudes it like toothpaste, ready for the thrower or maker.

Mouldrunning has also been mentioned, described by Scriven as 'labouring like little slaves', but many girls started their factory lives in this way not so long ago. Mrs Wenceslas began working in 1947 for a woman cup-maker as her mouldrunner:

> I had the job of taking the two moulds off her, and taking them up steps, all on shelves, like a room like this, but all shelves in and red hot pipes. And I used to have to lay them all on the shelves, for dry. Then I'd have to take two more moulds, which were red hot – they'd been against the pipes – run back to the woman before she's made the other two. Then I used to have to take the two cups out that were drying, put them on boards at the side of me, in threes so that you'd got about three and a half dozen on a board, then take these two moulds and run round the other side to give her two more moulds; then make up all the clay and stick them on, so that she could just pick the clay up and throw it in, for make her next two. So you were really working hard. It was damned hard work.

Making, dipping, casting, handling, finishing: women can do and have done some of the most skilled and central operations in potting. They have done some of the heaviest work, and they now do work whose skill is often not recognized until one tries it oneself.

A generation of women were given opportunities for better-paid, more skilled work, not only because of the absence of men in the First World War, but also because of the traditional cheapness of employing women. In 1924, for instance, according to the Wethered Report, men flat-pressers (who made plates) earned 70s 5d for a 47 hour week, while women flat-pressers earned 47s 9d.[41] Men casters could earn 66s 2d for a 47 hour week, and women 36s 5d for the equivalent hours. But even where they did the same work as men, the assumption that men's financial responsibilities were greater kept women's wages down. Even in the 1950s we find the General Secretary of the National Society of Pottery Workers, Harold Hewitt, asserting that women paid lower union dues and got lower pay 'because they do not have the same responsibilities.'[42]

The idea of the male breadwinner and the family wage has been widely discussed in relation to union wage bargaining.[43] In the pottery industry it is the other side of a continuing theme which has always asserted that women's duties are primarily domestic. If we return for a moment to the nineteenth century, Dupree quotes a response to the regularization of hours over the week as a result of the Factory Act: 'The female workers are looking forward to the happy time when they can be certain of being home to their domestic duties.'[44] Burchill and Ross, in their very useful *History of the Potters' Union* (1977), refer to the Hollow-Ware Pressers who, in their return to the 1867 Commission 'stated that "Women are better occupied at home" '[45]

In spite of this, it should be clear that the potting industry has relied very heavily on women and girls for their cheap and skilled labour, using them especially when trade expanded, or when a shortage of labour – after the Factory Act of 1864, or during the First World War – threatened to interfere with production. The position of male potters on the question of women's work and wages is not a straightforward one. Both Scriven and, later, Charles Shaw in his autobiography, *When I Was a Child*, present the mid-nineteenth-century picture of male heads of potting departments being paid, and then paying their sub-employees, women and children, later, in the pub, where they got change for the wages.[46] This picture is complicated by the fact of all-women departments and by the often non-family character of the potting shops: in other words, that a man would have been paying wages to an unrelated assistant, boy or girl. If we thus see male potters as independent workers rather than as fathers or husbands of female workers, then their interest would have been served by women's low wages, since this kept overall production costs down and enabled them to have higher wages as men.

At the end of the nineteenth century their separate interests are clear in the conflict generated by the introduction of machinery. Burchill and Ross say that the 'jolly' was in general use by the 1880s and that, 'Although opposed by most of the men, they found that if they did not work on the machine, women would be employed to use it.'[47] The trade union was opposed to women doing men's jobs during the First World War, but it was agreed that this should happen, and that men returning from the war should have their jobs back.[48] Where the inevitability of women doing men's jobs was accepted, the union wanted them to be paid men's rates; it rightly feared that women would be used more and more, since it was cheaper to employ them. In some trades, like casting, plate-making and earthenware cup- and saucer-making, women had taken over from men by the middle of the Second World War.[49] In 1935 there were 37,635 women and 30,902 men employed in the industry; in 1981 the proportion of women had fallen below 50 per cent. Their former skills, burdens and responsibilities are all but forgotten; but, in the chapters which follow, these forgotten women will describe their real history and not the myths of women's work which both pervade the industry today and provide a justification for their lower wages.

Notes

1 The work of Richard Whipp and Marguerite Dupree makes an important and very useful exception. More of them later in this chapter.
2 Part of this chapter is based on my article, 'Sexual segregation in the pottery industry', which appeared in *Feminist Review* No. 21. Winter 1985.
3 F. Burchill and R. Ross, *A History of the Potters' Union* 1977, pp. 29–30.
4 Burchill and Ross, 1977, p. 173.
5 Department of Employment, *Employment Gazette*, April 1984; Male average hourly earnings in 'bricks, pottery, glass, cement etc' were £3.46 at April 1983 for men of 21 and over. The comparison is for women of eighteen and above. Men of 21 and over earned on average £154.28 for an average 44.5 hour week, while women aged 18 and over earned on average £92.51 for an average 38.4 hours per week. The 1985 *Employment Gazette* also gives the 1983 figures.
6 I am grateful to Alf Clowes, General Secretary of the Ceramic and Allied Trades' Union for supplying me with figures from the British Ceramic Manufacturers' Federation's 1986 wage census. It was pointed out to me at union headquarters

that, in sanitary-ware, men had higher wages because of the *former* heaviness of their work.

7   Veronica Beechey, 'What's so special about women's employment?' *Feminist Review* No. 15. Winter 1983.

8   Simeon Shaw, *History of the Staffordshire Potteries*, 1970, p. 210 (first published in 1829).

9   Samuel Scriven, *Report on the Employment of Children and Young Persons in the District of the Staffordshire Potteries* (written in 1841 and first published in 1843), reprinted in *Children in the Potteries, Parts 1 and 2*, 1975.

10   Scriven, 1843, evidence no. 44.

11   Scriven, 1843, evidence no. 293.

12   Quoted in G. Woolliscroft Rhead and Frederick Alfred Rhead, *Staffordshire Pots and Potters*, 1977, p. 291 (first published in 1906).

13   Lorna Weatherill, *The Pottery Trade and North Staffordshire, 1660-1760*, 1971, pp. 112-13.

14   Weatherill, 1971, pp. 96-7.

15   I am grateful to Pat Halfpenny, Keeper of Ceramics at the City Museum and Art Gallery, Stoke-on-Trent, who kindly sent me a transcript of Thomas Whieldon's Notebook. To 'flower' means to make flowers out of clay, something which women still do today in the pottery industry.

16   John Baddeley's Day-Book; and Weatherill, 1971, chapter 7, *passim*.

17   A. Finer and G. Savage, *The Selected Letters of Josiah Wedgwood*, 1965, p. 36.

18   Finer and Savage, 1965, p. 75.

19   Shaw, 1970, p. 193.

20   I quote from these papers by courtesy of the Trustees of the Wedgwood Museum, Barlaston, Stoke-on-Trent. I am concerned here only with the early material.

21   Weatherill, 1971, p. 33.

22   F. Celoria, 'Working and living conditions of nineteenth-century potters in Staffordshire', in Geoffrey Godden (ed.), *Staffordshire Porcelain*, 1983, chapter 23.

23   Scriven, 1975, p. 14.

24   Scriven, 1975, p. 15.

25   Ibid.

26   Scriven, 1975, p. 14.

27   Ibid.

28   Burchill and Ross, 1977, pp. 29-30.

29   Scriven, 1975, p. 14.

30   Scriven, 1975, p. 15.

31   Richard Whipp, *'The women pottery workers of Staffordshire and trade unionism, 1890-1905'*, MA thesis, Warwick University, 1979, p. 128. It may be that Dr Whipp has reassessed his position on this question, but I have been unable to discuss it with him.

32   Scriven, 1975, p. 17.

33   Marguerite Dupree, *'Family structure in the Staffordshire potteries, 1840-1900'*, D. Phil. thesis, Oxford University, 1981, p. 145. I am very grateful to Marguerite Dupree for permission to quote from her thesis before its publication.

34   Dupree, 1981, p. 144.

35   Scriven, 1975, p. 118.

36   Dupree, 1981, p. 336.

37   Ibid.

38   Quoted in Dupree, 1981, p. 338.

39   Whipp, 1979, p. 27.

40   Whipp, 1979, pp. 24-6.

41   Burchill and Ross, 1977, p. 176.

42 Burchill and Ross, 1977, p. 211.
43 See, for example, A. Coote and P. Kellner, *Hear This, Brother: Women Workers and Union Power*, 1980; and H. Land, 'The family wage', in M. Evans (ed.), *The Woman Question*, 1982.
44 Dupree, 1981, p. 338.
45 Burchill and Ross, 1977, p. 148.
46 Charles Shaw, *When I Was a Child*, 1980, chapter 8 (first published in 1903).
47 Burchill and Ross, 1977, p. 154.
48 Burchill and Ross, 1977, p. 166.
49 Burchill and Ross, 1977, pp. 224–5.

CHAPTER 3

Small Cottages, Large Families and Small Means

'Cottages', the brick terrace houses with two rooms upstairs, two down and a back kitchen and back yard, line the old streets of the city. The view is always changing, the road winding up or down, so that a collection of factories or a slag heap, or some decaying industrial remains can divide street from street like separate villages. The local authority has been rehousing people for decades, and even now a terrace will be boarded up and suddenly disappear in a muddy wasteland of bulldozed bricks and little fires of broken timbers and window-frames. As a result, the city is ringed with council estates, and on the eastern side the hillsides are strung with the endless red-brick semis of Chell, Bentilee and Abbey Hulton. Beyond Longton, where most of the remaining potbanks are concentrated, an estate called the Meir has taken all the fields which the older women remember. Women who now live in council houses often have the worst tales to tell of the housing conditions of their youth, and those from big families the worst tales of overcrowding, lack of amenities and furnishings and sometimes lack of food. Interviewing took me both to the older terraces and to the newer parts of the city.

Mrs Box, who was born in 1904, lives in one of the old terraces leading up to the familiar vista of a grassed-over slag heap. She takes me into the next street to gaze into a marl-hole and the brickworks which hollowed it out. Down the road, a developer has 'modernized' a whole terrace, inserting ugly, too wide windows and featureless pea-green doors fit for an office suite. The big house of the original developer (some seventy years ago) has gone. A giant 'home improvement centre' dominates the distance, but in a street nearby a farrier is shoeing horses.

Mrs Box modernized her house in the past, perhaps in the 1930s or 1940s, putting stained glass and lead in the windows, and a door, high-waisted, with a letter-box and long vertical panels. Having climbed her two steps, I am in the front room admiring its square-armed three-piece suite and its glass-fronted cabinet full of china pieces given by friends. There are two pretty art deco tea-sets, and on the window-sill some delicately coloured vases and pickle dishes, which she herself made. Going through to the living-room, a coal-effect electric fire is burning, or at least the light is on; there are framed photographs of people in 1940s clothes. The kitchen and downstairs bathroom are tiled in the large tiles more fashionable in the shops a few years ago, and in the living-room there is a fine celadon-coloured fireplace surround, from the factory where Mrs Box worked for many years. The house is an unusual period piece; Mrs Box married late, and no children scrambled over the sofa, or wore out the carpet. Nothing needed to be changed, least of all the house, which husband and wife never outgrew.

At the other extreme is Mrs Gregory, born in 1915, and living comfortably with her husband and two of her grown-up children in a council house they are planning to buy. The kitchen has fitted units, a new tumble-drier – very different from the kitchens she has had in the past. She sits by a coal fire on a plastic pale-ochre three-piece suite – changed when I visited her again four years later. Brown-and-white flowered wallpaper cheers the walls, and she sits, ready for business, in her overall. On the wall are photographs of herself and her family dressed as if in a Western, the relics of a never-to-be-forgotten visit to her daughter in Canada. Mrs Gregory's present ease, the well-equipped kitchen, new decoration, ample chairs, warmth and holidays, the comfort of retirement, contrast strongly with the discomfort, hunger and overcrowding of her youth.

The women born before 1920 usually came from large families, unless their parents' marriage was marred by the death or serious illness of one of the spouses during the child-bearing period. These women were born before family limitation was common in working-class families. They often describe their mothers' continual child-bearing and frequent loss of children, and the overcrowding and poverty which were commonplace in the early part of the century.[1]

The mother of Grace Hewell (born in 1917) may serve as an example. She was a dairy-maid at a big house in the countryside near the Potteries. Married at 18, she had sixteen children and reared twelve, with a gap of about two years between each child; she lived to be 82. Her husband, who was a baker by trade, turned miner and then road-mender when there was no work to be had in the baking line. The problem of men's erratic employment, or long-term unemployment, recurs again and again in these accounts, and forms the bleak backcloth to their lives between the wars.[2]

Mrs Farrier (born in 1902) came from a household of fourteen. She described her mother thus:

> She worked as a lathe-treader . . . She did it from when I was a little girl, then of course, when the family grew, she gave it up for a while. And she used to tread the lathe for the things that they use in hospital laboratories, mortars and pestles. She did that kind of work, which was very, very heavy, and then she had a rest period because the family was growing . . . There was nine of us, and me mother took to two of her brother's children that were left orphans, that made eleven of them, and me granny, that made fourteen of us in one house, but we never seemed to get under one another's feet. . . . We lived in a terraced-type house with parlour,

living-room, back-kitchen. . . . We had two bedrooms, Mother and Father in one – oh yes, that was the holy of holies! – then there was me grandmother and us six girls in two beds, two big double beds . . . In one great big bedroom we had four beds. The lads were curtained off, and the girls and me grandmother were in another half.

The same story of children sharing beds, and beds filling all the available space, is repeated again and again. Sometimes it sounds quite cosy, as when Mr Hilditch (born in 1901) describes his two-up-and-two-down home: 'We used to be four or five in a bed. We were like little animals all snuggled up together.' But one has to remember that it is not so cosy when one of the snugglers wets the bed; and as they got older, the cottage, however small, had to be adapted to provide the necessary respectable separation of boys and girls and the 'holy of holies'.

Grace Hewell describes her home: 'It was only a small cottage where we lived. The boys used to have one bedroom, the girls another, and my mum and dad had the front room turned into a bedroom.'

Mr Hilditch's mother was a 'skivvy', or housemaid, before she married her husband, who worked in a brickyard. Mr Hilditch is not quite sure how many children she had; she died having the last one when she was only 39 or 40, and 'she was having them as quick as rabbits'. Eight or nine were living at that time, but there were other children who died, and he is not sure how many.

Mrs Barnes (born in 1911) had a father who was killed in the First World War at the age of 28, but her mother married again and had thirteen children. Eight of them lived in a one-up-and-one-down cottage with no inside tap. Mrs Barnes pitied her mother:

> There was no tap – used to carry water from next door. I wouldn't like to go back to them days . . . She used to take other people's washing in. She never could [go to] work, she was either carrying a baby or suckling a baby or something all the time, because she had thirteen . . . All the women did in those days; there was no birth control. And men didn't consider them either. They were just chattels, I should imagine. None of the men that I know, anyway, considered their wives, because they were all having babies, and big families were born in those cottages . . . They reckoned they were safe if they were suckling a child, that they wouldn't be able to have another, but as soon as they'd finished suckling on the one, there'd be another one there. Used to have one every twelve months, sometimes . . . two years to twelve months. She lost two in the first few months, and then she had four miscarriages, but they were developed, you know, she could tell the sex of them. But a poor soul she was . . . Well, wasn't she? With children like that and no prospects, skimping from mouth to mouth all the time, and taking people's washing in for a few coppers. People don't know they're born today![3]

Death, whether it be of child or adult, was a common childhood experience.[4] Mrs Neale (born in 1911) lost her father when she was 15. He was an ovenman and suffered from chronic bronchitis, brought on, the family felt sure, by the flint used in bedding the saggars. Her mother had had eighteen children, losing all but the last five.[5] Mrs Bede's (born in 1908) mother, who was married to an engineman on a potbank, had ten children, but reared only four. Mrs Box (born in 1904) was the only child in her mother's family to survive. Her mother's other children died as babies: 'They used to have what they called little fits, you see, convulsions.' In fact, a number of problems attended Mrs Box's birth, and her mother was in hospital for three weeks. She lost twin boys seven years later. She had started work as a spoutmaker at the age of 12 when her father (Mrs Box's grandfather) had died, and she continued working for the same firm for fifty years. Mrs Box's father was a biscuit placer.

Mrs Box mentioned the problems of paying for her mother's ill health and Mrs Champion (born in 1916) also talked of the financial burden of ill health: 'Of course they didn't know anything about hypertension and blood pressure in those days, and of course she had to pay for the doctor, and it just went on and on, and she had a stroke at 27 which took her right side.'

Mrs Champion's mother had been a gilder and her husband a farrier, until he too became unemployed in 1922. Their family was atypically small, no doubt because of her mother's chronic ill health, but they too were poor. Mrs Mason's (born in 1903) natal family of two daughters was small because her parents had married late, in their thirties, but here again childhood was remembered as 'very, very poor', even though her mother had worked as a spout-borer, working 'all the years' until her daughter started work. Mrs Mason's father, who worked in a marl-hole, used to have to be collected or intercepted from work on Saturdays, 'in case he went in the pub and spent his wages'.

To have an irresponsible father was an affliction for his family; to have a father out of work or in irregular work was a more common affliction; but to lose both father and mother (and thus any possible step-parents who might take on the responsibilities of the dead parents) was the worst fate of all. Mrs Parker (born in 1919) was only 4 or 5 when her mother died at the age of 36. She had had five daughters, and as Mrs Parker described it: 'She died over my youngest sister, and she had white leg and milk fever.' Shortly afterwards, their father, a miner, also died, at the age of 42. He had been gassed in the war, and Mrs Parker described his illness as 'a gas stomach . . . ulcers, and he couldn't keep his food down'. After their father's death, the daughters, only one of whom was old enough to work, had to look after each other. An aunt lived across the road, another one not far away, but they were basically on their own. Because they had no parents and one of them was already sickly, they had to take whatever work was going, however unhealthy it might be. As a result, she and one of her surviving sisters suffer from dust in their lungs.

Mrs Bentley (born in 1916) lost her 29-year-old mother when she was 3. Her father, who worked as an oddman on the bottle ovens, married another woman. She had two children after the age of 40, but was sickly and died at 50. Mrs Bentley's life was a constant reshuffling of who should look after her, where she should live, or where eat and where sleep. She had one brother and two half-brothers, and what had to be negotiated was not only some care for her, food and shelter, but also separate accommodation since she was the odd girl out. Three boys could share a room, but she had to go and lodge with an aunt. After her mother died, she, her elder brother and her father went to live with her

Figure 3. Looking after a younger brother in the 1920's.

father's mother, who looked after them. Her father then remarried, and her stepmother came to live with them. Her grandmother then died, and her stepmother had two children. Because there were only two bedrooms, Mrs Bentley was sent up to sleep at her stepmother's sister's house at night until she got married, but taking her meals at home, and doing a lot of the work at home.

Sleeping at a relation's house like this was not a rare situation; Mrs Goodrich (born in 1918) used to stay at her grandparents', who also minded the children during the day when father and mother were at work. Again, the explanation was that there were two brothers and only one sister, and that it was only a two-bedroomed house. The extended family had to be brought in to assist the nuclear family to reach the required minimum idea of decency, where money would not stretch to a higher rent and a bigger house. Where the first child was illegitimate, she was often entirely 'granny-reared'.[6]

Mrs Gregory (born in 1915) lived in some of the most cramped living conditions as a child, with hard-drinking, violent parents and little enough to eat. She was the eldest of six children, but knew that her mother had had more: 'Of course in those days it was nothing for a woman to have a baby and lose it.' Her mother had had triplets and twins, and a baby just over every year. But the death of infants was not all; her father died of pneumonia when he was 39; he had done six weeks' navvying for the council because he could get no work, and had come in 'wringing wet from head to toe'. Before and after his death, the family shared a cottage with another widow and her family. This woman, Mrs Crabtree, was like a second mother to Mrs Gregory as a child: her own mother treated her harshly, beating her with the buckle-end of the belt, but she could turn to Mrs Crabtree for comfort if she was ill or unhappy. Mrs Crabtree was a widow with five grown-up children, so there were thirteen people living in the little terrace house. The whole family of Mrs Gregory's parents and six children had the front bedroom, while Mrs Crabtree was able to separate the generations and the sexes in her own family, having the far back bedroom to herself, her boys in the back bedroom and her girls in the middle room. Everyone shared the downstairs living-room, but the parlour was kept sacrosanct: 'It was a parlour and it was kept as a parlour, yes, there was nice furniture in. If there was any weddings it was used, if there was any funerals it was used, or if anybody was courting, there was a fire put in on Sunday afternoon, you see.'

Mrs Gregory's mother, Sarah, continued in potbank work in spite of her continual pregnancies, because her husband could not get work. From Mrs Gregory's descriptions of her father, one can build up a picture of a man who would stay in bed until lunchtime, then go out to the pub, smartly dressed with a white knotted handkerchief and polished boots, who would play cards, gambling away the rent money and even (on one occasion) the furniture, who was having affairs with other women and who would knock his wife about when she was angry with him. There is never a note of criticism in these descriptions; but of the mother who, it will be remembered, was having a baby every year, working full-time on a potbank and sharing lodgings with twelve other people Mrs Gregory remarks: 'I think she made it hard on herself'. She apportions the blame to her mother because she did not put up with it all more patiently:

It was terrible to go back home and hear the quarrelling of me mother and father, and the fighting and that, and the way my father knocked my mother about. But, on looking back, for the things my mother said to my father, she shouldn't have said half she did. If she'd have just coaxed him along. Say, if he'd come in and had a drop too much to drink, Sunday, she'd fetch his dinner out of the oven, and he'd say, 'Come on, Sarah, sit by me. Now come on, get a fork and have a bit of my dinner with me.' Well, instead of my mother going sitting beside him and perhaps having a forkful of dinner off his plate, she'd throw something at him, or perhaps throw a jug of water on him or something like that: 'I'm not sitting with a drunken sod.' She liked a drink herself, don't get me wrong, but because my father had been out on his own – and I'm not saying perhaps he hadn't been out with other women, because probably he had, and it's not very nice, but I think if mother had been a little more lenient with him, he wouldn't have strayed from home . . . He didn't like my mother going out to work, but he didn't work, so somebody had got to earn some money somewhere.'

Mrs Gregory, like many of the other women born in the first two decades of the century, remembered the desperate effects of unemployment. She had vivid memories of the pawnshop, showing how precarious were the finances of these families, and how nothing was safe from being pawned or sold by their mothers.[7] Mrs Gregory, Mrs Farrier and Mrs Barnes tell the experiences of elder daughters in big families, who were growing up when the family was most in need and with most mouths to feed without wages coming in. Mrs Farrier (born in 1902) described her grandmother going to the pawnshop:

My grandmother used to go in style. Her used to put a clean white starched apron on and two bows at the back and a little neck-shawl on, and the parcel neatly tied under her shawl. She used to say, 'There's no disgrace in borrowing money off your own property: you're not taking anybody else's and you're not being dishonest.'

Every week, 'shoes, bedding, anything they could lay hands on' would be pawned to get food.

Adolescence would bring particularly sharp moments of grief, recalled in the loss of a particular favourite piece of clothing or shoes. Mrs Farrier described her own experience:

And when we grew up, you know, when we started growing up and we had new shoes, we dursen't take our eyes off them. We've hid them, we've hid them everywhere, but she's found 'em and they've gone. We've hidden them in the copper, put the lid on top, but she's found 'em and took 'em. 'Mother, where are me shoes?' 'I've borrowed them till Saturday' – we used to get paid Saturday – 'You shall have them back!' Then you'd sit and cry a bit, because you'd been [to] work with cardboard in bottom of your shoe. 'You shall have 'em back!' And we had 'em back if she had to make another bundle up for fetch 'em back.

Mrs Barnes's mother (with eight children in a one-up-and-one-down cottage and a husband out of work during the Depression) also used the pawnshop a great deal:

Anything that was pawnable used to go at our house. One Charity Sunday . . . I'd got ever such a nice suit – where it had come from I don't know; I think she'd bought it second-hand from somewhere – and she allowed me to wear it that day with a white blouse, and I thought I was Lady Docker . . . I wore it in the morning, and I wore it on stage at the dinner-time, and I wore it again at night-time . . . and oh! I was as proud as a peacock! Put it in the drawer, never thought about it again until the following Sunday, when I came to go to chapel.

'Mum, where's me costume?'

'Whose costume?'

I said, 'The costume I wore last week, that one as you bought me.'

'Didna buy it for you.'

'Well, where is it?'

'Didna buy it for you.' It'd gone to pawnshop, hadn't it? It never come out again. Only wore it one day. Those were the days!

Mrs Barnes also mentioned forms of saving, the 'maxims', clubs and 'diddledums' which enabled them to save for sheets, pillow-cases and blankets:

They used to draw chances, run for twenty weeks . . . 1s a week. You could buy a pair of blankets for £1 then. And they'd draw the chance, and whatever week it fell on, whatever chance it was, it was their chance that week – one to twenty – if you drew a one, you had it the first week; if you drew twenty, you had it on the last week. And as soon as they got them, you never saw them on the beds: they'd draw the chance, they'd go in the pawnshop, or they'd sell them to somebody else for so much.

There were clubs for everything: 'You'd go in a club for have your hair permed and go in for have a photograph taken.' In 'tin clubs,' you took it in turns to be able to buy things for the house from a shop. In 'diddledums,' you saved by paying in twice as much every week, from tuppence to fourpence to eightpence and so on, until at the end it was all given back except for a discount for saving the money for you.

Mrs Mason, Mrs Powell and Mrs Box also discussed the ever-needed pawnshop. Again it took the best clothes from Monday to Saturday, without the husband's knowledge. Mrs Mason remembered a woman who would charge people sixpence for taking their parcels to the pawnshop: 'They'd take neighbours', put 'em in a clothes-basket and take 'em . . . Good money that was! Mouldrunning for pawnshop!'

Mrs Madeley (born in 1898) emphasized that it was the married woman's job to deal with money, even during the pit strikes of the 1920s: 'You'd got to pay your way whether you worked or not, and my ring had to come off and go to pawnshop because I couldn't pay my rent.'

The pawnshop could involve some ingenious ways of making money. Mrs Gregory's mother took in washing; she washed the towels for the factory across the way. But having washed, dried and ironed them as quickly as possible, they too went in the pawnshop until Saturday.

Mrs Gregory and Mrs Bentley both characterized their parents as feckless and hard drinkers. The difference, said Mrs Bentley, between herself and the old people was in paying for things. She and her husband only had what they could afford, while the old people sent you to the door to tell the rentman you would pay double next time – but next time never came. Similarly, Mrs Madeley (born in 1898), almost a generation older, described her mother as 'brought down by drink'; she, like Mrs Gregory's mother, was widowed with a big brood of children, and they were very poor. Mrs Madeley had to earn well for her mother from the age of 13, and like Mrs Bentley started her married life with nothing. In fact, she started in debt, or with her bed 'in trust' and her ring and clothes 'on the never'.

Mrs Gregory was equally poor. She used to be given clothes by a girl who lived across the road: 'As a matter of fact I got married in a dress that she gave to me. And my mother, when I got married, would not let me take a pair of underpants with me: I went as I stood up. And my mother sold everything of mine or gave it away.'

Here we enter on the diversity of relationships between mothers and daughters, and the importance of that link in a young woman's life. Mrs Gregory's mother was not a selfless widow, devoted to her children at the expense of her own life; she foisted the responsibility for her children on to her eldest daughter, making her look after them when she was needed, instead of going to school, or having her help with the washing, mangling and ironing. Later, after the age of 14, when she was going to work, she would find her mother at home at lunchtime, sleeping off drink; and in the evening she would find a loaf of bread and a note: 'Fetch two penn'orth of chips between you.' She would have to carry this out, fetch two pennyworth of chips between the five children, feed them and see that they were clean before bed. She, in effect, had to do the mothering, which Mrs Crabtree had done when they all lived together. Her mother's reliance on her daughter was not only in services, but in money, and Mrs Gregory had to continue giving her part of her wages, even after she was married: 'She wasn't annoyed at me getting married, she was annoyed at me taking money out of the house, because she could spend! We hadn't a lot, but what we'd got she really went through, you know.'

Mrs Gregory's mother was the extreme case of the mother insisting on the child's debt to her family and to herself as its manager. Other women told me good-humouredly that they had had no joy from their children, because as soon as they had left school they had gone away to college or into the army and then got married. Children's wages brought a brief period of affluence in a couple's life, some recompense for the years of work and scraping along to raise a family. When the family was young, however, mother, father and children were all involved in providing whatever money or services they could to improve the family's situation. Mrs Gregory resented her chores as a child:

> I used to have to go home from school at dinner-time and take my grandad's dinner to the factory, and then come home, have me own dinner and go to school. Fetch a quarter of coal in and go back to school, you know. Kids were a drudge. The oldest child was a drudge in those days.

Certain things were almost 'stock' memories, such as daughters taking their father's dinner to him at work. Others which recurred amid laughter and agreement were references to the pawnshop (especially pawning a father's suit, or his shoes, and putting a brick in the shoe-box instead), the warmed brick in the bed instead of the hot water bottle, the tin bath before the fire on Saturday nights, the coveys of children in bed, some at the top and some at the bottom, and chores like scrubbing the bare wooden floors, in the days before they could afford lino, or the endless day-long chore of washing with dolly tub and dolly peg and the huge mangle. Everyone knows and shares these as a stereotype of the way things were, but of course individual experience varied, and families were not equally well or badly off.

The daughters who were drudges have no fond memories of their mothers. Mrs Bentley, who refers to her stepmother as her mother, remembers vividly a double exploitation, both financial and for her labour at home. She would give her mother her wages, and also go cleaning for her mother's sister, giving her mother the sixpence which she received for that, but she also looked after the younger children (her half-brothers) and did the family washing after work and all the cleaning. Her mother did not want her to get married:

> I was afraid of getting married because of leaving me mother. I'd a good hiding day before I got married, you know. On the Friday as I was getting married on the Saturday, and I cleaned all up and everything, and she suddenly started throwing tins of peas and things at me – I was bruised to death, wasn't I? But I think it was because I mean I'd always done the cleaning and the washing and the kids, you know.

Mrs Bentley was 23 when she got married and had been courting several years; she was not a child, but as a child she had missed school to look after her younger brothers, and work had not emancipated her from her responsibilities, only increased them. Marriage was an unwelcome interruption in all this, as far as her stepmother was concerned. It is perhaps not surprising that some daughters who had been drudges were pregnant when they got married: only thus could they be sure of being able to leave home.

At the opposite end of the spectrum, Mrs Bede (born in 1908), a younger child in a family of four, remembers that she never had to do anything at home. Her father was in regular work as a boilerman on a successful and famous potbank. She remembers plenty of pretty clothes as a child and toys – a big doll and a pedal-scooter bought for her by a working elder brother.

Her mother did not go out to work, but she bore ten children (rearing only four). Mrs Bede said: 'They never went out in them days . . . Mother was always at home.' Hers is a much more comfortable childhood, although she described her family as 'just ordinary'. Mrs Bentley, at the opposite extreme, in a family with coats rather than bedclothes on the bed and cardboard in her shoes, also emphasized that 'We weren't on our own. There was other people exactly the same.'

Grace Hewell (born in 1917), whose mother had sixteen children and reared twelve, had a father who found difficulty in getting work in his trade as a baker. Grace's experience, in spite of the big family and unemployment at home, is not of exploitation, but of continual mutual services between herself and her mother throughout her life. She was not kept at home to look after the younger children (she was the second eldest daughter), but she was expected, as were the others, to do jobs after school: 'We always had to go to school, and you had your jobs when we came home . . . Lots of jobs, I seemed to be helping with washing, mangling, ironing and – even when I was 17.' She also gave her wages to her mother until she was married. During the Second World War, she used to take her children to go and eat with her mother, and she and her mother took it in turns to mind the children (her own and her mother's) while one of them went out to work. She too paid her mother for minding them, and worked a full day to be able to do so.

Grace Hewell is at the end of our period, married during the Second World War. Mrs Farrier, born at the beginning (1902), had the same kind of relationship with her mother, who also reared a big family and minded her daughter's children. Mrs Farrier remembered their chores as children: 'We had to get on our hands and knees and scrub the floors – no wall-to-wall carpeting then – and we had some rush mats, and they used to look very clean.' She, like Mrs Hewell, talked of a very happy childhood in spite of the chores, which included washing bottles for the ginger beer which her mother had fermenting in the parlour:

> None of us could do anything until we'd washed all those bottles clean, no matter where you wanted to go, or what you did. 'When you've washed the bottles you can go. And the longer you jibbed about it, the less time you had to go where you wanted to go.' Very strict with us, very strict, but we didn't have [an] unhappy childhood, we had a good happy childhood, I'll say that.

Material circumstances – which included the extent of family support given by husband, parents, brothers, sisters and children – as well as individual character, determined how well a woman managed to cope with her children and her financial responsibilities. Some of the mothers of women born between 1900 and 1920 went out to work, particularly if they had a small family or no man's wage coming in. Others, like the mothers of Mrs Barnes, Mrs Madeley and Mrs Gregory (who were all widowed young, though men's unemployment, not their death, was the problem), took in washing. So did Mrs Powell (born in 1898), who lost her mother when she was 12. 'I washed when I was 13 . . . I used to do a basketful for half a crown, take washing in . . . washing and ironing for half a crown.'

Other mothers sold things. Mrs Box's grandmother took in washing, but also baked and made ginger beer and toffee. Mrs Mason's mother-in-law and Mrs Madeley's mother made oatcakes. Mrs Farrier's mother used to do a roaring trade selling ginger beer. Many mothers earned a little money minding children for five or six shillings a week; it was not expected that people would do it for nothing, even for their own daughters – everyone had to use their time to make a living. Some women (in the grandmother, mother and daughter generations) went out cleaning. One, in later years, worked as a cook, others in an electrical factory, or as machinists, the rest on potbanks. If a man was fit but unemployed, he too might sometimes add to the family's fortunes: Mrs Barnes's father used to shoot, bartering game for butcher's meat, and the whole family was involved in making and mending nets to catch rabbits. But more often the unemployed men are shadowy figures, making themselves useful at home, sometimes taking the children out, sometimes cooking, often walking about trying to find work, or fetching their dole.

The other source of income in which the whole family might be involved was coal-picking. Many people told me that they had gone coal-picking during the miners' strikes in the 1920s. They picked outcrop coal, sometimes guarding their spot for fear someone else would have their coal, and taking their dinner to whoever was guarding it. Mrs Madeley borrowed a donkey to cart her coal through the streets, while her husband did the digging in 1926, but she has a photograph of herself coal-picking, as a girl, in the 1912 strike. These recollections, like those of soup dished out at public houses, are memories of the hardest times.

The oldest people seemed to recall some of the worst experiences, and indeed Mrs Roper's father, Mr Hilditch, (born in 1901), could remember standing outside potbanks as a child, begging for food:

> There used to be a gang of us. There used to be one chap, he used to bring cake every Friday, and he always gave it to different ones . . . but we always used to share it out . . . quite a crowd. There was no disgrace in it then, because it was a natural thing to do.

Mrs Farrier (born in 1902) mentioned several times her grandmother's stories of the days when they were 'lighting candles for warm their hands', but her own memories of the later inter-war period are stark and vivid. They throw into relief the inhumanity of the treatment of the unemployed, and also the pitiful housing conditions in which a young family was obliged to live:

> Half the time he wasn't working, see. Unemployment was vile, those days. Sometimes we'd both be on the dole together. I'd meet him going – I'd be coming back and meet him going, and sometimes, if me benefit was running out, I'd come home crying, I'd no money.
> [Can you remember what you used to get for benefit?]
> I did, by God – 12s 6d a week . . . During the 1930s, 12s 6d . . . And the men used to have 15s, and half a crown [2s 6d] for each child – and I had five! They were lads, 12 and 13 – could eat their heads off! Half a crown! . . . We had about 38s between us for seven of us. That was it, 38s. And then there might be some as don't remember this, and they say it won't happen again, but the government even reduced that; they took some of that off us. It came from 15s to 12s 6d.
> [That was very hard.]
> Hard? It was cruel! And there'd be thousands of people outside the dole, standing in the snow and – this is no lie – queueing to get in and sign your name. It used to be a day's work go up that dole. It used to be a big queue of men up one side and a huge queue about a mile long, all down that lane, where the dole is at Longton. They'd all be queueing down there. They say it's bad enough now, but those days it was wicked. Your feet and legs would be soaking wet – no wonder me legs are like they are.

Mrs Farrier started her married life living in the parlour of her mother's house. By the time she had three children, she had gone into lodgings in part of a neighbour's house. She moved next to a flat over a dairy, and finally had to move into the garage under the house, because the landlord needed the space. She divided the garage into two rooms with a long curtain made of fourteen yards of red serge, and they kept warm with a fire; it had once been a bakehouse. Nobody wanted them, but they had nowhere to go:

We had Lady Cynthia Moseley – now that's going back a bit, isn't it? – Lady Cynthia Moseley and Mrs Copeland . . . at them times, before our council houses were finished, there was a big piece of spare ground in Fenton. People were living in pigeon-cotes, old caravans, sheds, hen-cotes, everywhere, because there was no houses. So she came once . . . And she came inside. She said: 'Oh, my goodness!' And I never forget, I started crying, else I never, never broke down or anything – life was too tough, you were hardened to it. And I never forget Lady Cynthia Moseley saying, 'Well, never mind, my dear, your baby's beautiful and clean,' she says, 'and at least . . . you've made it look like a home.'

[Why did she come?]

They were slumming it, weren't they! They didn't do anything to help us. They could only report. And then there came a sanitary man, because we had to share a lavatory, or go round the street and share a lavatory with about six or seven more that lived in two little cottages. And oftener than not, we'd just have cut across a corner and gone me mother's for use her toilet. And that's how it went on.

Mrs Farrier is not unusual in describing how wonderful it was to get her first council house in 1930, with running hot and cold water.[8] Other people, like Mrs Hewell, remarked on the electricity in these new houses, which again made life seem so easy and convenient: 'We'd got no light upstairs. The downstairs we had lamps, oil lamps. Of course when we went up the Meir and we'd got electric, we thought we were in heaven. Just switch on, you know.'

The terrace houses often had a lavatory across the backyard, and many of them had no running water. They would be emptied at night-time, sometimes all the excrement having to be carried through the house to the waiting cart. Mrs Barnes and Mrs Powell came from areas where this was the norm, but Mrs Mason remembered a better system at her home: 'We were posh, we had a chain!' But still the lavatory was down the yard. Mrs Dove (born in 1902) recalled the early days:

I can remember when there wasn't water toilets, you know . . . They used to come and empty them . . . night-soil men. Yes, they'd come and empty them. Well, I lived in a cottage across L—, and they'd got those then. And they nearly always came when you were having your breakfast as well. I used to call it sweet violets when they used to come . . . It was like a metal tank, I think, [pulled by] horses in those days.

Recalling this aspect of living conditions experienced by women who were born in the first two decades of this century is not merely anecdotal. We began by looking at childhoods remembered in large families, or at women who bore many children and who were accustomed to losing them. At the turn of the century, the record of one of the Potteries towns was unbeatably appalling for infant mortality, as J. Briggs's *History of Longton* (1982) pp. 74–75 makes clear:

In a number of years Longton headed the table of towns with the highest infant mortality in all England and Wales, reaching at the turn of the century the staggering figure of 327 per thousand, or only a shade better than a 1 in 3 survival prospect. Behind that figure lay poor sanitary systems, including even those of recent construction, inadequate diet, and uneducated mothers, ignorant of their children's needs.

Two factors have often been argued as crucial in accounting for figures like these in industrial areas: the first is appalling living conditions, especially the lack of sanitation, and the second is neglect on the part of working mothers. The latter, of course, was an often heard cry in Victorian England, which both required women to work as cheap labour in factories, and lamented their lack of maternal care. Briggs (1982), pp. 69–70, speaking of the establishment of Longton Cottage Hospital, describes two doctors who, in 1897, attributed the ill health of the borough to these different problems:

> [Dr Dawes said] that the remedy for ill health lay not so much with the hospital as with the inhabitants of Longton. There were still too many cesspools in the borough and there was need of a better system of flushing the borough sewers. Of the 819 deaths in the borough in that year 478 were of children under 5, including 320 children in the first year of life. Another Longton surgeon speaking in the same year declared 'the high death rate of infants would continue so long as mothers work on the pot banks and put their babies out to nurse at such a small charge . . . and are fed almost entirely on boiled bread and water, sago and biscuits, a poor substitute for milk and inadequate to sustain the lives of young babies'.

It is worth remembering that many of the mothers of women born in these two decades did not go out to work at all, while we have vivid accounts of women like Mrs Barnes's mother, who bore and lost children in the most overcrowded houses with no running water or sanitation.[9] Sometimes women worked just for a few months of the year, in between births; they did this because without their wages they could not keep the children who survived. Mrs Gregory's mother's pattern was of this kind. Mrs Farrier, in the 1920s, also worked when she was pregnant, and it was heavy work at that time:

> You see, when we'd done our ware, we hadn't finished with it. When it was put on those boards . . . we used to have to carry that to the placers to put in the oven. And if they'd shot a load of coal up in the middle of the [pot] bank, you used [to] have [to] balance your board on your shoulder and climb over that. And we used to laugh and joke about it. I'd be pregnant, as big as I could be, carrying a board up there. 'I'm carrying one mountain and a man over another,' I'd say, 'Here we go!' And some of the placers would take pity on me . . . and they'd come and take it off me shoulders.[10]

Mrs Farrier would work until the eighth month, and go back to work when her baby was a month old. Her brother used to bring her baby up to the potbank where she worked, 'And I could sit private round the corner and breast-feed him. He used to say, "Milko! Feeding time!" ' Obviously, she was not making do with bread and water laced with an opiate, as many Victorian working mothers are said to have done before her.[11]

Mrs Farrier may have been an unusually caring mother; my research cannot answer the question as to whether women were sufficiently 'ignorant of their children's needs' in the Potteries towns to cause the high infant mortality rate at the turn of the century. What is clear is that slum clearance in this district revolutionized the lives of women in the 1930s and after. Just keeping clean – people, clothes and houses – was an almost impossible task in a smoky city full of bottle ovens.

Keeping miners clean in the days before colliery showers was a well-remembered nightmare, even for Mrs Mason, whose first husband was killed in the pit:

> They used to come home in all their dirt just like a chimney-sweep. And then their underpants . . . we used to have to wash them – used to be terrible. But just before he was killed . . . they'd just opened new baths where he worked at Sneyd Colliery . . . showers – you've seen 'em on television, haven't you? . . . So that relieved us a bit. But oh, when they used to come home in all the pit dirt, oh, sweaty underpants, dirty, you know, with coal dust! Terrible!

The importance of achieving cleanliness in houses where every drop of hot water had to be heated on the fire is not to be underestimated. Mrs Farrier spoke repeatedly of how clean her mother kept the house, going through it scrupulously every Saturday. Mrs Box's and Mrs Mason's mothers had strict routines of housework, involving their daughters, who all had their jobs to do. Their daughters still kept to some of the rules – Mrs Mason, for example: 'We worked in rotation. My mother used to wash on a Monday, same as I do now; I keep to me mother's rules . . . And I iron Tuesday morning, then I've got the rest of the week to do what I want.' Mrs Box also had her chores after school:

> Used to have to have the table set and a fire going for when our mother come in from work in those days. We always had to clean, do something I mean, so much work every night. Used to get up early, six o'clock and wash . . . We used to wash on a Monday, finish it off, bedrooms Tuesday, parlour Thursday, and then all the kitchen on a Friday, and your back road at back, because you had to do your shopping a bit on a Saturday afternoon. Then you had a bath on the hearth in a little tin bath.

Arguably these routines were a methodical way of struggling against very difficult odds. The relationship between dirt and disease was, then as now, imperfectly known, but women who went out to work had little enough time to keep up with the effects of city grime. Equally, parlour-polishing and grate black-leading may have had more to do with competition between women and the attainment of high status within a community; the desire for approbation is the cultural imperative, and not the need for hygiene. But the two are melded together by Mrs Box in the sentence, 'I've always been brought up as cleanliness is next to godliness; you get a bit of both, you don't go wrong.' Mrs Box introduced it into the conversation at the first sign of criticism of these perpetuated routines, by Mrs Powell, who had rejected them on the grounds that 'I've come to this conclusion, duck, I'm more important than the house.'

Eighty years on, who are we to pass judgement on their standards of housekeeping? But in conclusion, one is bound to suspect that working mothers felt under some pressure to fulfill the ideals of housewifery which were mentioned in Chapter 2, the 'domestic duties' which were considered a woman's natural sphere. One must also conclude that before the advent of gas or electric kilns, women's responsibilities must have been onerous in the extreme, because of the all-pervading soot, even if they were lucky enough to have an indoor water supply and gas or electricity laid on. Mrs Bloore (born in 1909), comparing life in her youth with the present, commented again and again on how much harder it all was before. And in the Potteries hard work always means laborious, muscle-tiring, back-breaking work, such as the white-collar worker can scarcely imagine – especially the washing, which Mrs Bloore's mother would be doing all day long from eight o'clock in the morning until her daughter came home at five in the evening. No wonder, then, that children, and especially daughters, were brought in to take their share of the chores. Mrs Bloore and her brother, for instance, used to have to take it in turns to fetch coal from the wharf, to 'bring a half-hundredweight of coal up in a barrow'. Boys and girls, it seems, both had to make themselves useful, but older girls had the worst drudgery (which almost all informants recall spontaneously): the weekly wash.

Not all homes were spotless or hygienic. As a child, Mrs Gregory remembers the invasions of fleas, beetles and lice. Once a week, straw for packing would be delivered to the potbank across the street, and they would have to buy camphor balls for their beds, or be peppered with flea-bites. They were fortunate in her house, she said, if they drew a curtain and did not find a cockroach or a beetle on it. Headlice, too, were a problem which her grandmother, rather than her mother, would try to tackle. Mrs Gregory's mother, out at work and with her neglected brood of children licking bread and condensed milk for their dinner, would gladden the heart of those commentators who saw working mothers as feckless and ignorant. But the odds against her were enormous. She is at the opposite end, in the great diversity of housewives, from the households with small families and better accommodation, where cleanliness was more attainable.

If housing and amenities like an indoor water supply, a bathroom, gas and electricity improved, as the women born between 1900 and 1920 grew up and started to have families of their own, money continued to be a problem for many of them. Unemployment was very high in 1921 as a result of the miners' lock-out. At the end of 1932 unemployment in the pottery industry had reached 34.6 per cent, although a year later that figure had more than halved. Never-theless, the unemployment rate continued to be higher than the national aver-age for the rest of the 1930s. We have already mentioned poverty and the dole queue, but no description of living conditions would be complete without mention of the fight for dole or for benefit, which was part of many women's experience between the wars. This is the period which Mrs Farrier described after 1930 as the time when 'there was neither work, wages or anything, there was more meal-times than meals, if you can understand me'.

Mrs Mason could remember being put on short time, and taking her little son with her when she went to sign on for three days a week:

> And he broke his heart. He cried . . . Well, she was a tata [character], wasn't she?
> She said, 'Who does that child belong to?' I said, 'It's mine, why?' Her says,
> 'Well, when you come here, you come to sign on for work. If I've got a job for
> you, you're supposed to go to it.' And her stopped my dole.

Normally, Mrs Mason paid her mother 5s a week to look after her two children next door while she went out to work. She also remembered problems with sick-pay, in this case her mother's:

She was out on sick-pay, and what she used to do, [she'd] do her washing at night in case [the sick] visitor come. They used to come visit you them days . . . She came next day and visited mother. Her said, 'Let me look at your hands.' She said, 'You've been washing!' Stopped her pay! Stopped her pay! Oh, they were, they really were, wrong-uns.

Mrs Box described the same experience: 'If you were sick on the club, you could only have so much, but if you was to pick a shovel full of coal and put it on the fire, and the sick visitor come and visited you, your pay'd be stopped.'

Mrs Farrier's husband had been wounded in the First World War, and had a pension of 7s 6d a week during the 1920s, when they had two children:

And work got so bad then . . . And they wrote saying would he go for an examination . . . Well, it meant him losing work. Of course he didn't go, and . . . they took his pension off him. See, if he'd have gone there he'd have lost his job, because there was always somebody there waiting step in your shoes, see. He didn't go, and they took his pension off him.

Mr Hilditch also remembered the unemployment of the 1920s: 'From about 1922 to 1929 there was no work at all, none to do. That was when we had to walk from Burslem to Cheadle and back for unemployed . . . As we were walking up Victoria Road, people was throwing bread and cheese at us to help us on the road.'

Mrs Bede, who had had a comfortable childhood, was married to a salesman: 'He's sold everything – he's had to, poor devil, when the Depression was on!' She too went through hard times, but her priorities seem always to have been clothes rather than food: 'You know, when you're young, we starved up there – it was a bad time all round – walking along . . . dressed up to the nines, but we were starving, you know.' They had to live in furnished rooms, but if her husband did not sell anything, there was nothing to eat. She remembered that her husband used to be out all day waiting to sign his name for the dole, 'there was that many, you were all day getting in'. She dressed her baby in satin and lace, but fed her on Nestle's milk because she was too malnourished to breast-feed her: 'If you hadn't had good nourishment in you when you're having them, you can't, can you?' She was six stone.

Several women recalled the means test, which meant that a man would have his dole reduced if members of his family were working. Mrs Barnes remembered that her own and her sister's wages were counted, and their stepfather's dole was reduced accordingly. She describes a piteous situation:

He couldn't get a job. They used to have to go from place to place, to carry a little book, and they had to have the boss's signature on this book to prove that they were looking for work. Otherwise they didn't get [it], and it wasn't dole, it was means test.

Mrs Barnes's husband was also unemployed for seven years, and although she worked 'to help out', they were poor. She remembers it as 'hard times': 'I hope our children never go through what we had to go through – when we used to have to go to the market on a Saturday night just before closing, to get a cheap cut of beef or about six penn'orth of bits of meat to make a dinner. Those were the days.'

Mrs Box's father returned from a period of sickness to find that he and his team of placers had been fired; another, cheaper team had been taken on. When he signed on, he found that there was no money for him. His wife and daughter worked: 'And it worried him, because he was a conscientious man. You see he wanted work, but couldn't get it, and he . . . worried and worried, because my mother and I had got to keep him.' Shortly after this, he was found dead at the bottom of the stairs.

Jobs were constantly disappearing. Mrs Neale was courting her husband when the firm where he had done his apprenticeship closed down. Mrs Bentley's husband was repeatedly out of work when firms closed down.

Mrs Champion remembered that her father worked as a farrier until there was no work for him: 'I remember him finishing work, because that was when all the poverty started, all the trouble started, and he walked round and round and round for jobs, because there was no social security when his stamps ran out . . . you'd got nothing, you just got nothing.' He sustained an injury in his next job, and never really worked much after that, until during the war when, in spite of bronchitis, he was directed to a job which filled his lungs with dust. Eventually, he was invalided out, never to work again.

This catalogue of poverty, insecurity and suffering is enough to give some idea of the effects of the Depression on the families of women pottery-workers between the wars, and to show the background against which they went to work, brought up families and tried to manage their finances. Some, like Mrs Barnes, were brought up with just one ragged dress and clogs. Some shared their second-hand clothes with the pawnshop. Others, like Mrs Bede, would rather buy silk undies at sixpence a week out of their pocket-money than anything else. Some, like Mrs Madeley, would work all evening to be able to afford clothes. Differences in priorities and personalities are startling when people remember the pleasures and pains of sixty years ago. A woman like Mrs Madeley will remember a serge barrel skirt, a fox fur or yellow gloves worn before the First World War; a woman like Mrs Farrier will remember eating her supper alone in the parlour, a novel propped up against the sewing-machine, totally absorbed in the world of fiction. Mrs Gregory will remember the mangling which her mother would make her do, instead of reading a book. Mr Hilditch will remember the hunger which you just got used to, between Monday and Friday.

This chapter has concentrated on the difficulties, mainly material and economic, and the help, mainly familial, which the mothers of my informants, and my informants themselves, encountered during the first three decades of the century. Children will have appeared in this as both a curse and a blessing, and only in the case of Mrs Barnes's mother has the size of families been questioned. Those who commented on this subject suggest that they believed there was nothing much you could do about it. Mr Hilditch, for instance, philosophizing about the size of his mother's family, said: 'It's just one of those things that happen, isn't it?' Mrs Gregory, who came from a big family and had seven of her own, was candid about her ignorance:

I didn't know there was such a thing as contraception.
[Did you want to have a big family?]
Not really, but I didn't know how not to. I mean, my only thought was, if you don't have a family, you don't have your husband near you. I had no idea there was any way that you could prevent having a family. And I think some of the young people today are far wiser now than we were, they really are. We have never used any contraceptives. We had no idea what they were until perhaps this last ten years.[12]

Mrs Hewell, born two years later in 1917, had two children and consciously aimed at a small family in order to have a better standard of living. Her mother had reared twelve children. Mrs Hewell was still at work in 1981. She had originally gone back to work to replace worn-out towels and bedding; she and her husband now have a house of their own with a big garden, and take holidays in Llandudno and East Anglia. Her married children live within walking distance, and she looks after the grandchildren at weekends. Mrs Gregory still has two unmarried children living with her; they are trying to buy their council house, and seem very content. Some of her children have gone very far afield, but inevitably, enough children and grandchildren are near for her never to lack company. Other widows like Mrs Bentley, whose one daughter has gone away, would spend their evenings alone, were it not for the extended family: she cooks for her brother and his daughter, and she busies herself with fund-raising jumble sales and 'petticoat lanes'. In both cases, their children have moved to better their opportunities, but Mrs Gregory has the advantage now of children who have stuck to the Potteries and its limitations. The continuity of the industry has enabled families to keep together; but as we shall see in Chapter 4, it was the family, and in particular the authority and help of the mother in relation to her pottery-working daughter, which enabled women to serve the industry when they were needed.

Notes

1 In 1911 women in Stoke-on-Trent tended to marry earlier, to have more children, and fewer women were economically active than in a cotton town like Preston, where 45 per cent of the population were textile workers. In Preston 22.4 per cent of women aged 20 to 24 were married, 17.9 per cent of married women were occupied, and the marital fertility rate was 155.9 live births per 1000 women. In Stoke 31.8 per cent of women aged 20 to 24 were married, 12.5 per cent of married women were occupied, and the marital fertility rate was 203.2 (Diana Gittins, *Fair Sex, Family Size and Structure, 1900–39*, 1982). Marguerite Dupree, using the 1861 Census enumerators' books for Stoke-on-Trent, describes a mid-nineteenth-century pattern of marriage on average a year younger than in the country as a whole, relatively high birth and illegitimacy ratios and high death rates, with people marrying spouses of similar ages and often from the same neighbourhood (Dupree, *Family structure in the Staffordshire potteries, 1840–1900s*, 1981). Early marriage and high birth and death rates persisted into the twentieth century. In 1900 the birth rate in Stoke was 39.1 per 1,000, and the death rate was 25.3 per 1,000. The birth rate declined steadily through the 1920s and 1930s. In 1930 it had fallen to 19.9, in 1940 to 17, the same in 1950, to 15.5 in 1960 and in 1970 to 15.1 (City of Stoke-on-Trent, Annual Report of the Medical Officer of Health, 1930 and 1970). The birth rate for England

and Wales was 25.4 per 1,000 in 1920, 16.3 per 1,000 in 1930 and 14.6 in 1940. The two birth rates, local and national, were level-pegging at 15.6 in 1956, but as the national birth rate increased up to the mid-1960s the birth rate in Stoke-on-Trent did not keep pace, and even fell in the late 1960s.

2 In 1932, the *Pottery Gazette and Glass Trade Review* said that unemployment in North Staffordshire 'remained bad on the whole with much short-time working'. The proportion of insured workpeople unemployed was 25 per cent at 24 November l930, and 29.8 per cent at 23 November 1931.

3 In *Round about a Pound a Week*, 1979 (first published in 1913), Maud Pember Reeves also describes Lambeth women (about 1900 to 1913) nursing their babies for a year as 'a safeguard against pregnancy'. Undoubtedly this works, but with diminishing certainty as the months go by, and only with truly demand feeding, such as is rarely found except in the Third World today. Victorian and modern attitudes to the breasts – as seductive rather than nourishing – have led to the need to breast-feed in private as if attending to a slightly embarrassing bodily function.

4 In 1901 the death rate for Stoke-on-Trent was 20.9 per 1,000. In 1921 it was 14.8, and in 1931, 13.1. In England and Wales as a whole the death rate was 12.1 in 1921 (City of Stoke-on-Trent, *Annual Report of the Medical Officer of Health*, 1921). At the outbreak of the First World War almost 10 per cent of all deaths were from tuberculosis; the same was true in 1921, and a further fifth of all deaths were attributed to bronchitis and pneumonia. In Longton, where some of my pottery-workers lived or had lived, the mortality rate was even higher at 26.5 per 1,000 of the population in 1901. Life expectancy for anyone who survived his or her fifth birthday was an average of forty-six years (J.H.Y. Briggs, *A History of Longton*, 1982). Nationally, between 1901 and 1912 life expectancy at birth was 51.5 for men and 55.4 for women (Diana Gittins, *Fair Sex, Family Size and Structure, 1900–39*, 1982, p. 210).

5 In 1900 deaths under the age of one year per 1,000 live births stood at 159 in England and Wales. In Longton the figure was more than double this. The infant mortality rate was 207 per 1,000 for the whole of Stoke-on-Trent in 1900; in the 1920s it varied between 134 in 1921 and 87 in 1928; in 1930 it was 70, in 1940, 61, and in 1950, 43. In 1950 the Medical Officer of Health noted in his report that 'The infantile mortality rate has been more than halved since 1926.'

6 In 1920, 4.8 per cent of all births in Stoke-on-Trent were illegitimate, which was similar to urban Lancashire; in 1930, 4.22 per cent, and in 1940, 3.1 per cent (City of Stoke-on-Trent, *Annual Report of the Medical Officer of Heatlh*, 1920, 1930 and 1940).

7 It seems that families used them much more regularly in Stoke-on-Trent than in Elizabeth Roberts's Lancashire towns (Roberts, *A Woman's Place*, 1984). Melanie Tebbutt, in her study of pawnbroking and working-class credit, *Making Ends Meet*, 1983, describes the long history of pawnbroking among the working class in cities. She gives an account of a riot in August 1842 when 'a crowd of at least 2,000 surrounded the shops of three pawnbrokers in the Potteries, demanding to have their goods returned without payment'. Two of them obliged, but the third had his premises ransacked. Four men were transported afterwards for this offence (p. 28).

8 The city corporation's programme of slum clearance and house-building meant that in 1930, for instance, there were 327 new houses built by the corporation. In 1939 they built 515. In 1911 and 1921 there were 22 people to the acre in the city; in 1929, in the extended area of the city, there were only 13.18 people to the acre. The population was about 279,200 in 1930 (City of Stoke-on-Trent, *Annual Report of the Medical Officer of Health*, 1930).

9 The *Annual Report of the Medical Officer of Health* for 1921 notes that the rate for deaths from diarrhoea under two years per 1,000 births was 43.7 in Stoke-on-Trent in that year, and averaged only 19.3 in ninety-six large towns in England and Wales. In 1914, 1,150 privies and pail closets were converted into water closets. In the

following year the *Annual Report* for 1915 shows 190 deaths from diarrhoea and enteritis, a fall from 368 in 1914. In 1917 the figure declines to 67, and in 1939, to 16.

10 Margaret Llewelyn Davies, in *Maternity: Letters from Working Women*, 1978 (first published in 1915), wisely points out that the heaviness of domestic work should be emphasized as much as factory work in any discussion of the causes of infant mortality, and also the mother's poor nutrition (pp. 5–6). Mrs Farrier did not to my knowledge lose any of her children, while Mrs Gregory's mother, who also did potbank work, lost several, and so did Mrs Box's mother. All three worked in the more tiring clay end.

11 In *Life as We Have Known It*, 1977 (first published in 1931), Margaret Llewelyn Davies recounts the same pattern of baby-minding in 1931. Mrs Yearn's mother had to go and work in the mill, because her husband was laid off work in bad weather (this happened to husbands in the Potteries, who did outdoor work like labouring on building sites). The eldest daughter minded the children, but Mrs Yearn's job 'was to take the baby into the mill to be fed twice a day' (p. 102). Potteries seem to have varied a great deal as to whether they allowed children on to the factory; some still allowed them to accompany their mothers in the 1950s.

12 Margery Spring Rice, in *Working Class Wives*, 1981 (first published in 1939), remarked from her data on the health of 1,250 women for the Women's Health Inquiry Committee that 'contraceptive advice seems practically non-existent' (p. 44). Roberts (1984) says, speaking of Preston women, that 'Nothing has emerged from the oral evidence to suggest that women weavers were noticeably more informed on sexual matters than other women' (p. 102), and 'There is little evidence that women discussed sexual topics in the mill.' In the potbanks, there seems to have been talk but little knowledge about contraception.

CHAPTER 4

Mothers and Daughters: Going Out to Work between the Wars

We've earned our corn, haven't we? You're entitled to have your bonnet on and go out (Mrs Powell).

The pots of the late 1920s and 1930s are some of the most lively, the most daring, the brightest and occasionally the silliest that Staffordshire ever produced. This was the age of teapots covered in crazy paving and sundials, of ceramic Snow Whites, of potted pixies and motor cars and of Laurel and Hardy transformed into cruets. It is also the period of fine art pottery, from William Moorcroft and Charlotte Rhead, for example, of the bold but (at that time) inexpensive patterns of Clarice Cliff's 'Bizarre' ware, and Susie Cooper's more simply decorated, functional tea and coffee sets. It was a time when the potbanks vied with one another in new and daring ideas to keep themselves afloat. Many went under without the benefit of a flourishing American market, after the Wall Street Crash. As in the 1980s, there were cuts in wages, short time, job losses, but also a depth of poverty into which, as yet, the present-day unemployed have not sunk. In this chapter we shall look at work in the potteries between the wars. We shall see that here too the link between mothers and daughters was important, and we shall describe the work itself, as it was recalled, in terms of skill, companionship, style of management, wages, conditions and industrial diseases.

Among the women born between 1894 and 1910 only two were still working in 1981, a gilder, Mrs Bloore (born in 1909), and a freelance modeller, Jessie Van Hallen (whose name I will not disguise, because she was too rare a phenomenon). Mrs Bloore had started work at 13, going into service for twelve months, because one could not work in a factory under the age of 14. Her mother had worked in a brickyard, trimming bricks, but had stayed at home when she married and became the mother of six children. Mrs Bloore's father and three of her brothers were colliers, whom she recalled coming back from the pit 'as black as night'. She could also remember hard times, queueing up for soup at a public house, picking outcrop coal during the miners' strike and her husband unemployed after the birth of her son.

She had started an apprenticeship as a gilder, and had had an allowance stopped out of her wages for her training until she was 21. It had actually taken her about six months to learn to gild. She had married at 21, sharing a big house with one of her brothers. After her son was born, she had gone back to work when the baby was six months old, and her mother had looked after him. Mrs Bloore used to take him down to her before work and fetch him in the evening. It was a kindness, but also a business arrangement: '[I] used to give her 6s a week; that was a lot of money. Still, you had to go out them days – there wasn't much work . . . so you had to plod along.'

When they moved to another area, the boy would go up to a neighbour after school, until she came home at night; she worked until five-thirty. She could remember the big iron gates of the factory being locked in the morning, so that you could not go in if you were late. The factory had been closed and taken over by the government during the Second World War. Sent by the dole to her present factory, a family firm, she had stayed there forty-one years. She did not want to stop now. 'It's just as nice to me now as then,' she said. 'I don't think you can have better bosses anywhere than X—'s.' She had also lived in her present council house for about forty years, and now had her son and his family next door. She had been widowed at 55, her husband dying of cancer; he had been a thrower.

Since Mrs Bloore had been in paid employment over a period of fifty-nine years, she was well placed to compare working conditions in the decorating end during that time, particularly in an independent firm which had not been taken over by one of the two biggest groups of potteries, Doulton's or Wedgwood's. Two aspects stood out in her description of the past: how much harder the work had been, heavier and more laborious, but also more skilled (she had learned to do skilled work which was not done today), and secondly, how much cleaner and better the factory was nowadays. She recalled that she used to do all her own fetching and carrying when she was young:

> We used to get ten dozen cups, ten times twelve in a basket of cups, and you carried them . . . No, it isn't as hard. Everything is more modern . . . now you've got a canteen, haven't you? Well, before, we had a stove-pot . . . you had to have a saucepan and boil all your water on that – light the stove-pot – and we'd got no electric. It was all gas with mantles, you see. Everything has been modernized . . . Toilets, you've got six lovely toilets down there and wash-basins; you never had them. That's another thing. You had one old sink, and everybody used it . . . That's a new factory to me.

To Mrs Bloore, modernization and automation in the factory meant the end of back-breaking labour – the end of kilnmen going into red-hot bottle ovens, shirtless and with a wet towel on their head, to check the firing, and the end of the old method of dry transfer printing which had been replaced by water-slide lithos:

> It used to be really hardwork . . . They used to get a cup, and they used to get size in a cup and a brush, a paintbrush, and they used have to paint all that with size, what they call sticky size . . . They'd do about ten dozen, then they had litho sheets, that you had to cut by hand, cut all round them and trim them. And then

you put your litho on that size, which is tacky and sticky, press it out, then you
used to rub it with a sponge, and then you used to get a soap sponge and soap it off
and wipe it. Now today, as you know, you just put that slide sheet in water . . .
Take it out, put it on and it's done – and yet there was all them processes years
ago . . . It's nicer today. It's not as hard work. I mean, they had to size it, stick it
on, rub it, soap it off . . . [It's] more easier today. Nicer prints, nicer colours.

Some people would not have agreed with her about that. The question as to
whether the ware is better as a product with the new methods is not so easy:
quicker and therefore cheaper, certainly; but some people said that the 'slide-
off' litho prints did not last so well on a cup or plate as a transfer print rubbed on
in the old way. Mrs Bloore's own job is one of the few which has not had the skill
taken out of it. Her husband's job as a thrower is almost obsolete in industrial
pottery. A jollying machine does the work almost everywhere except in one
part of the Wedgwood factory at Barlaston where prestigious ware is made;
Mrs Bloore was of the opinion that a jolly could not make ware as thin as a
thrower. Automation had reached her own department, and a young woman
worked fast and furiously and with a terrible clatter of plates on the automatic
plate-gilding machine, which disturbed the peace of the decorating department.

Jessie Van Hallen (born in 1902) was a freelance modeller, designing and
making figures, and in the 1930s she managed the figure-making and flower-
making departments at Sir George Wade's factory. Her life makes a striking
contrast with almost all the other pottery-workers to whom I spoke. She came
from a family of engravers, and was encouraged by her parents to go to Burslem
School of Art, and also to study figure drawing for a few months at West Ham
Polytechnic. Her father used to take the figures she had modelled with him
when he visited potbanks, selling engravings. He took her with him as well, and
thus got her started as a freelance modeller. Whereas Mrs Bloore began by
earning 6s (30p) a week, and 30s (£1.50) when she was fully trained, Jessie Van
Hallen was earning £5 ('a fortune in those days') for a model which might have
taken her only a few hours. She worked for various potteries including
Moorcroft and Coalport, and did an enormous amount of freelance work.
When she had married and had two children, Sir George Wade came and asked
her to be his modeller, so she got a nanny for her children and worked for him
for about ten years.

On this family firm, she recalled having a very good relationship with the
experienced women who worked for her as casters and figure-makers (at a firm
like Doulton's now, of course, the figure-makers are men). This sort of
personal relationship between manager and potter was something valued and
described to me by a number of older pottery-workers:

> I used to go round every day, every morning, and talk to them all . . . They were
> very nice girls, and they worked very well. And the women casters, they were older
> women, because they were experienced casters, you know, figure-casters – and I
> got on with them very well. And if I'd been away for a weekend, I had to come
> back and tell them all about it, and who I'd met, and what I'd done and so on, you
> know. We were very friendly. We got on very well together.

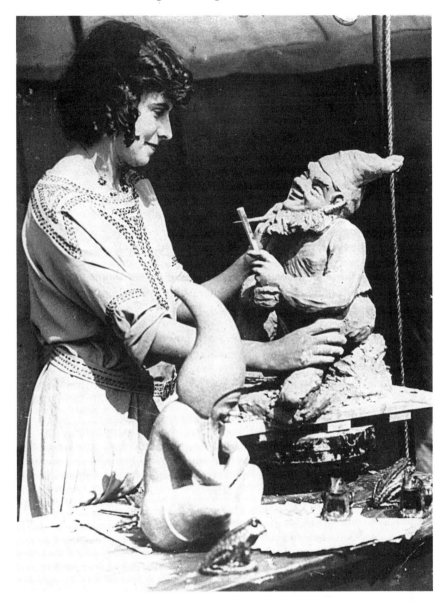

Figure 4. Jessie Van Hallen modelling garden ornaments at Southport flower show
(Kindly lent by Anthony Hallen)

Mrs Van Hallen had full responsibility for the figures, and would watch their progress as they were casted, stuck together, fired and painted:

> They were paid piece-work, a lot of them, and you got some that would, as you might say, try and get away with things. But when we made figures, I used to go into the figure clay-making department, and I used to look over every figure and sign it, so that if there was anything wrong with that figure after it had been fired, I was responsible for it. So if I saw anything wrong with a figure, I'd tell them to sponge that off, or take that off, or you haven't stuck this arm on right, and they'd just have to break it, you see, and not count it.

Like many others in the pottery industry (particularly decorators), she lost her job when the Second World War came, and potteries started producing for the war effort. She wept when she received the letter giving her three months' notice, but she continued to work for various potteries and to freelance, and indeed was still working at home when I met her.

Both these women had enjoyed their lives and enjoyed their work, and had no thoughts of retiring from using their skill. Both had had small families. Mrs Bloore had worked when her son was young, because men's work, including her husband's, was so erratic. She had depended on her mother to help her when her son was a baby, she and her brother had rented a house together when she was married, and her son was next door to help her, if necessary, in old age. The family had thus helped one another, and she and her husband had helped the pottery factories through the white water of the 1930s.

Mrs Van Hallen's family were also significant for her. Her father helped her to sell her first models, but would not let her go to a London college of art to study for several years. Her husband helped her: 'My husband has always been the sweetest man there is. Yes, he's lovely. And he just let me do my own thing.' She had a nanny for her children rather than family help, but her children remained around her in houses nearby, and maintained closeness across the three generations. When I visited, the grandchildren were in the garden, knocking tennis balls against the windows. In her relatively well-off family context, it was the father who had contacts and who was important; for most of the women working in the potteries between the wars, it was their mothers who had the contacts. The most usual way for a woman to start work was to leave school at 14 (or 13 before 1918) and for her mother or a female relative to 'speak for her' to get her on to a factory.

Most women had enjoyed school, whether they were good at it or not, but one or two had not been allowed to attend regularly. They had been kept at home to help their mothers, and 'it took the interest out of it'. Mrs Gregory's mother, for instance, with a big family, did not approve of her daughter wasting her time painting at school: 'You're not going, and that's it! I can find you something better than that to do!' She had said, referring to mangling or ironing. Mrs Hewell's mother, also with a large family, was also scornful when her daughter, at 16, had been singing at the 'dole school': 'I could have been singing over the ironing!' She was obliged to go to this government-run school when she was unemployed.

Most, but not all, went to school and remembered it happily. Mrs Barnes enjoyed school and did so well that her books were shown to the other children. Her grief was that she could not be put in for a scholarship, since her parents were too poor. She was too ragged in her one dress and clogs. Mrs Roper felt that poverty counted against her: 'We were made very much aware in my schools that we were poor; always nice and clean, but sometimes I had nice things, sometimes I didn't . . . I always felt that there was a lot of favouritism' Better-off ones were given more care, she thought. Several dismissed school rather briefly, saying that they had not been clever. Mrs Bloore (born in 1909) remembered the sexes being separated by a wall, and learning knitting and sewing, cookery and laundry, practical subjects, but not much in the way of arithmetic, essay writing or academic subjects, which she thought were much more difficult nowadays. Painting, in fact, was not an idle accomplishment as Mrs Gregory's mother seemed to think; it was the means to an elite occupation.

Mrs Bede (born in 1908), whose father had a job in one of the most famous factories, went to classes free for a year at Burslem School of Art, and then decided to take a job straight away as a paintress, although she could have had a further year at art school. Her father took her book of work up to his factory, and she was sent for to train as a freehand paintress. It is noteworthy that on this path to an élite training it was men who were the contacts to give her training at the art school and the factory.

A paintress who worked for A.E. Gray, a 'decorating bank' (a pottery which did not make ware, but decorated it with some of the most exciting hand-painted patterns produced in the 1920s and 1930s), described being picked out in the same way in 1931:

> I was taken on as apprentice freehand paintress . . . You were chosen to work there by the decorating manager, who went round the schools, asked for the children's painting-books and sketch-books . . . and he would examine your painting-books and then choose from what he saw, the apprentices, you see.

Although it was not unusual to become a paintress and to go to evening classes at the art school, it was unusual for a girl to become a modeller. Jessie Van Hallen described how a male modeller might quite often be a mouldmaker as well, working on the factory: 'And when I took things they'd sort of say to me, "Well, who's taught you to do all this? You're only a girl!" They didn't realize that I'd been at the college of art so long, and I'd learned so much beforehand.'

To have further full-time education like hers was very exceptional, and the only other woman pottery-worker whom I talked to who had not started work by the age of 14, was Mrs Dove (born in 1902). Her father had a bakery, while her mother, who had been a handle-maker, stayed at home after marriage and had two sons and a daughter. Mrs Dove left school at 13, but having a more finan-cially comfortable background, she learned shorthand and typing, before get-ting her first job in the office of a potbank at the age of 16, through a relation of her mother's. A mother's contacts, even in this case, were very important. The modeller and the two above-mentioned freehand paintresses were exceptions to the normal pattern of leaving school and starting work. For the majority,

Figure 5. Casting dolls heads c.1910 (from the Ernest Warrillow Collection at the University of Keele, by kind permission of the librarian)

Figure 6. The decorating shop c.1910 (from the Ernest Warrillow Collection at the University of Keele, by kind permission of the librarian)

unless their mother was already dead, or had long ago left the industry, the way to get a job was through the people one's mother knew in the industry. Mrs Farrier, you may recall, started to work for her mother, who made pudding-bowls, working as her assistant. Mrs Box first went on to the pottery where her mother worked, and made the ceramic tops for sterilized milk bottles, but she learned from her mother how to be a spoutmaker: 'Then an old lady that was a spoutmaker, she was too old and giving up, and the manager asked me mother why not take me and learn me, and if she learned me, I'd no need pay the fourpence in the shilling that we had to pay for learning.' This was an apprenticeship for press-moulding the spouts of teapots, before they went over to casting teapots.

Mrs Neale's experience indicates that the way of going into the printing department was the same. A neighbour, who was a printer, needed a paper-cutter:

> So he come up and asked me mother if I'd like go work with him. So when I come from school – I was on the verge of leaving, like – and me mother said, 'I've got you a job.'
>
> I said, 'Why? Where? What have you been doing?' like.
>
> She says, 'Mr Clarke has been up and wants to know if you'd like to go work with him, paper-cutting.'
>
> I said, 'I don't like that man.' I didn't.
>
> She says, 'Well, you're going whether you like him or not,' me mother said – because, like I said, we got no dad. 'Can't keep you on nothing' sort of thing, you know.
>
> Of course then I has to go. You know how mothers were, them days. You couldn't say you weren't going, you just got [to] go.

Mrs Barnes also got her job as a dipper's assistant through three aunts who spoke for her; they already worked on the factory. Mrs Gregory's mother found her daughter a job as a 'looker-over' in the greenhouse, which is the place where ware was put to dry before it was fired. Later, her mother got her a job as a mouldrunner for a woman she had known and worked with herself, warning her daughter that she would live to regret it, as it was such hard work.

Undoubtedly, the girls without mothers to help were at a particular disadvantage. Mrs Bentley's mother was dead, and her stepmother was a sickly woman who did not work in the industry. Mrs Bentley had to fend for herself, and go round the potbanks (this was about 1930) looking for a job. Mrs Hewell also had problems in 1931 (her mother had been a housemaid in the country); she wanted to be a paintress, but there were no jobs. Mrs Parker, whose mother and father had died when she was a child, also had to take whatever work was going, and went into dusty occupations.

The women who were born betwen 1921 and 1930 had very similar experiences of starting work. Mrs Furnivall (born in 1921) started as a gilder in 1934; a friend of her mother's, a 'warehouse lady', spoke for her, and she took her birth and leaving certificates to the decorating manager before she started her apprenticeship. Mrs Roper (born in 1923) had a mother who was a supervisor in the dipping house; she got her daughter a job there straight from school – there was no choice: 'My mother told me I'd got to go on (the pots), and it was the most money there . . . I just automatically went on.' Her mother needed the money, because her husband never had a lot of work, but Mrs Roper did not like working with her mother: 'I worked there two years. Mother, again, if ever I did anything wrong, she'd come up and give me a clout, so with that I thought it was best to get off.' She moved to another potbank, and became an aerographer, later a manager.

Mrs Atkins (born in 1923) first worked in a shop for a short while, but then was able to get a job at a print-works (making prints for pottery) through her sister. Mrs Adams (born in 1923) got a job straight from school, learning to be a caster. Her mother

> asked this lady if she'd take me on. She says, 'I'll give her a trial, a month,' you know how it is, so you've got to be a good girl for a month; you know . . . and she taught me . . . what she knew gradually. After about twelve months, you sort of go on a bench on your own . . . to earn your own wages, you know. I used to get about 10s 6d . . . She used to fill all the moulds with the slip . . . and I used to make the handles . . . she used to put on the jugs. I used to do the little bits of things and all the donkey-work as it were, fetch all the boards to put the work on . . . fetch clean buckets of water for her, and clean all, run about for her.

Mrs Havelock (born in 1924) also got her first job as a 'thimble-picker' through the female network, a friend of her mother's. (Thimble-picking was sorting out the little stilts which were placed between plates in the saggars when they were going to be fired in the bottle ovens.) She did not particularly like this job, but did it for fourteen years: 'I never bothered to look for another job because the lady that got me the job was a friend of me mother's.' Mrs Flowers (born in 1927) went to work in the white warehouse straight from school, 'Because my mother made me . . . and made me have a day wage job, because her said my money was there whether I worked or not.' She stayed there until she was 21. Mrs Caesar (born in 1927), who became a decorator in earthen-ware, got her first job through her friend's mother; she found out from the decorating manager that he wanted to take on some more girls as apprentices, and so the two girls started together. In 1941 her first wage was 17s, and she had to buy brushes and knives out of that, 'so that was my first week's wages spent'.

It is clear from all these accounts that being 'spoken for' was the normal way for a girl to get her first job between the wars, and that her mother was very frequently the person to place her, through her connections in the industry – unless the girl went into one of the élite decorating jobs as a freehand paintress. Sometimes these accounts also suggest that mothers were more than helpful, they were dominating; they made their daughters do the work that they chose for them.

Universally, all the girls gave their wages to their mothers and were given back 1s, or sometimes 2s pocket-money. The girls usually assumed that they must do as their mothers said; if their family was poor, then they had to go where good money was to be earned. Mrs Madeley, for instance, mentioned that she had had to leave a job, cup-handling, because she did not earn enough for her mother. Her mother, who had five children and a husband out of work, took the 10s a week that she earned from 7 a.m. to 6 p.m., lathe-treading, 'because we were poor', and Mrs Madeley then worked an extra four and a half hours (from 6.00 until 10.30 p.m.) for 2s 6d 'for buy me clothes.' This was during the First World War.

Mrs Bently, referring to the 1930s, said the same: 'You hadn't any choice, duck. We'd no choice because we'd got to go for the biggest penny in the pot'. Mrs Hewell also 'just took what there was' without any choice. At marriage, however, girls took on new responsibilities, whether or not they left home; and from the time that they were engaged they were usually allowed to pay board, that is to pay their mother a certain definite amount out of their wages, and to save for setting up a new home. The mothers, like Mrs Gregory's and Mrs Bentley's, who took their daughters' wages and gave them nothing to start off with, were quite exceptional.

For a girl leaving school, going to work on the pots was the most natural thing in the world. Frequently, girls had experience of potbanks as children. They would have gone on their mother's factory on a Saturday, when their mother was at work until midday, but also when there was no school. Some potbanks did not allow this in the 1930s, but children were going into some factories unofficially even in the 1950s.

Starting work, as we have seen, usually meant learning a skill, either formally as an apprentice for a number of years (as Mrs Bloore, Mrs Champion, Mrs Hewell and Mrs Bede did) or less formally in the clay end under an older woman, a maker or caster, for example, who taught her skill while the learner did lots of jobs for her. Mrs Farrier, Mrs Box, Mrs Gregory and Mrs Clarke learned this way. Money was deducted from the skilled woman's wages to pay for the young assistant. Learning this way in the clay end could be very hard work; the maker's assistant, the mouldrunner, had one of the hardest jobs in the factory. But an apprentice could also earn money running errands for the older, skilled women called journeywomen, and this could be an amusing and lucrative time. A girl who ran errands and did little jobs in the decorating shops was called the 'kale-girl' ('kale' means rubbish). Mrs Madeley, starting work before the First World War, could remember being sent out on fools' errands to get a kind of fat oil (which the paintresses used to mix with turpentine) which did not exist. The kale-girls were the babies of the workshop, there to have fun with and to do little jobs for the women on piece-work; they were on a day wage, and so lost no money when they went out to get people's breakfasts, chips from the chip shop or milk for their tea. Mrs Hewell (born in 1917) recalled this from her time as an apprentice paintress:

[You] used to hold your hand out and put a cup on each finger . . . Everybody wanted a ha'p'orth of milk, and you used to go to the gates, and there used to be a lady there with a horse and – well, a cart effort, you know. And these used to be about half full, these cups, for a ha'penny. Yes. And you used to fetch dinners and chips for them. We used to even have to fetch turps, take it in turn to fetch turpentine from Goods – you know how they bring it to the factories now – well, day-wage girls always fetched turps, prints and all that kind of thing, fat oil . . . Well, for quite a couple of month you do that, and you seem as if you're not learning anything much, you know, and then all of a sudden perhaps [you] have a new girl, and you 'go down', you see, sit at your bench. And there's none of this running round and looking round. You had to really keep eyes down, you know.

The journeywomen used to supplement the apprentices' 6s a week when they did these jobs. Mrs Champion described this on a decorating bank in 1930:

> You'd fill the urn every day, tea urn, water for the journeywomen to go and make their own pot of tea. Well, there wasn't regulations in those days for everybody to leave their bench and go in the canteen for food . . . And we used to clean a top of a trestle, wipe the chairs over and clean the lavatories once a week. And for that we went to every journeywoman in the factory, and they'd give us a penny in a cup, and it used to come to . . . 4s; there was two of you . . . so that made your wages up. So I used to take home 8s, which was a grand wage.

She gave them to her mother, of course, and had about 1s pocket-money.

Mrs Hewell described how, after about six months, they could tell whether you were going to be any good as a paintress, and they would put you on piece-work:

> And when I earned me own money, they took threepence out of every shilling I earned to pay them back for what they'd learned me. I mean, I only had 5s 9d a week . . . You paid that until you were 18; and then when you're 18, you only paid tuppence in the shilling. And then when you were 21, it was all your own money.

In the clay end, Mrs Farrier was apprenticed as a bowl-jollier, making bowls, but because of the shortage of labour (this was during the First World War) she did not have to pay for learning, as the paintresses did. The mould-runner, who assisted a bowl-jollier, had to run so hard during the course of a day, between the jollying machine and the 'stove' where she had to put the moulds containing the newly shaped bowls to dry, that her feet, and her footwear, would be worn out. Mrs Farrier:

> The woman I worked for was making, and I had to get the clay off, make it in a ball and throw it in these moulds as fast as ever I could, keep her going on her machine, see. And then you'd run, run, run with them – well, you went as fast as you could – into the stove, take them in and bring some more out with the cups in, empty 'em out, put 'em on a board ready for the sponger, see – and that's how it was all day over. By the time you'd finished, your feet were that sore you didn't even know where to put 'em . . . We hadn't used to work in our going-home shoes even if they had cardboard in: we used to wear 'trashers', any sort of old shoes, carry us through, like. And many's the time me and a friend as worked with me, we've got as far as the bridge in Stoke . . . and we've walked all the way up Stoke in our stockinged feet. By the time we'd got there, we've had . . . no feet in our stockings. So my grandmother used to sit, cut soles out of other stockings and make us a sole in a stocking again.

It must be said that not all the older journeywomen wanted to help the youngsters.[1] On one potbank where Jessie Van Hallen worked, the old ladies would hide their work when she came in, covering it with a cloth. Mrs Furnivall said that the paintresses would not show the apprentices how to do anything, and that you were left to 'grope your own way' at her factory. Mrs Bloore said how frightened she was as a kale-girl of the journeywomen, and did errands because 'you dursen't say no'. Mrs Gregory described how her missus tried to make her do twice the work of which a mouldrunner was normally capable. Mrs Adams said that your missus would perhaps give you threepence if you had behaved yourself all week (the firm paid the apprentice directly), but that sometimes the missus found a girl so useful that she did not want to lose her, and the girl might lose her chance of going on a bench of her own, instead of just being an assistant. These examples suggest that even though there was a network of contacts relying on kinship and friendship among women, it could not be counted on to blot out the self-interest of these older women, or a lack of sympathy for the young ones coming on. No doubt, as a woman got older and started to slow up, she might fear the skills of the young ones who would eventually replace her.

Although wages were very low in the 1930s, the wages and hours of work of women in the first decades of the century were worse still, and some could remember that their parents had worked as children, going to school for half a day and to work on the factories for half a day. Young people were the most exploited labour. Mrs Powell (born in 1894) worked at 13 from 7 a.m. to 6 p.m. in the transferring shop for 5s a week; Mrs Madeley (born in 1898) had 2s 6d a week as an apprentice cup-handler working the same hours, 7 until 6. Mrs Farrier's first wage as a mouldrunner was 5s 6d. Mrs Bloore (born in 1909) was better off, with 6s a week as a 14-year-old apprentice. Mrs Hewell and Mrs Goodrich (born in 1917 and 1918) started as apprentices with 5s 9d a week, as did Mrs Furnivall (born in 1921). When Mrs Roper (born in 1923) started work in 1937, the hours were from 8 until 5, with half an hour for dinner – there had been some small measure of improvement in hours and wages, but the real improvements in wages came after the Second World War, when the pottery industry was expanding and anxious to get labour.

People had to be very quick to earn a living on piece-work. Mrs Madeley (born in 1898) used to get tuppence, at the age of 15, for making twenty dozen handles. At 16, she went wheel-turning for a cup-maker, making 620 dozen cups for 10s a week. Mrs Box 'casted enough spouts to keep three handlers going, fifty times twenty-four every day'. She was paid tuppence for twenty-four spouts 'all good', that is ones that had been looked over and found to be faultless. Astronomical numbers of cups, handles and spouts trip off their tongues like auctioneers, after years of counting piece-work. Small pieces were counted as 'long dozens', that is at thirty-six to the dozen, so a board of three dozen cups would actually have a 108 cups on it, 'boxed' in pairs, rim to rim, ready to be fired.

In 1931 Mrs Bentley started work cutting off prints for tranferrers, and earned 7s 6d ($37\frac{1}{2}$p) a week; hoping to get more, she went casting and earned 9s a week. Her husband, the same age, began mouldrunning for funeral teapots (which could hold a lot of cups), and then worked for £1 a week for a woman who made teapot-lids, but the firm went broke. He worked for her sister on another firm, and the same thing happened. He then got a job as a saggar-maker's bottom knocker – making the bottoms of saggars – at 21s (£1.05p) per week, and in 1937 was a saggar-maker at 37s 6d a week. He then went down the pit, because there was no work on the pots.

Small wonder! Women working at the end of this period were earning from 10s 6d to 30s a week, while men were getting from 12s 6d (at 14 years of age) to 60s (at 25). Mrs Neale's wages in the warehouse were £1 a week, while Mrs Barnes, a trained and skilled dipper, still earned only 24s (£1.20p) for many years. Mrs Mason's full wage at 21 was 20s in the biscuit-warehouse, while Mrs Bloore's and Mrs Furnivall's wages as gilders were 30s (£1.50). Mrs Parker earned 22s (£6.10) as a skilled maker, having started at 4s 9d. Mrs Dove, for the privilege of working in the office, earned about 8s (40p) a week. It was inevitable that these and other women should get work in the pottery industry, while their husbands found jobs sometimes in the pit, sometimes in other trades and sometimes not at all. Only in certain very heavy jobs such as mouldmaking and oven work were men assured of their preserve in the pottery industry.

All agree that the work was very heavy for both sexes: Mrs Farrier used to carry clay in a wheelbarrow and, like everyone else, carried hundreds of boards on her shoulder – the six-foot wooden planks on which ware would be carried from one workshop to another about the factory. In the clay end, a woman might be carrying three dozen (108) cups on a board; another time she might be carrying seven chamberpots. Women like Mrs Havelock and Mrs Parker did all kinds of jobs on factories, and for Mrs Havelock this included drawing ovens, which meant taking the saggars full of ware which had been fired and emptying them. Mrs Roper's work in the 'glost' warehouse (where ware was put when it had been glazed and fired) also used to include emptying saggars. This was when she began work in 1937:

> We used to be there for eight o'clock, so we would get up about half-past six, just have a cereal and a cup of tea, and then go and catch the bus and go to work. You had to clock on, and when you put your card in, it has to say eight to . . . at them time it used to be five o'clock. And if you was a minute late, they used to count all these minutes up, and then take it off your money . . . You'd bought your own overalls . . . If you are in a dipping house – anywhere glaze is – they provide you with overalls. If you are in the clay department, they have to supply you with overalls, but in the glost warehouse, no, you bought your own . . . Two girls, myself and another one, we used to have to empty these great big round saggars of ware – pots and things like that – and we used to have to stack them on boards. Sometimes, because there was such a lot, you had to lift the saggars with the ware in, and put them on the floor. The worst of that job was it was very, very heavy. But apart from that, it got hotter and hotter, the ware did, so we used to have to wear these gloves, because the saggars were so hot, or the ware was so hot. Then you'd have your dinner, just half an hour, and you'd start work again, and you'd work then till five o'clock.

In the transferring shop, where there was a lot of hard work going on (sizing, sticking on prints, rubbing and washing off, you may remember), the problem was also the long hours. Both Mrs Neale and Mrs Bentley recalled having to stay late on Saturdays, Mrs Bentley as a cutter: 'On Saturday, when all the women had gone home, you'd got to scrub all their benches and sweep up. So, Saturday, instead of finishing at half-past twelve, it would be four o'clock before you'd sit at home.' Many of these girls in the various departments of the factories were sweeping, making fires, dusting for the manager, carrying heavy wads of clay or buckets of water, fetching food and drink and generally acting as servants when they started off. They were then cheap labour until they were 21 and, having then the right to a full wage, were a less desirable commodity. In 1931, more older women were unemployed.

Firms had their individual reputations. Mrs Parker (born in 1919) said that what mattered was the management:

> Some of the potbank owners like, some of the gaffers, they did look after the workers, and some of them didn't. Some of them just made you a rubbing rag. Some of them didn't care what you went through, or how ill you were, or anything, as long as they were getting work out of you. You see, it's all different now, it's all different.

Some people found their niche and stayed on a firm sometimes for as many as forty years, or very often for ten or twenty; others went from firm to firm trying to get more money, or unable to weather a storm of short time, which they could not afford. Smaller firms, or family firms, then as now, were liked for the fact that everyone knew everyone, and for a personal style of management. Mrs Furnivall much preferred her boss before the firm was eventually taken over: 'He'd come round every morning, and he'd know you by name, you know, and speak to you, like.' He also knew the work – these were bosses who knew the work from end to end through their experience on the factory, rather than from courses in management – and would not allow poor craftsmanship to go through: Mrs Furnivall was proud of the quality of work that came out of the factory. Working on another firm later, one of a group of factories, she was appalled at the way quality had been sacrificed to speed.

Mrs Neale, on the other hand, still working on a family firm at the age of 70, did not ever want to retire. 'No, no. I mean I'm happy at work. I've got some good workmates, you know, good work-friends. We have a joke, a cheeky joke mind you, or we have a laugh and a song.' She too valued the fact that the boss would come in and say good morning, that he would say how sorry he was if someone was bereaved and that 'If any of his workers have passed away, he always goes to the funeral. Always, always has done.'

Roberts (1984), in her study of Lancashire women between 1890 and 1940, is careful to question the idea of the deferential woman worker. She points out that instead of organizing to resist their employers, if they objected to working conditions, or had some other disagreement, they would take the individualistic line of a personal dispute or leaving their job and going somewhere else. In the potbanks it was similar: sometimes people moved because they had had a row with a manager. Only two of my respondents had been on strike, one in the second decade of the century, when she had just started work, and the other in the 1970s; mostly the union had avoided strikes, in spite of reductions in wages in the 1920s and again in the early 1930s. But many people believed, quite erroneously, that potters had never been on strike, and attributed this to the large number of women in the union. The women I spoke to, however, showed a keen appreciation of the difference between a good boss and a bad boss, fair treatment and exploitation. But they had been working at a time when firms were going bankrupt, factories were closing, and strikes against small employers, who were only just surviving, were not feasible. It is also worth remembering that workshops were separate worlds, not made to create solidarity: the clay end, the dipping house and the finishing end did not necessarily visit one another or mix at all.

The 'cheeky joke', a laugh and a song were very important: Mrs Box described how they used to sing 'When Day Is Done' at the end of the day in her workshop, Mrs Bede and Mrs Farrier used to sing for their workmates, and Mrs Gregory went from a relatively light job as a looker-over in the greenhouse to the rigours of mouldrunning, because of the fun they appeared to be having in the making shop: 'I could see all these other girls in this big room with these machines, with their arms going up and down, these mechanized things, and they were singing away, and I thought they were having a whale of a time!'

The jokes among the decorators included putting mice under the saucer with which a paintress would cover her colours over night. In the clay end, Mrs Madeley and her young workmates used to fill a saggar with water, drop a penny in it and try to get it out with their hands tied behind them. These must surely have been apprentice pranks, for a woman on piece-work had time to sing, but time for little else. Mrs Mason's boss was a hard taskmaster, who would lift up the women's long skirts with his stick to see whether they were hiding any work they had broken underneath – for which they would not get paid:

> As he got older he got a bit more calmer, see . . . He was one end of the warehouse and we were all singing, and he stood and listened to us. And he said – he clapped his hands – he says; 'Very good, very nice!' he says. 'I know you're working when you're singing!' He understood how singing and, later, *Music While You Work* could help the work along.

The personal style of management included works outings. Mrs Box still kept photographs of an outing to Alton Towers. For her, this was a treasured memory, a happy time: 'A lovely meal . . . nice gardens and everything to sit around and look at, and a little bit of the old-time dancing, you know, and things like that if you could do it, a little band to entertain you. He took us by bus and brought us back by bus.' There was also a photograph of Blackpool; seven bus-loads would go on the seaside outing once a year. The 'day out' was much more important between the wars; it was, after all, not until 1937 that pottery-workers received a week's holiday with pay. Before that, Wakes Week (the first week in August), the Potters' Holiday – a week without pay – would be a time when they were really pressed to make one week's money last for two. Mrs Mason could remember crying, not knowing how she would manage.

Among those who remembered 'real good bosses' was one of Sadler's workers, a man who had worked for this teapot-making firm before, during and for twenty years after the Second World War. This firm was 'like one big family', and like any good family it had its characters. The head of the firm was one of them:

> When I worked on Sadler's, the old man Sadler, he used to pick five or six of us, and then take us to Barlaston for do his garden, many a time. And he used to feed us, but there was always one thing about him: we used to find us own road [there] on the bus, but he always brought us back – but he always had us return ticket off us for the bus! He did! That's right! He used to come up my [work]shop and say, straight out like this: 'Got any tea, Alf?' I'd say 'What? Again?' He'd say, 'You're the only one as has tea, I'll tell you!' Then when he's having his cup of tea, he'd say, 'Got any matches?' He wouldn't buy any matches, and he was the head boss!

People preferred to know their bosses rather than to deal with personnel managers and the distant deities of multinational companies – but they were to come later. The easy-going privacy of firms in which the bosses ruled without the intrusion of health and safety legislation or of trade union power had its darker side. Mrs Parker told me that she would run from the union collector for fear of losing her job; some of the bosses were against their work-force joining a union; and to begin with, the union collected its dues from people at their homes and not on the shop-floor.[2] This was a matter of pennies – tuppence at first – on a Friday night.

Only some people belonged to a union, and even now, when everyone is obliged to join, attitudes to it varied among the older women. Mrs Farrier, who had always done very hard work as a bowl-jollier in the clay end, had no doubt as to its value: 'It would have been God help us if it hadn't been for the union. We were exploited then, but we'd have been exploited a damn sight worse.' Nevertheless, she felt that some of the union men had not served their interests: 'Some of the union men that were supposed to represent you would run with the fox and the hounds. They'd be in with the bosses, some of them would.' Mrs Bede, a paintress, could not remember the union on her firm when she was young; at any rate, she had not paid anything towards it. Mrs Neale recalled that her boss in the warehouse was against it. Mrs Barnes, the dipper, remembered that not many were in it when she was young, and that it took a long time to build. But she recalled some of the things which the union had got rid of: having to work overtime without pay or be given the sack, or being fined for leaving an unnecessary light burning.

The darkest aspect of work in the potteries between the wars was not in the relations between bosses and workers, in spite of pitifully low wages and under-employment. It was, undoubtedly, in the toll of sickness and death which was exacted from the workforce. A friendly potbank where the bosses were on first-name terms with everyone and where a family atmosphere reigned might at the same time be a killer workplace with cosy little corners full of dust, floors caked with dust, walls and ceilings coated with dust, just a bucket to wash your hands in and a comfortable little workshop for you to eat your sandwiches, with your nails full of dust, or colour, or glaze. This was not just true of the small potbanks, of course. Illness and death stalked the workforce of some of the grandest names as well as the little firms.

People remembered 'very dirty, grubby places'. Mr Hilditch, for example, was not alone in remarking on the beetles: 'Anywhere in a potbank in those days, you could get a guaranteed beetle race any time as soon as it got dark – thousands of beetles where they made clay by boiling slip.' He too praised the improvements in hygiene: 'They are more particular nowadays. You can't walk in a shop now and see it wet and dirty . . . there wasn't as many inspectors, and . . . these little, old-fashioned places didn't bother so much. But they are more up to date now, and it's a good job they are.'

The filth was not only in the workshops. Jo Tennant, who started work in 1930, described the view from Hartshill down to Stoke in those days: 'pitch black with smoke from the bottle ovens', like a 'dense fog' when you got into it, and behind the factories 'the banks of clay and slip, the slip that used to be all wet all over the ground and dry white', which used to blow on people's clothes and into their lungs.

People whose families desperately needed money were more likely to go into harmful jobs where the dangers to health were greatest. Mrs Bentley's husband died a year after my first visit; I remembered him well, sitting stiff and upright, his voice coming deep and exhausted, and his skin yellow with lack of oxygen, the invisible dust coating his lungs. His mother had been left a widow with five children, and he, as the eldest son, forever out seeking work in the early 1930s, had gone to work in a saggar-hole. This was a cellar where, in the dirt and dust, they made the big pottery containers in which the ware was fired. As the youngest one there, he had been put to 'grog-grinding', which was grinding up the old, cracked saggars and mixing them with marl to make new ones. There, in an atmosphere thick with the dry dust of pottery, this teenager's future of a slow, gasping death was settled. When I met him and his wife, they were trying to get him a better pension. Solicitors and doctors were asking questions about work and hygiene fifty years ago; Mrs Bentley, with more strength and more air in her lungs, was giving most of the answers.

Mrs Parker, whose parents had also died when she was young (her mother through child-bearing and her father through the long-term effects of being gassed in the First World War), also suffered from dust, and her sister too. She had done all kinds of jobs including packing in wood wool, a practice which is no longer permitted because of the lethal dust which rises from the fine wood shavings. Her sister had a pension because she suffered very badly from dust:

> She was a maker in the clay . . . The conditions were appalling them days . . . The floors were all covered with clay, dust, scrap bins everywhere . . . It was a very hard job, very hard job. And then you got dust working in the biscuit-warehouse, because it was flint off the ware, you see, when it came out of the oven, biscuit, in biscuit state. You see, later, they had fans and brushes . . . where in my days, when I was in the biscuit-warehouse, you brushed it off by hand with a brush yourself. There was no fan, so all the dust as you're brushing off the ware, you're getting down you . . . And then later on when the Factory

Act came out, they made them have these brushes and these fans at the back: there was an opening and it used to take all the dust that way . . . Before that, you used to sit down on a little stool, and brush the ware on your knee, with a pad on your knee, and brush it . . . with a little brush.[3]

Mrs Gregory described to me her work in the biscuit-warehouse in the 1950s, cleaning the ware in a drum, but without extractor fans:

And you were covered . . . [with] a white powder. We had to wear a hat, what they call a dust-cap, and a very thick cotton overall. And even then, your own clothes, they really were thick with dust. And your feet, your shoes . . . If you wore sandals, thinking you were giving your feet a bit of comfort, your stockings would get – it would be like walking on a dry beach . . . with stockings on.

Several of the older women who had worked in the clay were suffering from chronic bronchitis, or had serious breathing problems. People who had done fettling, scraping the rough edges off a pot with a sharp little knife, were vulnerable; here again, it was working with the pots before they were glazed that was dusty and dangerous.

Working with glaze in the dipping house was recognized as dangerous because of the lead content. Mrs Barnes (and later her daughter) used to have to drink a pint of milk before work every day; this was laced with Epsom salts to keep the bowels open. But on her factory neither she nor her boss took account of the possible danger of her working as a young girl in these conditions: 'I shouldn't have gone in the dipping house until I was 16, but I was rather big for me age, and I looked 16, and the boss said, "If ever anybody asks you how old you are, you tell them you're 16, and you can start Monday." '

It is this easy-going flouting of regulations, the breaking of rules in the family, which contributed to the warmth and the dangers, the kindness and the cruelty of the factories of this era. The girl could risk ruining her health in a dipping house, if she needed the money, just as mothers could bring their children into the dangerous environment of machines and dust and wet clay, if they could not afford a Saturday child-minder. The bosses, largely unfettered by inspectors or union officials, could turn a blind eye and do as they and their workers wished. Arguably, this was not paternalism but a kind of freedom; yet the freedom was, of course, based on their workers' desperate need for wages. Some of the older women, still working, seem to enjoy this freedom to risk their lives even today. Behind the 'No Eating, Drinking or Smoking' signs in a dangerous scheduled area, a woman may be quietly eating her sandwiches with her nails full of powdered colour. But few of these areas remain, and the important difference is that now she has running hot and cold water in her workshop, a cleanly laundered overall, extractor fans to take away the dust of her work and a doctor and blood test to check her health once a month. The long walks with buckets of cold water, the workshops teeming with mice and beetles, the scraps of clay in piles and the rooms covered in dust have been banished.

Notes

1 Elizabeth Roberts, speaking in *A Woman's Place*, of the Preston mills, says that her respondents underlined the importance of having a good missus. One said: 'If you'd a bad one, by hell you'd a bad one' (p. 48).

2 In 1917 the union became the National Society of Pottery Workers, a name which it retained until 1970, when it became the Ceramic and Allied Trades' Union. In 1917 it had over 15,000 members and appointed its first full-time woman organizer. The packers' and ovenmens' unions joined the NSPW two years later. In 1970 the membership was 31,567. From 1968 onwards works union representatives were allowed to collect union dues in work-time. In 1974 a closed shop was introduced, and membership rose to 44,404, of whom 53.2 per cent were women (F. Burchill and R. Ross, *A History of the Potters' Union*, 1977, pp. 161, 243, 245, 247 and 261).

3 Lead was dealt with first, and dust only in the 1960s. In 1913 a detailed set of rules were instituted by the government for the manufacture and decoration of pottery under section 79 of the Factory and Workshop Act 1901 (Burchill and Ross, 1977, p. 150). Lead-base glazes were prohibited in 1947, which contributed largely to the end of deaths from lead poisoning. The problem of dust was tackled after a 1962 report of the Inspector of Factories, which showed that deaths from pneumoconiosis amounted to 449 between 1957 and 1961, with 2,000 pottery workers disabled by the disease. A report, *Dust Control in the Potteries*, brought out by the Joint Standing Committee which advised the Factory Inspector on the pottery industry, made detailed recommendations for dust control, including ventilation, protective clothing and inspection (Burchill and Ross, 1977, pp. 231–2).

CHAPTER 5

From Ladding to Minding

Childhood in the Streets and at Home

Childhood has grown longer during the course of the twentieth century. The oldest of the pottery-workers, born before 1905, had started work at 13, some even at 12, if their family was particularly needy. But during their school years these often large families of children were not 'under one another's feet'; if they were not at school, nor doing jobs at home, they were out in the streets, round Burslem Town Hall, for instance, and the Shambles where the meat and fish markets were, playing in little groups and gangs at 'whip and badger', 'hare and hounds', 'ring toes' and so on. The first of these games involved jumping on one another's shoulders against a wall, another, running and hiding while the 'hounds' followed. They would play all sorts of games which made use of the 'plenty hiding-places' and lack of motor traffic. Mr Hilditch (born in 1901) described this before the First World War.[1]

Mrs Roper (born in 1923) also described a childhood in which parents were for the most part not at home. Children played in little gangs, charging one another with 'the ashbin lid and a brush', putting tins with string on their feet, playing hopscotch, playing out in the fields or in a wood, where they would swing on ropes 'like Tarzan', or dare one another to cross the canal on a plank.

Very often, in the first quarter of the century, child-minding meant nothing more than fetching children in for their dinner or tea. Mrs Farrier's grandmother looked after her granddaughter's tea and that of her brothers and sisters, and when Mrs Farrier (born in 1902) grew up and worked, her own mother looked after her daughter's children from the time that they were a month old. Mrs Mason was minded by her aunt Phoebe: 'When we came out of school we used to go to her house just round the backs, and she'd perhaps give us a piece of jam till me mother came home, something like that, you know, and me mother used to give her 5s a week for looking after us.'

Mrs Adams (born in 1923) was minded by her aunt Emie, her mother's sister, who was 'big and homely . . . and content to be at home with children'.

But in this case they went to their own house at dinner time. Their mother prepared everything beforehand:

> We used to have the . . . black-leaded grate, you know, with the hob on, and she used to have three basins with potatoes, meat and gravy on, and it was put, then, at the back of the hob before she went to work, and they were warm when we came home for lunch, and we just sat and ate that.

She remembered very little about being minded:

> I'd got me aunt Emie, you know, and I'd got me grandma top of the street, you know, and we were all right. I don't seem to remember much about it. [Did kids play out of doors a lot in those days?] Oh yes, gangs of us, in each other's yards, having little concerts and all that.[2]

Mrs Farrier's children were growing up at the same time as Mrs Adams herself, in the 1920s and 1930s, and she bitterly regretted, as a mother, never having seen such little concerts:

> I don't know whether me mother did me – I often sit here and think, I sit here hours and think – I often wonder if she did me a good turn or a bad turn with having me children, minding them. You miss such a lot of them growing up. You miss all the niceness of your children, when you're away at work.
>
> [What did you do then? Did you used to work right up to the seventh month or eight month, or something?]
>
> Oh aye, I used to be some time about the eighth month, I used to give over about four weeks beforehand, then I'd be back when they were a month old. Me mother used to have them right away, see. And when I've left 'em, I've gone [to] work crying. That's what I think about now. [She] used to tell you little stories, what they did about bringing their first books home and the words they were learning and that. Now, me mother knew all that, but I'd got to hear it second-hand, when I come home from [work].
>
> And then once when we did get a council house, and our Janet was going to school – her'd only be about 6 – some neighbours met me when I was coming [home], said, 'Maggie, your little girl, today, she's born to be an actress!' I said, 'Why?' She said, 'Oh, they've been doing *Snow White*' (or some – it was *Snow White*, I think, yes, it was). She says, 'And as the children have been acting it, she's been telling the story on the side of the stage,' she said, 'and she never faltered and made a mistake.' Well, why couldn't I have been there and watched it for meself, you know? Them are the things you think about. You miss all the niceness of them when they're little. And I'd say to every woman now, I would, stay at home and look after your kids, no matter what happens – a woman's place is with her children. That's what I think nowadays, now all that's past me, because you do miss all the niceness of them.

This is the sadness of a woman who spent only one month with each of her children and who worked a 47 hour week, because of her husband's difficulties in getting work. When (as from June 1919) working parents were at the potbank from 8.00 a.m. to 12.30 p.m. and 1.30 p.m. to 5.30 p.m. on weekdays and 8.00 a.m. to 12.30 p.m. on Saturdays, there was obviously a lot of time for children to have little concerts and games out of doors, especially in the school holidays. If they were not in the yards, or 'backs' as they were known, youngsters might be out walking in Trentham Park with a bottle of water and some jam sandwiches, the older ones looking after the younger ones, or they might be in the street, putting pins on tramlines 'to make scissors' (as Mrs Bloore did).

Within the family, some people remembered happy times, especially the Saturday evening. Mrs Farrier's mother used to get all the children to help her clean the house from top to bottom, but in the evening there was singing:

> We used to have a gathering nearly every Saturday night. Neighbours would come in, and there'd be a singsong, you know. And my husband – I can see him there just inside our door – and I was singing. I'm going back to the First World War now, I'd be about 17 or 18 – I don't think I was 18 – he'd come home. He was convalescing at Sandon Hall, and he came home. I always remember, he'd got hospital blue on. So of course me father [said], 'Now sing for us, Maggie, sing for us!' . . . I wouldn't sing for anybody, oh no. Anyway, I remember singing 'When the Great Red Dawn is Shining', and me husband said after, 'I said to meself, "Her's for me!" ' he said ' "If I'm going have anybody, I'm going have her!" '

Born fifteen years later, Grace Hewell also remembered the Saturday night:

> Although we hadn't got much, I think we enjoyed ourselves . . . especially Saturday night, when we used to have supper. We used to have either rabbit (me dad used to get about three rabbits at one week) or, another week, we'd have conger eel fish, you know, done in butter in the oven . . . and we all used to sit round . . . Saturday night was a – really . . . you used to look forward to it.

Courting, Monkey-Running, Dancing and the Cinema

When they got older, boys and girls met one another 'monkey-running'. This was walking around in groups of girls or boys, to meet groups of the opposite sex.[3] Like childhood games, it was unregulated by parents. Mrs Powell, Mrs Mason and Mrs Box all discussed together how they used to 'monkey-run' from one end of the town to the other. Mrs Mason met her husband this way: 'You know where I met my husband? We were monkey-running in Burslem Park, round the bandstand, backwards and forwards. And he used to stand on the edge, him and his pal, and he give me the eye, you know, the wink.'

Mr Hilditch knew about monkey-running in Burslem, Hanley and Tunstall. He used to go in a group of five or six: 'In Burslem it used to be walk up the top of the town and all round Queen Street and keep on circling round, and sometimes you'd go back the other way. And if you wanted meet someone special, you would turn round again, see, and go the other way.'

Mrs Roper, twenty-one years younger, could also describe it: 'It was just like Easter Sunday, you know. You just all come together somehow. And you met friends who, you know, you had a good talk [with]. If you liked a particular person, you had to go home with that one.' Jane Phillips, thirty-seven years younger than Margaret Powell, was amazed to discover that old ladies, over 80 years old, had been monkey-running, as she herself did in the late 1940s. Iris Wenceslas, born in 1933, also remembered monkey-running, but women younger than her, growing up in the 1950s with substantially more money in their pockets, talk more of pubs and cinemas. Mrs Atkins, who met her husband

walking in the park one Sunday, explained that monkey-running cost nothing
for young people who gave their mothers all their wages except a shilling or two
for pocket-money.

Mrs Neale, who lost her husband in a pit accident, remembered him lovingly,
and visited the cemetery with flowers every other week. She had met her
husband out walking in the usual way:

> Very nice, he was, he was real nice to talk to . . . you couldn't have any sharp
> words with him, because he wouldn't let you . . . He was ever so loving to live
> with . . . I've never bothered with anybody else. He was the only boyfriend I ever
> had in me life, and I've started going out with him – I was nearly 17. We met . . .
> down Trentham one Sunday night when we were having a walk, my friend and
> myself, you know. We met down there, and just got talking to him and his pal,
> and from then on – and yet it was nearly twelve months before I ever walked out
> with him – we kept just having a word or two and passing on, you know. And
> then my friend came one night, said she'd started courting my husband's friend,
> like, so he came and asked me if I'd go out with him. And I said – you know what
> we are at sixteen . . . I said, 'Oh, don't know what to do!' I said, 'Me mother'll
> give me good hiding'. You know . . .
>
> But anyhow, he says, 'Well, I'll come Saturday, and see if you've made your
> mind up.'
>
> Anyhow, I said, 'Well, how shall I know you're there?'
>
> He says, 'I'll give you a little whistle.'
>
> So at half-past six, Saturday night, you know, I could tell he was at bottom of
> street. Anyhow from that, we went to pictures, like, that night, and I went with
> him, like, till he – I was with him till he was killed in pit.

She courted him for five years, and was married when she was 22 in 1933; he
was killed in 1945. This was obviously a loving relationship, begun from the
strength of their own friends – the girl's girlfriend and the boy's pal – with no
rush while they got to know one another from the security (and demands) of
their natal families.

Most courtships were of this kind, although monkey-running was only one of
the ways to make the initial meeting. Quite often, husbands and wives met at
work. Mr Hilditch was 'chasing her [his wife] when her was 15 . . . on our
potbank. Yes, she worked on the same firm. Her was a stumpy little wench
then.' They were married when she was about 23. Mrs Powell met her husband
on a firm where she was in the warehouse and he was a placer. Mrs Farrier
originally met her 'destination at work', where he was in the sliphouse and she
a bowl-jollier; she married at 19.

Mrs Madeley's husband worked at the same colliery as her brothers, and she
used to pay her brother a copper or two if he would 'say what the young man
said'. He demanded threepence to deliver the messsage that the young man
wanted to see her. She married at 27, starting her married life just before the
1926 miners' strike, when she was picking coal off a tip to sell it so that they
could pay the rent. Mrs Dove's courtship 'went on quite a long time, years, you
know', because of her husband's possessive mother. They met in one of the
usual places: 'I was with some friends. I thought he said "good night", I
thought he was someone that I knew, but he wasn't. Anyway, and then he sent
word would I go out with him, by some friends of his that knew me, see.'

Mrs Champion was 18 when she met her husband under the pavilion in Hanley Park:

> I really knew very casually his friend [Albert], that he was with, and I said to my friend, Ada, 'Oh, there's Albert Normacott up there', I said. 'Come on, let's go see, have a talk with Albert Normacott.' And this young man – my husband as is now – was with him, and 'Albert' introduced me to Bill, you see. And he said, 'What are you doing tonight?' And I said, 'Oh, we're not doing much.' 'Well, we'll go out in a foursome.' And that's how it went on.

Mrs Champion did not go out with him continuously until they got married. Having been with him for two years, she was 18: 'But I didn't want to be tied down, I didn't at 18. I could tell he was very interested, but I didn't want to be tied down, so I said, "Oh, I think we'll have a rest, a change, and you go your way and I'll go mine." ' But two years later, still with her friend Ada, she met him again; he asked her the usual, 'What are you doing tonight?' and followed it with, 'Well, we might as well make a date.' After that, things went smoothly: 'I've gone with him ever since. That was 1937.'

Mrs Bede met her husband out dancing, with her friend, of course: 'I couldn't get rid of him. He kept popping up from out of the earth from nowhere.' She was actually in love with someone else, but this person did not dance, and 'I landed with Wilf, and you go on and on. Then he wanted me to become engaged.' She went out with him for three years, and was married at 21. Several women said they were not very keen on their husbands when they first met them, both among the older women and among the younger ones I shall describe later. Mrs Bentley is another example; she met her husband on a potbank: 'We met making tea, when we used to go down to this wash-place making tea, and I couldn't stand him! I used to look at him, I thought, "I don't fancy him at all!" And then suddenly he made a date, and I thought, "I'm not going!" ' (The husband chuckled in the background.)

So many women gave similar accounts of not really liking the look of their future husbands that I felt it must mean something, but I was not sure what its significance was. They might have been asserting their independence, that they had to be wooed and won over, rather than make an effort to win their husbands; or they might have been stressing the fact that externals, their husband's appearance or manner at first glance, were unimportant. It might have been that in fact they were not able to take the initiative in choosing a husband, since boys made the first move, and girls could only respond to the ones who offered. The first and not the last interpretation seems to me more likely, as girls initiated by encouraging or discouraging boys to take the first steps, and boys were obviously often frightened to ask a girl for a date, and would sometimes send an intermediary to ask on their behalf. Even the initial question – 'What are you doing tonight?' – could allow a girl to say she was washing her hair, or busy, before the boy actually took the plunge and asked for a date.

Another example of this type of meeting from a woman working between the wars is as follows:

I met him when I was 14 and I didn't like him, no, not at first . . . I don't know what it was about him. I was very quiet, and he wasn't. That would probably be it . . . Every Saturday and Sunday we had what we call monkey-runs . . . and you'd see hundreds of boys and girls walking up and down, and you'd probably know a lot of them. There were either two girls or four girls. No, you never saw anyone on their own. But I already knew Joe, and I already met him once or twice that way, and he . . . used to say, 'Now, stop round here and I'll see you home.' And I was 17 in August, and he asked me to go out with him in the September, and I just stuck to the one youth.

They courted for five years, although he was away in the war much of that time.

Mrs Gregory met her husband out bicycling when she was 18. They made a date and used to go cycling together. Mrs Furnivall, at 16, met her husband through her friend, who had noticed (in her friend's words) 'Some lovely boys in the next avenue . . . I've seen them moving . . . They're carrying clothes-baskets.' The girls introduced themselves as soon as possible, but this chance encounter led to a love relationship, with a wartime wedding: 'My husband, when he was in the army, he used to write to me, and he'd say, "If I could only get home, I'd work for you night and day", you know. He did and he has.' They were married when she was 21, again after a long courtship.

Freedom to meet as children and later as teenagers, on monkey-runs and at work, did not mean that girls had total freedom to go out with boys. Mrs Neale was frightened of 'a good hiding' from her mother if she went out with a boy when she was 16. Mrs Furnivall, who also met her husband when she was 16, was also frightened:

> Me father used to say to me, 'Oh, if I catch you ladding it', he used to say to me, 'I'll give it you. I'll knock your head off!' he used to say. I used to be frightened to death of him seeing me, you know, when I was out with him. Sometimes we'd walk and sometimes we'd go to the pictures about twice a week, you know. And sometimes he hadn't got any money – I used to give him some for the pictures, you know.

Coming-home time was strict.[4] Mrs Bloore had to be in at half-past nine. Mrs Roper's mother and her sister had been keen on dancing as girls (this would have been in the first decade of the century), but they had to be in for nine o'colock:

> And they used to be that frightened after nine o'clock, her and her sister, they didn't dare go in. And me grandmother had a strap, and she'd cut it down the middle like that, and that is what they got when they got in, used to make them black and blue. But she'd got five children and no husband – he'd left her – and I reckon she thought that was the best way to deal with them.

Mrs Havelock, in the 1940s, had a strict time for coming in:

> My mother wouldn't let me stay out in any case at night-time: half-past ten. If I wasn't at the backgate at half-past ten, she'd be having sixty fits. She used to keep calling me from the backdoor, 'Are you coming in? Are you coming in?' And I had to go in. There was no messing about – in the house and that was it.

In the 1950s Rosie Fenton's 15-year-old sister got into dire trouble from her father for being late home when she went out dancing. In fact, she had gone out with her mother, but her father was still furious that they were late, and had locked them both out, refusing to allow Rosie to let them in. 'Let them stay where they are, this time of night!' he had said. It was well before midnight, but 'She was only 15 then, and that was terrible for a girl of 15 to be out till that time of night.' When they were finally allowed in, their father tried to hit his daughter and gave his wife a black eye by mistake: 'She never wore his wedding ring, not for months after, wouldn't ever go up the local where they both went.'

There seemed to be hard-punishing fathers *and* mothers; in Mrs Gregory's natal home it was her mother. Mrs Gregory could go out only when her mother allowed her to: 'And I had to be in by half-past nine or I got the belt. She was a very extra hard woman, my mother was.' Certainly, growing up and going out to work did not stop this kind of chastisement, or the burden of work at home. Teenage daughters did not earn enough to live separately, and they were usually in their parents' power until they got married.[5] By the time Rosie Fenton (born in 1941) was growing up in the 1950s, however, she was describing the strict patriarchal father as 'very old-fashioned'.

Throughout the whole inter-war period, the range of entertainments where young people met (apart from chapel socials and anniversary Sundays) was monkey-running, dancing and the cinema. It seems that totally free entertainment, monkey-running, was killed off not just by young people having more money in their pockets, but also by traffic. Mrs Mason (born in 1903):

> I was 20 when I got married; we'd been courting then about two years. [I met him when] I was about 18, monkey-running along top of town. Them days we used to call it monkey-running. We used to walk from one end of the town in Burslem to the other, backwards and forwards like that, until there come a time when they stopped it – because traffic was improving, see, and you couldn't get that. So what we did . . . we made a way up to High Lane . . . we monkey-runned up High Lane. And of course that was all right . . . and then they started stopping that. So after that we monkey-runned in Burslem Park around the band stand. The band would be playing, and we'd be walking round. And I can see him now, me first husband . . . He and his pal would be standing there, and we'd be walking past, and he'd smile, you know, smile . . . But any road . . . we got as we got talking to them . . . and we asked them if they went dancing. By the way, during the [First World] War we could go dancing for sixpence a night, any night. So we asked them if they did any dancing, and they said they couldn't dance. 'Oh' we said, 'you want to come, we'll learn you.' Know where I learned them? In, it was Coliseum, Burslem, picture palace. And we did it in the passage, the very wide passage . . . we danced there . . . But anyhow we had some fun in them days, I know.[6]

Mrs Barnes (born in 1911) met her husband when she was 15, 'at Barber's picture palace at Tunstall under the clock', where she used to go on Saturdays for tuppence. She courted until she was 21, because her husband-to-be was unemployed. Mrs Neale also used to go to the pictures or the theatre, once on a Saturday and once in the week, while Mrs Bede was 'all films, duck. Should have been on 'em.' The cinema was an almost essential part of courtship.

Some families, like Mrs Hewell's and Mrs Box's natal families, were very much involved with a social life centring on their church. Mrs Hewell's family were Salvationists, and because of this she did not go to the pictures when she was young. Mrs Box used to go old-time dancing with girls and to socials at the Methodist chapel. Her parents had met while dancing to a concertina in the town hall; this would have been at the turn of the century. Mrs Box already knew her husband as a boy and later got to know him at work. This kind of significant meeting with an already familiar face, only possible in settled communities, was a frequent pattern; people met at work, but also out walking, or they knew each other through a sister or brother who worked with the other partner. Mrs Adams (born in 1923) worked with her husband's sister, and Mrs Madeley's husband worked with her brothers. Mrs Roper's mother and her husband's father worked together in the dipping house at the same factory.

Several of the women who were born in the 1920s had courtships lengthened by the Second World War. Mrs Adams and her husband wrote to each other throughout the war, and were married after demobilization. Mrs Havelock (born in 1924) courted for six years while her husband was in the Navy, and could see him only when he came home on leave. As with a number of other people, there were good reasons for putting off marriage: 'We knew we'd got nowhere live.'

Mrs Havelock mentioned that 'there used to be a special night for seeing your young man. The other nights you went out with your mates.' But he, nevertheless, had a certain priority:

> When he was in the navy, I mean I never knew when he was coming on leave, and he's come and fetched me out of a dance hall many a time – he always knew where to find me. But he wouldn't come in. I used to have to go out. I used to say to my mate, 'Oh, he's standing at the door, I've got to go.' I used to have to go out then, you see. I'd perhaps be just enjoying myself dancing, but he wouldn't come in. Just have to go out then and leave me mates in.

The passion for dancing (as with Mrs Adams, for instance, who used to have her hair put in curlers at work, so that she could go out dancing in the evening) was widespread, and continued in the 1940s. Elsie Barbour (born in 1930) used to practise dancing with her brothers at home, and then go out to the Majestic ballroom with her sister. To begin with, she was very nervous:

> I went to some club when I was . . . perhaps about 14 or 15. And a boy came, you know – all this trouble you'd gone to, a nice dress on, your hair done – and this boy came to ask me to dance, and I was that nervous, I nearly fell off me seat . . . But really, going or dancing with a boy was . . . so nerve-racking! . . . You never grew up, you didn't grow up until you were about 18, did you? Now when they're 14 they're grown up, aren't they?

She used to practise the quickstep, 'dancing across the lino' to the wireless, and was soon going dancing three or four times a week – not to make dates, but because of her passion for dancing. On one occasion, a famous dancer asked her to dance and to coffee, but she was so shy that she made an excuse to go to the cloakroom, and ran all the way home.

Weddings

Having met their husband-to-be at work, monkey-running, dancing or else-where, and courted until they were allowed to get married, the group of women born before 1925 usually married without much fuss.[7] Weddings were prob-ably not occasions at which families cemented relationships. The girl had chosen her own husband, nothing to do with her parents, and they were losing her wages and her labour at home, which was not necessarily an occasion for celebration, especially in large families. This was not always so, however, because the young couple might start marriage by renting part of the house, and if a child came along soon, the grandmother might also earn money by child-minding while her daughter continued to go out to work.

The first modestly detailed account of a wedding comes from Mrs Bede (born in 1908), who went up to Scotland to marry her husband in about 1927. He was a salesman, and they were in lodgings with a lady who gave them 'a big room to have our wedding in' and 'a breakfast and everything'. She and her husband travelled around together, living very much from hand to mouth, and she finally decided to come home to her mother. He went to his mother's (who was too strict for Mrs Bede), who found them rooms when Mrs Bede discovered she was pregnant. The landlady where they lodged now was 'all right . . . but she used to have money off me for the gas and all that, and then they'd go the pictures, and when I was bathing Susan, the gas used to go out, see. They used to get off to the pictures with the money, instead of putting it in the gas.'

Mrs Madeley (born in 1898) came, unlike Mrs Bede, from a very poor background, with (you may recall) her father out of work and her mother selling oatcakes about the streets and washing potbank overalls. Mrs Madeley worked very hard to help her mother, and did not marry until she was 27. But even then she married in poverty, owing money on her bed, her clothes and even her ring.

Mrs Farrier (born in 1902) began her married life in her mother's parlour (see Chapter 3) and went into lodgings after three years – a terrible time when she had to live in a converted garage without a lavatory. As with Mrs Bede, the landlords themselves were on the premises and consituted a problem. They would complain about the noise from her children, and she would be driven to take the sqeakers out of toys, so as not to annoy them – and the children would be furious!

Mrs Dove (born in 1902) and Mrs Box (born in 1904) both married rather late in life in the 1940s, and their weddings were simple affairs, but they could afford honeymoons. Mrs Dove said: 'I didn't have any fuss with it.' Her parents were already dead. She was married at the local Methodist church, had something to eat at home, and they went off to North Wales for a short honeymoon. Mrs Box married a collier who was working on munitions at the time they met. They had 'a plain wedding' (there was rationing), but a friend made a cake, and 'close friends' (mostly relatives) came. They went to the seaside for a week, and then her husband moved in with her and her mother.

Mrs Mason (born in 1903) had a vivid memory of her church wedding in a much poorer family:

Now in me father's day – I'm going back to when I got married now, duck – my father was drunk at breakfast time; bottle of stout was only tuppence a bottle. Pubs were open at four o'clock in the morning, weren't they? You could go to the pub at five . . . I got married on the Sunday morning . . . I always say I was poor, which I was, but you got used to it. We walked [to] church, which wasn't far; we walked, six of us . . . and when we come back it was breakfast time, but me father was drunk.

Mrs Mason and her new husband went to live with her mother when they were married, and once again they got a house through her mother's influence with the landlord. Her mother paid 4s 6d ($22\frac{1}{2}$p) a week rent for one of his terrace houses, which was 'a lot of money to your mothers and that, when they hadn't got money coming in'. No doubt, a daughter in the parlour had helped to make up for the loss of her wages. Mrs Mason's husband was a thrifty young man, from a thrifty family, and had saved £10 – 'Oh, a fortune, wasn't it, them days!' So they were able to buy furniture:

> We had a bed and bedstead on terms, so much a week . . . and we had a seven-piece suite for less than that £10. And it was a sofa as let down one side . . . and two armchairs and four ordinary chairs . . . in leather, duck, and it filled the room up. It was marvellous! So after we'd finished paying for the bed, I managed, I paid for a sideboard. We had a sideboard to go . . . down along the other room, and that made the little place, you know, look full up then, them days.

Mrs Mason lived in a poor area of Burslem. Mrs Bloore's (born in 1909) mother lived in a house with no electricity or gas, and paid 6s (30p) a week rent. After she was married, Mrs Bloore shared a big house with her brother. Like Mrs Farrier, she eventually got a council house, and lived there very comfortably.

Mrs Neale (born in 1911) was married in 1933. Her mother had 'had to struggle' because her husband had died when she still had three children not working. But Mrs Neale's husband 'helped and we had a nice wedding. His mum had a wedding cake made for us, and bought us all the bedding, you know. She was real good.' Mrs Neale lived next door to her mother when she had small children, and, as we shall see, this was very convenient.

Mrs Barnes (born in 1911) did not get on with her stepfather, but could not marry until she was 21, because her parents wanted her wages. They went into lodgings with a friend of her husband's in a parlour and an upstairs room, until later they were able to get a house down the street. The difference between her start in life and that of Mrs Farrier, Mrs Box, Mrs Mason and Mrs Neale, for instance, is very clear: most mothers did what they could for their daughters, helping them with somewhere to live, even if it was only a portion of their own house. It has already been mentioned that Mrs Gregory (born in 1915) and Mrs Bentley (born 1916) lacked this kind of support. Their mothers were angry at losing their daughters' wages.

Mrs Bentley recalled her wedding with wry humour. She wore a 4s coat from someone her aunty knew who was much better off, a dress for 2s 6d and 'six pennyworth of flowers for me hat. And that was me wedding-gown.' She paid for it by doing cleaning for the aunt. The morning of the wedding, she had to clean her mother's parlour and kitchen, then have a wash in the back kitchen and, as she put it, 'come down in all me glory. So, we're walking through the door, and me mother says, "Well, you'd better come back for a cup of tea, but there's nothing eat." '

Mrs Bentley sent one of the boys off to a little shop to buy two ounces of boiled ham and four scones for elevenpence ha'penny (under 5p), so that when they came back from the registry office there would be something to eat. She then had to go and clean the flat that they were going to live in. A 'well-off' aunt had given them a red plush seven-piece suite (full of dust) and an old carpet, and she had bought a 4s table. Mr Bentley went off to fetch his 'things', his working shirt and his pit trousers. His mother had said, 'I didn't bother mending them because I knew you were getting married. You can mend them.' Mr Bentley was married in his dead father's best suit and shirt. He then drew their 'worldly wealth' out of the post office, and with 16s bought groceries and a set of saucepans to cook with.

It is obvious from this account that the couple's families did not 'go to town' in well-wishing and providing for them, but they were both very poor families. Just as Mrs Gregory's mother sold all her daughter's clothes when she got married, so Mrs Bentley's mother could not rise to the occasion even to make them a ham sandwich. Mrs Hewell (born in 1917) had a better start in life with a more caring mother, but right up to her wedding she always handed over her wages to her mother, and only collected a few things together by buying them every week out of 3s pocket-money. The wedding was held on a Saturday and, as usual, at home, rather than in a hall or hotel. But her mother still had a lot of little children:

It was held up at my mother's, yes. We couldn't afford to have a room. We had two settees because it was a big family. And the children were sent to the pictures, and as they came back, me mother had got bags of sandwiches and cakes, and they were all sneaked upstairs. They were up there, and then me mother went up there, and she saw everybody was all right, and washed and got them off to bed. But then somebody put their foot in it. She said, 'Anybody as wants to see the presents, it's in the front bedroom.' And somebody went and walked in the back bedroom by mistake, and they come down and they said, 'What are all those children upstairs?' she says. 'There's about four at the top and three at the bottom.' My mother says, 'Ooh!.' And they went mad over it and said, 'What lovely children!' . . . And my mother had tried to hide them really, you know. They weren't a bit of trouble.

To summarize, it seems that the weddings of these pottery-workers in the 1920s and 1930s were mainly low-key events at home, with friends or relatives. They were mostly in church or chapel, varying in effort with the strength of the relationship between mother and daughter, and sometimes between mother and son. Mrs Roper's wedding makes an interesting exception. She came from a close community where everybody knew everybody. She had a church wedding, to which her parents invited a lot of their friends and 'too many' relatives – since those who were invited brought all their family with them; there were too many for them all to come back to their little house. This wedding, like Mrs Hewell's, suggests an event in the community; both sets of parents knew one another, the fiancé was acceptable, and they all worked together at one time. The couple had courted by letter for some time during the war, and the parents were prepared. For the first two and a half years following the wedding, they lived with the bride's mother and father.

In this chapter we have seen how much young people were left to themselves in the first three decades of the century – left to organize themselves and play in groups as children, and later to go out gregariously in groups of their own sex, walking, or to the cinema, or dancing, so that they would meet members of the opposite sex. Having agreed to go out with someone, they stayed with them until the relationship developed into an engagement, or was dropped. Some people married and started having children in their teens, tending to have large families, but most people had long courtships.

Low-key weddings underline how individual was the decision to marry, how little the girls' families were involved in their choice of husband; but they often continued to live with parents, particularly the bride's parents, in preference to lodgings.

Undoubtedly many of these marriages were love-matches, although some girls seem to have been unenthusiastic about their boyfriends at the outset. They appear to have grown to like them gradually, rather than to have experienced the *coup de foudre*. On the other hand, long courtships meant that people knew at least what to expect of one another, in terms of personality. In a minority of cases, women seem to have married their husbands out of compassion, or even pity, particularly older men who had no one to look after them. Marriage, as we shall see, was thought of as providing a man with someone to look after him, his food and comforts, and to manage the expenses of the home, as well as to look after the old, the sick and the very young. For a woman, it meant new burdens of work, new financial responsibilities and, eventually, a home of her own. These are the practical aspects; but marrying wisely could mean a loving and enjoyable partnership, while marrying unwisely (as we shall see in Chapter 7) could be a torment and, at worst, a death sentence.

Notes

1 Phyllis Willmott in her autobiographical *Growing Up in a London Village*, 1979, p. 33, describes the way street games like skipping would have a season in her London suburb in the 1920s. C. Forman, in *Industrial Town, Self portrait of St. Helens in the 1920s*, 1979, Granada, London, also describes the seasons of street games in St Helens just after the First World War; 'whip and top' was a winter game and 'ring games for girls were played in summer' (p. 119). Michael Glasson's *City Children: Birmingham Children at Work and Play, 1900–1930*, 1985, describes street games in some detail, including 'kick the can', which was 'an energetic form of hide and seek', 'tip cat', in which a scrap of wood would be hit up and down the road and marbles, cigarette cards, conkers and skipping games.

2 P. Willmott, 1979, also describes these little concerts, particularly *Cinderella*, in the 1920s and early 1930s (p. 31).

3 Elizabeth Roberts, in *A Woman's Place*, 1984, also describes what she calls 'promenading' in Lancashire, when 'at an appointed time at the weekend, groups of young men and women paraded up and down hoping to catch someone's eye' (p. 71).

4 *York Memories: Nine First-Hand Accounts of Life in York, 1900–1939*, 1984, published by the York Oral History Project, describes the monkey-run in York, a strict father who would not let his daughter go out with a boy, and beating with a belt and buckle, so that none of his daughters should have the chance to have an illegitimate child: 'He wasn't going to have trouble brought home.' Roberts, 1984, talks about subtle changes of status which happened when a girl was earning wages, including more freedom in coming-home time at night (p. 41); but in Stoke this does not seem to have been the case. Diana Gittins, speaking of girls in Burnley who were weavers, suggests the link between morality and family finances: 'It is tempting to wonder the extent to which fear of premarital pregnancy on the parents' behalf was a fear of social disgrace or a fear of losing valuable income and unpaid domestic help. Similarly, it could have been that on a daughter's part, premarital pregnancy was as much a deliberate attempt to gain independence from her parents as a manifestation of ignorance or carelessness'. (Gittins, *Fair Sex, Family Size and Structure, 1900–39*, 1982, p. 72). The evidence from my study would support this.

5 Roberts's study also points to the difference between responsibility and power (1984, p. 10). Young people in her Lancashire towns had responsibilities thrust upon them at an early age, but they were dominated by their parents 'until, and even beyond, their own marriages'. This describes the situation in Stoke as well.

6 Roberts, 1984, says that, among working girls in her areas, dancing 'became almost a mania in the 1920s' (p. 69).

7 This was also true of the Lancashire towns which Roberts studied, where weddings were usually 'a very low-key affair' (1984, p. 82).

CHAPTER 6

Case Studies of Marriage between the Wars

Having been duly married and lodged, how did these new couples get on? Many of the women born before 1925 told me how the work at home had been organized, how the shopping, cooking, housework and child-minding had been sorted out, how the money which came into the house was managed and how they spent their leisure. Plainly, at that time, the ideal, if not the reality, was of the wife who did everything at home. Mr Hilditch, for instance, said in praise of his wife (whom he had married in 1923) that he had never even had to pour out his second cup of tea, 'She always brought it', and 'I didn't know what cleaning was until I was on my own.' But there was some variation from household to household, especially among men on shift-work. In general, however, work at home was women's work and responsibility.[1]

Three of the women born before 1905 talked together about this, and agreed that, when they were young, women worked harder than men. Mrs Mason put it succinctly: 'You'd got your own work to do, your children to look after, and go to work.' Another of the three, Mrs Powell, added: 'We never went out either, an' all, duck . . . You had to be Cinderella. You never went out!' Mrs Powell, however, stressed that her husband was 'a hard-working man, hard, very hard'. He worked until he was 76. Certainly, men's heavy manual work tested their strength and endurance; the war had injured some of them, and work had injured and diseased others. This had important effects on women's lives, since many women acted, at one time or another, as nurses to their fathers and/or husbands. Households, dependent on these women as nurses, frequently went through at least one period as a three-generation family, with a daughter looking after an ailing parent of her own or her husband's.

Few of these women stayed at home after they were married. Mrs Powell and Mrs Gregory worked at home, looking after other people's children. Mrs Dove was required to give up work to make her husband's dinner, and Mrs Champion's and Mrs Atkin's husbands did not want them to leave the children. Going out to work was a way of life for women under 25, whose domestic tasks, nevertheless, were always seen as their primary obligations. I was, in any case, interested in women pottery-workers, and it was those who had worked in the factories whom I interviewed.[2]

In the case studies which follow, we shall note the continuing importance of the mother–daughter relationship, even after marriage, a mother sometimes providing somewhere to live, sometimes company when a daughter was at home with her baby, very often providing child-minding services when a daughter returned to work. We shall also note the great diversity in the roles of husbands at home – from Mrs Neale's husband, cooking for his wife when she was confined, and Mrs Barnes's husband out with his gun in the fields, bagging their supper, to Mr Adams looking after the children and cleaning the brass, and Mr Roper out with his shopping-bag. We shall also note the gaps, the things which they would *not* do, in the domestic world which was essentially seen as their wives' responsibility.

We shall see the gradual lengthening in the time that women could spend at home with their babies, before they went back to work. For Mrs Farrier and Mrs Mason, a month was all they could hope for. Mrs Furnivall, Mrs Adams and Mrs Roper, two decades on, were able to spend two years at home. We shall also note that the reasons for going back to work change over this period. In the 1940s Mrs Havelock goes back to work to buy a house, and Mrs Hewell to replace her linen and furnishings; but Mrs Neal works to buy her children necessaries, and Mrs Farrier works because there is work only intermittently for her husband in the 1920s and 1930s.

We shall also describe the varying patterns of money management, in which most usually the wife has responsibility for paying for groceries, rent, bills, clothes and 'clubmen': the variety lying in whether or not all the wage-packet is handed over for her to accomplish this and, later on, how much is left to the husband (or occasionally the wife) to save for holidays or large items of expenditure. We shall also see to what extent leisure is shared or separate in these households, and how gradually holidays can be afforded as occasions when couples can spend time together. These are for the most part small families with much closer relationships than the parents of my next group of pottery-workers, brought up mostly in the 1930s, 1940s and 1950s. Many of them, having worked hard all their lives, brought up their children to seek other kinds of work. In each generation, we shall find the same thing.

Mrs Powell did all the housework in her home, but she had had a break of twelve years from paid employment, while she looked after her own and her sister's children. Mrs Madeley had no such freedom, she went back to work only three weeks after the birth of her child, whom her mother looked after. Her husband was a miner, later suffering from pneumoconiosis. When he gave up work eventually with dust, he would sometimes do cleaning for her, for she continued to work full-time, cup-handling until she was 67, and then making tea on a potbank until she was 76. She emphasized that she had had to work very hard all her life. She never went away on holiday on Wakes Week, the first week in August, because she was working and looking after her husband, and she used to have a rest. They would go out to a pub together and have half a pint and a sandwich, and enjoy themselves. In this household, husband and wife went out together; in others, sometimes this was the case (particularly on a Saturday night, and when the children were older), and sometimes men went out drinking alone; more will be said about this later. Mrs Madeley was, in old age, very much against drink, having seen its ill effects in her family, and now took strength and comfort in the Salvation Army.

Mrs Powell (who was church, not chapel) described her husband just going out for the last half-hour at night, not longer: 'They couldn't afford, duck.' Simply true as this might seem, some men went out – and some women – whether the family could afford it or not. But, unlike some of his contemporaries, Mr Powell used to hand over all his wages to his wife and not just give her housekeeping.

Mrs Dove and her husband had separate tasks in the home. He could not cook, she said, but he did odd jobs and repairs in the house, while she did most of the housework. She left paid work in 1946 when her husband, who was not a potter, became self-employed – so that she could cook his midday meal. They had no children to be minded, and her leisure was more reading than going out. They were Methodists.

Mrs Farrier's husband sometimes worked in the sliphouse, sometimes in the pit and sometimes not at all. Like so many men at this period, he could not get regular work. But he had also been wounded in the First World War. She describes him painting their converted garage with 'wallop', making a little hob with two biscuit tins and some bricks for her fire, and putting up the rail to hold a curtain of fourteen yards of red serge, which made it into two rooms. More surprisingly, she describes a little pin-cushion that her husband embroidered in wool-work cross-stitch in blue and pink, 'For Baby, 1921', for their first baby. Their babies came thick and fast, but she had to give them all to her mother at a month old, and so endeavoured to live near her. The mother-daughter relationship continued strong and indispensable, mother and daughter often eating and working together at home, and the two households were not really separate until she got her first council house in 1930.

Mrs Farrier used to sing in concerts, particularly during the Second World War, when, like so many women pottery-workers, she went to work on a munitions factory. But, as was the case with Mrs Mason, Mrs Dove and Mrs Gregory, she also used to love reading. As a young girl, Mrs Farrier used to read while she was eating:

> As long as I'd got a book propped up in front of me – the others would be round the table – and I always used to have me dinner in private. I used to go in the parlour and push the machine, sewing-box, to one side, put me plate there, knife and fork, or a spoon oftener than not (we weren't well off in the way of cutlery). I used to prop me book up and sit there, all on me ownio, eating . . . I never was one for going out a lot, but I used to love reading. I used to lie on me belly in bed with *The Man in the Iron Mask*, I remember that, and Charles Dickens's books – Little Nell, Peggotty, David Copperfield. I used to love 'em!

Mrs Mason used to read later in life. She would read in bed while her husband watched the TV, 'if there was anything suitable for men on the box'. As a young woman, she was married to a miner whose entertainment used to be playing billiards, when he was on 'noons'. (Mrs Powell's husband was the same, or he liked to go bowling.) Mrs Mason and her mother were also an inseparable unit, especially when her first husband was killed in the pit. She was pregnant:

> He was killed in the pit at 35 . . . That was a shock . . . I was pregnant then, and the child – shock did it, I filled all full of water, I think it drowned, you know . . . It was dead anyway when it was born. And, do you know, I wanted that child – I did so want it with him going and all, you know, being a little girl, I did. I really wanted that child. Well, I haven't got it, have I? Somehow the Lord works mysteriously. I suppose he thought I'd got enough, left with two as it was, you know, and that, so that died . . . We worked almost up to the last month, them days – they don't today, they make them finish . . . And I was back again before the baby was a month old. When I had the baby, you had four weeks off to have this baby, and you have four weeks what you call insurance pay – which was only 12s a week, them days. And as soon as that month was up, you'd either got to start work, or go down to Stoke and be examined again. And they would only sign you off and say you were fit. Well, I never went; I went back to work, because my mother lived next door, and she had . . . the baby. She had both me children . . . when I had them. I had the first one, and I went back to work before – I went back to work with the second one just the same – and they were a month old. We worked hard, really hard, them days, duck. We had to do to make a living.

There were no holidays away. Mrs Mason had never seen the sea until she was 20, the summer before she was married. She and her fiancé went with her future sister-in-law and her young man to Blackpool; her husband's family used to go there every year. She continued working after his death, and later married again. Her second husband worked out of doors and had a vehicle, so he was able to take her and fetch her from work, but then, of course, 'her' work started.

Their financial arrangements seemed fair at the time, but in fact favoured her husband. He paid the rates and the electric bill, while Mrs Mason, from her wages, paid for the coal, the gas and all the groceries. Including stepchildren, she had nine in the household to feed, and she said: 'I kept them all.' Unbeknown to her, he was able to save out of his wages: 'I always thought he was very, very poor. That's why I took to him, because I felt sorry . . . for him, and of course he was saving money while mine was going, what bit I'd got with working.' The money which she did not know he had went to her stepchildren, and a 'little bit' for her. She used hers to put into a bond 'towards burying me', 'because, reading in *The Sentinel* . . . it takes such a lot of money to bury you these days.'[3] Thus, in this family, because the wages were not put together, the wife's wages kept her husband and stepchildren, and effectively provided them with an inheritance via her husband. A life insurance went to her: 'So he did me a good turn that way, granted. I know he didn't leave me a big lot of money, but that goes to me. I draw that and I'm highly satisfied, you know. So, in a way, I can't grumble, can I? Much?'

As was the case with many other women, Mrs Mason's work at home included looking after old and sick relatives. She not only nursed her husband through an illness, but also looked after her husband's father, who had been in hospital: 'And whether he took to me straight away I don't know, but he says, "Flo, let me come home!" So I had him at home, see, as well as the rest . . . And do you know, he wasn't that much trouble.' She had him until he died.

Mrs Box lived contentedly with her mother for many years; her 'young man' had died after straining his heart at work. She eventually married her husband much as Mrs Mason had married hers, out of compassion: 'I didn't really want to get married, but after his mother died he seemed a bit lost. And then his sister, she remarried again . . . so he kept on and on until I eventually said yes.' They lived with her mother, and both paid their board to her mother, who was the manager, until one weekend she could no longer do it. She said to her daughter: 'Keep it, keep it all, and you do it all now. You've got to start.' Her husband gave her £3 to £4 a week, depending on his wages, and kept what pocket-money he wanted. Her mother,

> when she was well enough, did pretty fair of the housework, but I did the other when I came home from work. [What about cooking?] Well, Mother did the cooking. Yes, she did the cooking. But my husband could cook for himself if it was necessary. [Did he do any housework or anything?] Oh no, not really. He was all outside [working] and getting money in.

This was a very compatible marriage, even though its start may not sound very romantic: 'We shared, shared in everything. I mean, we'd got really a lot in common, you know.' Leisure was mostly shared, but partly separate. Mrs Box and her mother used to go to the Methodist church together (which was not his faith), and then she and her husband would go to see his sister. He 'used to, like, go and have half a pint of beer across the public there, with a friend as lived down the street. Used to go about ten minutes to ten and be back in again just turned ten.' When they went on holiday, she used to pay for the hotel, while he provided the spending-money (this was a very common pattern among couples, when holidays started to be more common). In public, he would have been the provider, paying out for them both for meals and whatever they wanted. They used to go to south coast resorts, sometimes taking her mother and aunt too, and enjoying the fact that he could read Latin and explain the history of churches to them. Inevitably, as with the preceding women, she nursed a relative, in this case her own mother, who was bedridden for eighteen months before she died.

Mrs Bede might seem to be more independent of her mother, since she married and lived away from the Potteries, but she returned to her mother one Christmas, when she felt too far from home: 'I'd had enough. I said, "Charlie, I'm going home." I was crying because I could hear 'em singing Christmas carols, and I thought, "Ooh, I'm going home." ' She stopped work for twenty years, but used to do some decorating from home.

Mrs Bede's husband was plagued with one hopelessly brief job after another. All too often he seemed to be going out and trying to sell things in soaking weather. She paid 12s 6d rent, and lived on £1 6s (£1.30); it was she who did all the shopping, the managing and the rest: 'Charlie never did anything. He'd become a sick man, years – nearly all my married life.' She nursed him for years: 'I used to have to go out in street to see if I could find anybody help me get him off the floor. I've had lots of worry like that. I've lived in ambulances with him, you know, continually.' The early and late years of her married life form a sad contrast, because her husband at one time played in a dance band, and she remembered, 'How he danced!' Dancing and going to the pictures were what she loved, but once again, her role became gradually that of nurse to a slowly dying man.

After she married, Mrs Bloore and her husband shared a house with her brother. Her husband worked as a thrower (when he could get work), she as a gilder. As in so many households, the young couple were not really separated from an extended family by marriage. She had only one child, and went back to work when he was six months old, putting him into her mother's care for 6s a week, and later to a neighbour, who would see to him after school. She said that she and her husband used to do the housework between them at night, but she added that she did the cooking, the washing and ironing, the nappy-changing and baby-bathing. She mentioned only his skill in turning the mangle and washing the dishes and the windows. The arrangement, however, suited her, and she said: 'As long as you're happy, that's all that matters.' Each knew what the other earned but 'just used to have what we wanted'; this was not very clear to me, but was certainly, in retrospect, satisfactory. Her husband was ill for three years, before he died of cancer when she was 55; she also looked after her parents, but did not want to impose on her own children.

Mrs Neale, who, like Mrs Mason, lost her husband in the pit, had a loving relationship which has already been mentioned in some detail, but the picture which she recalled was still of herself doing all the washing at night, while her husband read the paper. It was his job, however, to get the water hot in the boiler. Like all the husbands in this group, he had problems getting work and had gone into the pit to get more money for his growing family. He had done an apprenticeship, but been made redundant at the moment when he would have gone on full money. All too often these memories of the 1930s find their echo in what was happening while I was doing my fieldwork in the early 1980s; Mrs Furnivall's son, a potter on a well-known firm, had just been made redundant in the same way. An apprenticeship is of course an investment in the future; you have low wages in the expectation of being paid as a skilled man or woman at the end of your training. It is amazing how little bitterness people show when such investments come to nothing, and they try something else. This is not an isolated case.

Mrs Neale volunteered a good deal of information about her confinements and her arrangements for childcare, both of which again show the combined importance of the husband and the mother in a young woman's life. In the following passage, one also glimpses the links between and importance of neighbours, and the innocence of a young woman who knew very little about what to expect from maternity:[4]

> Didn't hear much about being in hospital then, you know, not like today . . . I'd the first one, George, in the City General Maternity Home, but the other three I had at home. Well, we used to have to pay for midwife then, not like today, we

had to pay them ourselves. Betime we'd paid them we'd got nothing left at all, not like today when they have all this money to get everything with . . . 30s then . . . Them days, you know, we couldn't get out of bed for a fortnight, you'd got to stay in for the fortnight . . . and then you'd got to stay indoors for about another fortnight, before you could go out . . . It was just like being in prison. I think it's a better way today, though, meself. You did have a rest, but you got restless, you know what I mean?

I know my husband used to cook dinner, give me dinner . . . and I used to real enjoy it, with him getting it ready. I know, one Sunday he give it to me, and I ate it all, and he looked at me and said, 'I thought you were bad!' because I've ate all this dinner, you know, but I was really ready for it . . . I breast-fed George, but not the others after. I had our George in City General Maternity Home like I say. Well, when I come home, I'd only been at home about two days – oh, and this breast come out like that! Oh and it did ache, you know, and I never told anybody. And being first baby, you know, I didn't really know, because you weren't as wise, them days, as they are today, you know what I mean? We weren't taught, them days, like they are today. And I was in lodgings then down by Longton Cemetery, and I came up me mother's this particular morning, because me husband had gone work, like, and I'd got baby, so I took him out of pram, and put him on Mother's sofa – sofas then. And as I was putting him down, I must have caught meself.

And Mother must have seen me wince, so she says to me, 'Have you got any pain on you?'

And I said, 'No.'

Says, 'I think you have,' her says. 'I've seen your face go.'

Anyhow, she made no more todo, picked me sweater up . . . oh, Mother went mad! 'Oh my God!' she says. 'However long have you been like this?' Anyhow, Mother sent for next-door neighbour – in them days, you know, they helped one another – and she says, 'Mrs Poole, will you take our Winn down doctor's?' Because doctor's was only bottom of the street, then. Her said, 'Oh, her *is* in a state!'

The doctor asked whether she had been feeding the baby and said, 'It's a wonder you haven't poisoned him!' All the milk had 'gone bad', and she was three months, going backwards and forwards every day to the hospital – after they had opened her septic milk abscesses. She recalled that she was able to breast-feed her second child only for a month, and had to bottle-feed the other two, as 'I hadn't got milk enough for those.'

Mrs Neale went back to work when her child was four months old, even though her husband was working, because 'wages was nothing, nothing at all . . . You'd got to go, to give your children that little bit extra, or else . . . you couldn't afford to give them anything that you'd really like. So . . . I'd rather go to work than see them go short of anything.'

During this period the Second World War was on, and food was on ration, so there was little enough:

When you'd had your limit off your ration book, that was it – you'd perhaps have a quarter of tea for the whole family, perhaps you were allowed 1 oz each, same with butter, same with cheese, and you could perhaps get about 2 oz a head each sugar . . . But it was terrible them days. If you had egg, you'd got to have dry egg-powder – oh, it was terrible, terrible. In fact, the night as my husband was killed, his supper was in the oven (because we'd got oven, then, to our grates, like, then). And even that night he was killed, there was a bit of bacon and this dried egg on the plate waiting for him. Couldn't get eggs or nothing – and 'prem', what we called 'prem', you know, like luncheon meat they call it today. Well, he always said he'd got a prem belly. He got that much prem, he used to say to the lads, 'Look at your dad's prem belly!' you know, because you just couldn't get anything else.

The children had more meat because Mr Neale would not eat any meat, and more cheese because, as a miner, he had an extra ration; but she felt they were deprived, both of nice food and of toys.

Mrs Neale used to leave her children next door with her mother while she was out at work. They would have their tea there, and then she would fetch them home and make her own tea. 'It's been real hard work,' she said, 'but I always say, God's been good. He's kept me well enough do it, you know. I haven't been able [to] have much pleasure . . . Coming home, you know, sitting in me home, and I was quite satisfied.' When the fourth baby was born, an aunt who lived 'up on the corner' had him from the age of seven months: 'When you look back you wonder how you've done it, you know. I've sat up in bed at nights, when baby's been teething like, Margaret [a toddler] on one arm, baby on the other, and I daren't . . . go to sleep.'

Mrs Neale's mother was particularly good to her, 'clung to me' as her daughter put it, because she too had been widowed young and understood her daughter's difficulties. Mrs Neale's father died of chronic bronchitis (he was an ovenman), but they believed it was pneumoconiosis, a disease which was not talked about, she said, in those days. She and her mother both had the same pensions, '10s for self, and 5s for the eldest, and then 3s for the other three'. Mrs Neale's mother's mother and father lived nearby, so the link in the maternal line was very strong, and Mrs Neale used to clean for them, being obviously very fond of them: 'Sometimes you wish they were here again.'

It is not surprising that links between women were more long-lasting at this period. In the First World War, and in peacetime industry, men were so dispensable. Her mother lost three of her brothers in the First World War, and another was badly injured, while her husband was a victim of his work, as was her son-in-law. Women had influence in getting houses and in getting jobs; they were pivotal in the family. A daughter could comfortably go into her mother's house with her husband when she was married, and her mother or father could comfortably go to her when they were old, since it was the women who gave the character to the household.

Mrs Barnes's father, like Mrs Neale's three uncles, was also sacrificed to the First World War, at the age of 28. Her husband died in his fifties, but his youth was marred by unemployment. He used the freedom imposed on him, however, to spend more time with his little children, and would take them for miles on the back of his bicycle. Perhaps because of Mrs Barnes's strained relationship with her natal family, he took the place of a grandmother for child-minding, while his wife was at work. She and her husband saw very little of each other, however, when he was working shifts on the railway. Mrs Barnes said: 'It didn't bother me, it didn't make any difference. He was there and I was there. It was the money we wanted in those days. We were poor, you know. Even though we both worked, there just wasn't any money.'

Her husband retained a close relationship with his own mother and brothers and when they all died in quick succession 'It made [his] world just crumble around him.' He lost interest in everything, drank heavily and became very ill with diabetes. This was the end of a very active man who had loved his garden and his dahlias, and who, with his dog and his gun, 'used to ramble for miles and miles'. He had done this in the 1930s, bringing home all kinds of game – rabbits, pheasants, pigeons, snipe, grouse, wild goose, woodcock and duck: 'We've had it. I cooked it, cleaned it, everything. His gun was always busy.' He used to pay for permission to bag these, and he would net rabbits at night, and sell them door to door, or barter them at the butcher's for bacon or meat. On winter's evenings he would have them all making nets at home. In this household the father on the dole became more of a father through child-minding (instead of a mother or aunt), but hardly less of a provider, through his gun, his nets and his ferret.

Mrs Champion, who had been a paintress before her marriage, did not tell me much about her work at home, but she did not go out to work after she had her two children. Her husband was in an 'up-and-coming trade' and had strong views: 'I didn't go to work. No, my husband wouldn't let me go to work. He says, "You have children and you rear them yourself. Other people are not rearing them, getting into other people's ways and habits." So he wouldn't let me go.' This was an attitude we shall find later with other husbands after the war, and it suggests that the women's husbands dominated their lives in an important way.

Mrs Gregory, who, like Mrs Barnes and Mrs Bentley, could not count on help from her mother, married a helpful husband and a helpful mother-in-law. She had children regularly, not knowing how to prevent them (see Chapter 3), and while she went out cleaning or working on potbanks (and her husband was also at work) her mother-in-law would help mind the babies. A missus for whom she worked, saucer-sponging, gave her advice about pregnancy and confinement, and she had, in any case, very easy births. She gave a very detailed description of how they used to dress the baby in binder, muslin nappy and 'barra', and how little boys wore dresses until they were about 2. Then they would be put in little 'buster-suits', and this event, the beginning of true masculinity, would be marked by a little party to which close relatives would come. Her detailed account shows her agreeable dependence on her mother-in-law in sharing the child-minding, but also the problems; her mother-in-law had different ideas about fresh air, for example, and tried to preserve the baby from it at all costs. A mother with a child-minder who was not her own mother came into contact with other ideas about and ways of child-rearing – just as Mr Champion said. Working mothers experience the same problems today. Mrs Gregory had the added problem that she did not get on with her father-in-law, yet was obliged to live in his house, because there was nowhere else.

Mrs Gregory married a man whose father had come from the countryside, who was a miner, and whose mother had worked in a factory. Mrs Gregory hated and feared drink, having seen so much of it with her parents and grandparents – her father, for instance, said that you weren't drunk unless you couldn't crawl home. She married someone who was not a drinker or a violent man; nor would he allow her mother's hand to be raised against her any more. The responsibilities of the home were his wife's: she did all the work while the children were growing up, and in retirement she shared the cooking and cleaning with her grown-up daughter. He looked after the garden and the car. When I visited them, he had been out in the shed using his circular saw, which he had made out of a treadle sewing-machine, but he made us a cup of tea and gave us some shortbread which their daughter had baked.

Mr Gregory was a family man and enjoyed his children. He had changed nappies, bathed and fed them (when she did not breast-feed them herself; she breast-fed each child until he or she was 2). When they were older, he would play football with them, or they would go train-spotting. They were not well off with seven children, and had no money to spend on entertainment, but they used to do quizzes and play games at home.

In Mr Gregory's home, his father had always handed over his money to his mother:

> They always handed their wages over in those days. And if he wanted anything, say to buy pigeons, he used to ask Mum for the money. I can't ever remember my father keeping any wages back . . . I followed exactly the same, yes. I have never kept anything. No, we have always been over and above board, share and share alike.

This seemed an eminently companionable marriage, based on segregated, but not rigidly so, roles and pervaded by kindliness. Mr Gregory said: 'We have always understood one another's feelings and needs.' Nevertheless, one of their children remembered arguments over money which were the almost inevitable accompaniment to a large family and a small wage.

Both of them were very fond of children, and when their own children had gone to school Mrs Gregory became quite wistful. On the advice of her doctor, she took other people's children in to nurse, from when they were babies until when they went to school. This must have been easier than when she went out to work and had to come back to 'her' work in the evening. But she also tried to make it interesting and varied for these children, with outings on some days and work on others. She was also one of those women who are called upon or go to help when a woman in the street is having a baby. She was, after all, very experienced after her own seven confinements.

Although her husband was a family man and they had lived for years with his parents before they got their own council house, Mrs Gregory was obviously the pivot of her family. 'I don't like to be dominated,' she said, 'and I don't like to dominate. I like a little bit of compatibility if I can get it.'

Mrs Gregory was adaptable when it came to working. She had been a mouldrunner, a glue-maker and a warehousewoman on potbanks, a machinist in the rag trade, as well as a cleaner and nursewoman. Mrs Bentley also adapted to what was available and best at the time, and in the 1940s had given up working on the pots to do market work with an aunt. Before that she had worked on a teapot factory with an old lady whose husband had died, and when they came to get their first two-up-and-two-down house (with a mortgage of 7s 6d a week) this lady came to live with them. She stayed with them, living as family, for twenty-two years, having one of the two bedrooms.

Mrs Bentley did all the shopping and cooking. She had had to give up pottery-work and stay at home when her mother and father became ill, and she eventually had to look after her father and two half-brothers. Once again, the married daughter's obligations as a carer (for people in whose house she had not even slept as a girl, since there was not enough room) superseded all others. But on Saturdays her husband and daughter took over, and she was able to work in the market. Her aunt used to buy white ware and decorate it at 'a small, very broken-down old place up at Tunstall. And she would decorate it on a Monday and Tuesday, and they would go to the market Wednesday; she would decorate Thursday, and she would go to the market Friday and Saturday.' Decorators, working part-time or on their own account like this, were not unusual. Mrs Bede used to do outwork, and I met other decorators and flower-makers who worked at home. Outwork, washing, doing cleaning and taking in lodgers were important ways for women to supplement a man's wage if they had to stay at home.

In babyhood Mrs Bentley put her daughter out to nurse, while she worked on the pots. Money was all important, and sacrifices had to be made; the parents, for instance, always shared a room with their daughter, because of the old lady who lodged with them (compare Mrs Furnivall, above). But there were perks as well: growing up during the war, the daughter was 'right bonny, because she could have biscuits and chocolate, black market' through her mother's contacts in the market. Mr Bentley felt that his daughter, who had later gone to university, did what he should have done; he had been one of the ablest pupils at his school, but he had been unable to take up the scholarship, because his mother had been left a widow with five children, and he was the oldest. He had gone from job to job in the worst of the Depression, taking whatever work he could get on factories and in the pit. His own health had been sacrificed to it, and he died of pneumoconiosis.

One can see from these accounts of people's home lives how industry and illness not only marred or shortened the lives of old people but affected the opportunities and burdens of the young. Family feeling meant that a woman would go out to work first of all for her mother, then as a married woman, for her children's sake, but she might also have to give up work for a sick parent's sake. Her time and her energies had to be divided and to adapt rapidly to earning money on a potbank; or helping a daughter, sister or friend to earn money (while she herself earned money as a nursewoman) while she looked after her own children as well; or becoming the only available nurse to a sick husband or parent. Although proud of their skills as pottery-workers, women obviously had to go in and out of the industry as these more insistent demands were made on them. Although not always in the workshops themselves, they helped to keep them going – just as their own mothers helped them to go out to work – and it was they who picked up the broken husks of men, to nurse them at the end of their lives. When, in the 1950s, Harold Hewitt asserted that women got lower pay because they did not have the same responsibilities as men (see page 25), he had no thought for the way the pottery industry, with its (still) low wages and its (still) dusty workshops, depended both on women's labour and on the fact that they would at intervals leave work – to take on the responsibilities of caring, when their families needed them. The elasticity of women's labour, the fact that they could be hauled back temporarily to busy workshops that were short of labour, was as necessary to the health of the potbanks as it was to their families that they be called home at other times for other responsibilities.

The other women born between 1917 and 1925 contain in their life histories both elements of a new way of life and elements of the old. Mrs Hewell's marriage did not exclude her mother. She used to go up to her mother's house with her baby, most days, while her husband was away in the Second World War, and she paid her mother to mind the youngest, at 4 years old, when she went back to work again. Her husband did not see his first boy till he was 5 and missed all his 'little ways', but he was a proud father when he returned, pushing his second child in a pram. In what was to become a common pattern for the division of labour, Mrs Hewell did all the housework and the shopping, but her husband, when they eventually bought their own house, did most of the alterations, because he could 'put his hand to anything'.

Mrs Hewell and most of the women who brought up their children after the Second World War were not so hard pressed as the older women. It was no longer financially necessary for most of them to go back to work full-time when the baby was a month, or at most a few months old, as it had been in the 1920s and 1930s. But Mrs Hewell returned to work – as Anna Pollert, in *Girls, Wives, Factory Lives*. (1981), described women in a tobacco factory returning – to replace household necessaries, little realizing that she was going to have to go on working so long. Mrs Hewell now felt the relief of having paid off their mortgage, being able to sit in her garden with its roses and fruit-trees. At first, when they were both working, her husband gave her his wages, and she 'gave him what he could have, you know, pocket-money. But as the years have gone by and . . . we've sort of got better, we decided that he would give me so much, and he could save some. And he'll always save for the holidays, no worry about holidays.'

This, of course, was Mrs Mason's situation. The pattern of money management seems to be that women are allocated responsibility for money where there is scarcely enough, or not enough at all, to go round; but as soon as there is money to spare, the husband takes over. Gradually, as wages have improved, it seems that women are losing some of their traditional power and responsibility in the home. But in some households men who did not hand over their wages, just giving their wives housekeeping, still delegated responsibility to their wives. They kept their wives short of money but in charge of bills and groceries, rent and clothes, so that they could themselves go out drinking. This pattern, imposed on the wife, continues in some households to this day. I describe it in Chapter 7.

The pattern of caring for the old continues. Mrs Goodrich was a decorator and married a placer in the bottle ovens. Like many others, she looked after a parent, in this case her mother, until she died.

Mrs Furnivall and her husband together were the carers for her father, when he came to live and die with them. Her father did not want to go into a home, and so she and her husband had given him one bedroom, their son the other, and had themselves slept on a put-you-up in the sitting-room for twelve years. This was a father who had sat by the fire while his wife, recovering from a mastectomy, had done the washing and turned the mangle. This was the man who had gambled away any money he had earned. But he assumed rightly that his daughter would see to him, feed him, administer pain-killers and change his diapers until he died.

Mr Furnivall had been a plasterer for twenty years and then had several different jobs. He had helped his wife a great deal in caring for her father. In money management the same sharing and understanding applied, with Mrs Furnivall as the manager at home. Mrs Furnivall had the wages, but 'he used to have his pocket-money, what he wanted out – I didn't tell him what to have. He used to have it out, and give me the wage-packet. I saw what he'd got every week, you know. And, mind you, I always saw that he had everything he needed . . . He's always been well dressed.'

Mrs Furnivall stayed at home (she was a gilder) until her little girl was 2 years old, towards the end of the war:

> Then a friend of mine – she used to live next door but one to us – she said, 'Have you ever thought of going back to work?' And I said, 'Not till Joanna starts school.' She said, 'Oh, I'd love to have her!' you know, and she was ever such a nice person . . . They were advertising for gilders back [where I worked], so I went back again, you know, not meaning to do long, but I stayed.

She paid about £1 to the neighbour out of her £5 or £6 wages, while her husband was earning £8 as a builder. They were able to save for a little house not far from her mother, and to buy furniture with his £25 demob money. They had started their married life in her mother's house, so the fact that she went out to work had given them independence and freedom. In the new home, like Mr Hewell and many post-war husbands, Mr Furnivall did a lot of the alterations himself, and thus saved them a good deal of money.

After some time they had a second child, and again, when he was 2 years old, Mrs Furnivall put him out to nurse, this time with someone who was an old friend of the family. She went back to work, she said, because the pottery sent for her. Potteries needed labour in the mid-1950s and sought out their old hands, putting pressure on them to leave their homes again:

> They sent for me and asked if I could do – they were that busy – if I could do a bit. And I said, 'Well, I'll just come afternoons.' And I used to go half-past one till five o'clock, just afternoons at the beginning. Then, you know, they kept on and on, wanting a bit more, till I was doing a full day, eight hour again, you know.

She worked 'definitely for the money' so that they could get a nicer house. Like Mrs Hewell and many younger pottery-workers, the prospect was opening up for her, through a double wage and a smaller family, of better living conditions, ample food and a good education for her children. But times were changing in the early 1980s, and after two decades of improvement her husband was about to be made redundant. Like the men of his father's generation, he was worried about their future.

With Mrs Roper (born in 1923) we are among those women who were below retiring age in 1981, when I did my fieldwork. Mrs Roper was still working full-time in the pottery industry in a position of some responsibility. She too had a small family – like Mrs Furnivall, Mrs Goodrich, Mrs Hewell, Mrs Bentley and Mrs Champion – a pattern which was to become eventually the modern pattern of families locally (see Chapter 1), smaller than the national average. In Chapter 7 I shall describe a number of large families, out of which came pottery-workers still anxious in the 1940s and 1950s to get as big a wage as possible as early as possible, for their mothers.

Mrs Roper, herself an only child, began her married life in her parents' house. After two and a half years her husband's mother died, and they moved in with his father, to look after him until he eventually died of cancer. In the meantime she had two children and went back to work: 'I decided as I couldn't live on the money and I started to work, and I have worked ever since.' Her youngest child was 2, and he went to a nursery, while the eldest went to a lady who took her to school with her own child; thus she was able to do school hours. She said she had regrets about it, and 'I would have rather have seen them grow up a bit, and not gone to work.' But at the same time, 'I wanted to make sure as they had the chances that I never had.' She, like several other women with small families, did not want her children to work on potbanks as she had done; she wanted them to be able to choose: 'I believe in children being given the chance of being and doing what they want.'[5]

The financial arrangements in this household (where the husband had gone from potbank work to shift-work on a public utility) were similar to Mrs Mason's and Mrs Hewell's. But they had joint accounts, which should crucially have given Mrs Roper as much spending power as her husband:

> What we do is Jack gives me so much, but I use my wages. I pay all the road, I pay for everything out of my wages, but if I want new clothes, coats or dresses, or shoes, or a suite of furniture, make no mistake, Jack pays for all that. Same with holidays, Jack pays for that. I mean, we've got joint accounts, and if I wanted anything I could have it, but the way we work it, as I have found it, it works very well.

Mr Roper did the shopping, the decorating at home and also the cooking during the week, because he was at home, and she was out at work. Husbands who could and did cook for their working wives were something I was to meet on many occasions with younger working women. They scarcely met except at the weekend: 'As I come in at five to ten-past, Jack goes out at half-past. We don't see much of each other.' Like Mrs Barnes, Mrs Roper was philosophical about this; for many women, not just in Stoke, shift-work is a fact of life. Mr Roper also shared in the cleaning; he would hoover upstairs, and she would do the 'furniture pasting', the polishing. But child care had not been shared: when the children were small, looking after them was Mrs Roper's job, and when she was older, she had had to help with her bedridden mother.

Mrs Adams also had two children, and went back to work when the youngest was a little over 2 years old. She worked school hours, while one was in a nursery and the other at school. During the holidays, she was able to stay at home herself, or her mother would come down to see to them, or later, a cousin's girl, who was 14. She did not feel she had missed out on her children, because she was able to do part-time work, and this had just fitted in with being with them after school. Her husband had shared in looking after them, unlike Mr Roper, in bathing and dressing them, and doing 'anything as was necessary'. This gave her a freedom which the oldest women had not had – to go out and leave him in charge, while she went to the pictures:

> I used to go there every week; didn't matter what was on, I used to go there, you know. He'd come in from work about quarter-past five, and I'd already had my meal, and I used to dash out, 'I'll be back for nine!' you know. And I always used to sit in the same seat, but it was a night out, and I used to go and see the picture.

She used to do 'her' washing sometimes very early on a Saturday morning, and she also did the shopping on her way home from work, and all the cooking. They used to do the cleaning between them, always with a vacuum-cleaner, and not a brush, as the older women specified; she had been the only one on her street with a fitted carpet. Her husband used to clean their brassware too, and sometimes clean upstairs, if she did not have time. Gradually, it seems, the idea of what was strictly women's work was breaking down, and although it might differ from household to household, a husband might think that looking after the children, cooking or cleaning was not inappropriate for him to share.

For their leisure, Mr and Mrs Adams liked to go dancing, and Mrs Adams liked to sew; they had at one time or another followed up their interests separately at evening classes. They now lived in a council house, but had been through a period in lodgings and a period of home ownership before their house was compulsory purchased by the council. They had started their married life in rooms with a friend of her mother's, people with whom they got on very well: 'We had the front room and the front room upstairs . . . And they were great! We had both our children there . . . And the day we moved into X—Street, neither of us had any tea. We were crying because we'd got to leave one another. But, you know, they were smashing people!' After their house was demolished they were rehoused, and they now preferred to spend their money on holidays abroad.

Mrs Adams felt that her wages had been very important, because although her husband had a secure job it did not bring in big wages. Their pattern of income management differed from some other people's, since it was Mrs Adams who kept her wages as savings. She paid all the bills out of the house-keeping money which he gave her every week. His pocket-money, she said, was just for taking her out. Like Mrs Box, she paid for the holidays, and he provided the spending-money; they seemed to be able to have whatever they wanted: 'I go out and buy whatever I want, or if he wants anything – oh, yes . . . I'm not skinny with meself or Ted, you know. Whatever we need and what we want we have.'

The area where they now lived was an example of sensitive rehousing. Their neighbours were the same ones who had lived in the old street, and although they did not mix much nowadays they could still depend on one another: 'If we need them, or if they need us, you know, we are always available.'

Mrs Atkins had been working on the pots for only twenty-five years. During the war she had been in the fire service at a munitions factory, and had loved the work, but when she married for the first time, she stopped work. Her husband was an engineer and did not want her to work at all: 'He'd got a good job, and he thought, you know, I'd got enough to do at home.' But her sister had had too much work to do alone on the potbank where she worked, and had told them, 'Probably me sister will come, but she'll only do part-time.' Once again, with women's labour in demand – potbanks too busy to fulfill their orders – women could call the tune, or at least to the extent of doing the hours which suited them. She worked from 9.30 a.m. to 3.00 p.m. for seventeen years, while her son, who was 4 when she started, went first to a nursery school and then to school.

She had started her married life living with her husband's grandmother in a big house, and she 'was at home to do the work then'. Her husband had died, and after a period of widowhood she had married again. This time she was the one who was working, and her new husband was retired. He used to get her meal ready for her for when she came in, and he did the gardening and cleaning the windows. She did the rest of the work at home, 'because I'd rather do my own'. She was not really obliged to go to work, since she had a pension from her first husband, and she had bought their rented house, improved it and sold it, so that she now had a bungalow. Life was pleasant; they went dancing several times a week, and they were looking forward to a week, as they did every year, at Blackpool.

Mrs Havelock (born in 1924), the youngest in this group of women, has in her lifestory elements of the old and of the new way of life which was more typical of pottery-workers since the war than between the wars. She, like some of the oldest women, put her child out to nurse – but in a nursery, not with a child-minder – at seven months; but the reason for her starting work again so soon was a modern one: 'Because we wanted the house, didn't we, we wanted a house of our own, you see, and he didn't get a big wage. I mean, when I've first got married, he was only getting £4 a week wages, and I was only getting £3.'

Although they were living with her mother-in-law, she preferred to put her daughter into a nursery: 'And then her grandma had her when she was old enough to go to school . . . And her and her grandma were inseparables, you know; her grandma loved her, and she loved her grandma.' When they eventually moved away, her daughter had to learn to be independent. She was 11 years old, and her mother was anxious, but felt it was time:

And I gave her a key, told her to put it away safe, to let herself in. And I said, 'If you don't want to let yourself in here, go into Mrs Jones, next door.' And I thought then was the time for her to be independent on herself. And she used to sit in here hours, hours and hours. She would never go out through the door. She never played in the street.

The ideal of childhood was obviously changing to something more private. This account is a far cry from the children of the first decades of the century, playing in gangs in the backs, or out in the fields, or looking after one another, having little concerts or picnics.[6] Left to themselves, these early children had grouped together; children of the smaller, modern family were more solitary, staying in their parents' hard-earned houses, while their parents were out working to keep up the payments on their better standard of living. From now on I was to meet more and more women who were in privately bought houses, or who were buying their house from the council. Their children were loved and important to them; but, for them, to be good parents meant making sure that their children could be more successful than, even different from, themselves. They valued themselves above all as providers, and wanted and expected schools to give their children an education, horizons and opportunities that they did not have. In their own homes the ideals of many women aged 40 and 50 were to go far beyond the dreams of their mothers but also, in another sense, not nearly so far, because their aspirations stopped at the front gate. As we shall see in Chapter 7, the house, like a wall-to-wall carpeted stage set, was to become for many the achievement to be sought above all others.

Notes

1   The clear-cut differentiation of roles in working-class marriages is similar at this period to that found by Roberts (1984) in Lancashire. Roberts says that 'The majority of men believed that they proved their masculinity by never doing any domestic chore which could be construed as belonging to the sphere of women . . . But most women shared this view' 1984, (p. 116). What is interesting in the Potteries, however, is that this differentiation could not be based on a clear division of responsibilities such that the wife was the manager and the husband the provider. Most of these husbands had great difficulty in being any kind of a provider (including Mr Hilditch, whose wife worked much more consistently than he was able to do). Women were providers, managers and workers in the home. In Roberts's Preston sample, where there was a large proportion of married women in full-time work, 'the husband usually helped with domestic chores' (p. 118). Roberts says that they had to help their wives 'because otherwise it is doubtful if their wives would have survived'. Among my respondents born before the Second World War are a number of daughters whose mothers quite simply did not. They died young.
2   In 1921, 58 per cent of occupied females in Stoke were in the pots; 79 per cent of pottery-working women were under 35; over a third were married or widowed. In 1931, 64 per cent of occupied women worked in the pots.
3   It was traditional in Stoke, as in other working-class districts, to insure against a death in the family by paying so much a week (Mrs Mason had done this formerly). Thus funerals could become occasions, almost street parties, much more so than weddings. Lady Bell, in *At the Works*, 1985, (first published in 1907), describes the importance, among ironworkers, of paying for a good funeral in Middlesbrough, Yorkshire. She quotes a widow saying 'with pride after her husband died that she

had "buried him with ham", meaning that the assembled company who came to the funeral had had sandwiches of the best description . . . A funeral', she adds, 'indeed is one of the principal social opportunities in the class we are describing. "A slow walk and a cup of tea" it is sometimes called' (p. 77). One of the pottery-women I had talked to (born much later), who had come from Wales, said that sandwiches would not have been enough there, a proper sit-down meal was *de rigueur* if it was not to be a pauper's funeral.

4 Oral historians like Jeremy Seabrook have long lamented the loss of the working-class community where people helped one another. Elizabeth Bott, in *Family and Social Network*, 1971, asserts that feelings of solidarity are strongest in long-established areas with a dominant industry or a small number of traditional occupations (p. 103). The important factor is whether or not people feel they are socially similar to one another. Her description would, of course, fit Stoke rather well, and people often referred to the way that they used to help one another in the old days. The impression I have been given is that it has changed since perhaps the 1950s, and the reason given is that people do not know one another (because of moving into new areas), or that they are too busy making (or spending) money. Helping one another, however, often meant helping in childbirth or illness, because people could not afford proper medical care. The present government is perhaps seeking a revival of this kind of community spirit. Elizabeth Roberts states that the neighbourhoods displaying the most solidarity were the poorest (*A Woman's Place*, 1984, p. 195).

5 In Chapter 8 I describe how the daughters of Mrs Roper and Mrs Adams had fared in adult life, as well as the daughters of younger pottery-workers whom I also interviewed. Mothers and daughters did not always see things in the same way, and their accounts of the past emphasize different aspects of their childhoods. The past does not quite dissolve before one's eyes, but one begins to feel how important it was to have talked to a number of people about the same period and events.

6 Phyllis Willmott, in *Growing Up in a London Village*, 1979, describes the difference in the 1920s between her own family, in which the children were allowed to play in the street, and the more 'fussy' mothers with only one or two children: 'There were only about two dozen children of much the same ages in our road, but not all of them played out as much as we did. Some mothers, especially those with only one or two children and with a whole house to themselves, were more fussy, and let their children out only occasionally' (p. 162). The large and the small family are two different worlds of experience existing at the same time.

CHAPTER 7

Handleless Cups, Hard Drinkers and New Three Pieces

Before the Second World War there were 67,000 workers in the North Staffordshire pottery industry in 327 factories; when it ended, there were only 31,000 workers left in the industry, and at least 120 potteries had closed.[1] For this reason, if for no other, I have divided the experiences of women who worked in the industry before the war from those who started work during or after it. Many women did new work during the war; the government wanted them to work on munitions, and women like Mrs Farrier, Mrs Box and Mrs Neale were released from their potbanks to work at the Royal Ordnance Factories at Swinnerton and Radway Green. Others were on factories which had switched to war work and, like Mrs Adams, were for the first time making insulators instead of tableware.

There were restrictions on what potteries could produce. For the home market, a quota was introduced, restricting manufacture to two-thirds of the value of what had been produced between 1 June and 30 November 1939. Since prices had risen, this meant that in practice they could produce only half the volume of what they had produced in this period.[2] In 1941 the Board of Trade announced plans to concentrate production into fewer factories, which were granted 'nucleus certificates', and those outside the 'nucleus' were to close or market the products of the more fortunate. On 1 June 1942 decorated ware was banned from the home market. The *Pottery Gazette* published a list of firms licensed to make undecorated earthenware, which became quota-free. It commented caustically (in a report on the House of Lords debate on child labour in the potteries) that 'Now there is an acute shortage of tableware it is being realized, even by government officials, that we are not yet back to the level of pigs; we need cups and plates for our food and drink.[3] The *Pottery Gazette* also published a photograph of 'Miss Ida Nicklin, once a decorator, [who] is now busily casting teapots'. At her factory, Howard Pottery, which made Brentleigh ware, production had gone over from fancies to utility ware, and 90 per cent of operatives had to be retrained; decorators had to consent to work in the clay end, and the sacrosanct divisions had to be broken down.[4] Apparently, another government brainwave was to introduce cups without handles, but the advantages of cups as opposed to tea-bowls had been felt by customers in the early nineteenth century, and there was no sign of their reverting to Chinese tea-drinking; the handleless cups did not sell.[5]

The intervention by the government in the industry, the experience of working on munitions, the rationing of food and clothes and the rising cost of living all affected women pottery-workers; but the disruption of the war cannot be said to have changed family life in the way that it disrupted their work lives. Certainly, boyfriends and husbands went away – courtships were lengthened or cut short; husbands like Mr Hewell returned from the war to get to know children whose babyhood or infancy they had missed. Certainly, there was better housing available in the city, but this had been a long and continuous process of building: 4,337 new dwelling-houses were certified for habitation between 1921 and 1929, and after 1925 the number built never fell below 500 a year.[6] Certainly, during the war, women went into every area of work in the potbanks that had been male preserves; they casted everything, they made all but the biggest plates, they even drew the ovens; the heaviest work was not beyond them. But, as we have seen, before the war the industry had been very reliant on women. Even if the ideal was of women whose work was at home, it was normal for women to go out to work. In 1935 there were 56,185 employees in the pottery factories, and more of them were women than men.

The Second World War did not suddenly show women new horizons, a world beyond the white-stoned step. What we shall find is that, in the 1950s and after, for the first time they were able to put their children first, to call the tune and to work part-time when it suited them. We shall also find a very striking division between husbands who acted as partners to their wives (both of them doing paid work *and* unpaid work in the home) and those who said they did not want their wives to work, or kept up the fiction that it was unnecessary, refusing to do any chores at home.

The women who started work in the 1940s and 1950s were born between 1925 and the war itself. Family life in the 1930s and 1940s, as they describe it, has to be placed alongside what the older women said about their married lives and it was intriguing among these, and younger women whom I talked to, to compare how several mothers and daughters described the same events. I describe some of these daughters in Chapter 8. Some of the older women I have described, marrying in the 1920s and 1930s, were achievers with small families, bringing their children out of the prospect of factory work and, through education, into jobs as teachers, business men and women, skilled trades people or white-collar workers. The next generation of pottery-workers I talked to, born between 1925 and 1941, came mostly from large families which had much in common with the big families remembered by the women born before 1925.

One continuity in the family life of the older and younger women I spoke to was in the early loss of mothers.[7] Jane Phillips's (born in 1931) mother had six children and died of strokes aged 48. Iris Wenceslas's (born in 1933) mother, with eight children, died aged 45. Pam Tunstall's (born in 1937) mother, with nine children, died at 54. Jill Rugeley's (born in 1939) mother died of cancer at 39. All these women died with dependent children. Infant mortality fell steadily in the 1930s and 1940s, but the death rate moved erratically in the same period: 11.9 per 1,000 in 1930, 12.3 in 1935, 13.2 in 1940, 11.9 in 1945 and 11.4 in 1970. Deaths from diarrhoea and enteritis had gone down to 16 in 1940, but deaths from cancer – the new scourge, which was to continue its unrelenting increase in every decade – were 407. By 1965, 19.6 per cent of all deaths were from cancer.[8]

There were, as before among the women I spoke to, fathers with pneumoconiosis. Mrs Eagle's (born in 1940) father was a miner and suffered from dust. Mrs Caesar (born in 1927), Mrs Kazak (born in 1931) and Mrs Thomas (born around 1939) all had fathers who were miners and who died of pneumoconiosis. Such cases as these were not the last final flourish of the disease; the 1970 Annual Report of the Medical Officer of Health announced 250 newly identified cases of pneumoconiosis.

Another feature of these families in the 1930s and 1940s is one of life-style rather than health; it is in the number in which there were arguments over money and drink, sometimes but not always associated with violence. If there were no arguments, it was sometimes because wives took money from their husbands without their realizing it. A certain type of father persists seemingly from generation to generation: he is in a 'manly' job into which women may not venture; he keeps his wife short of money, and spends most of what he has on drink; he often has numerous children; if his wife remonstrates with him, he can be violent. Having written the above, I was amazed to discover how similar it was to the type of husband whom Elizabeth Roberts (1984) describes in her Lancashire study as the Victorian type: it also bears comparison, of course, with the hard-drinking costermongers whom Mayhew describes beating their common-law wives.[9] Roberts's description is of a minority:

> but a minority which cannot be ignored, producing as it did untold physical and psychological misery. All the husbands in this group had a keen sense of what was 'manly'. This almost invariably included heavy drinking, demanding total obedience from their families, expecting and getting the best food available in the family, and spending an inordinate proportion of their wages on their own personal pleasures, whether it was on clothes, jewellery or gambling. They almost inevitably had very large families, and in some cases tormented their wives even further by accusing them of having affairs with other men.[10]

The following is the childhood of a woman pottery-worker in the 1940s:

> It was rough when we were kids because my mum and dad used to fight like cat and dog, terrible, horrible fighting, you know, horrible . . .
> [What did they used to fight about?]
> Oh, my father having a drink – because he used to have a lot of drink then, you know. Sunday dinner, he'd come in and he'd – my mother used to bake every Sunday, you know, hundreds of little cakes and big tarts, enough to last the week for all of us. And he'd come in, and he'd throw them up the wall, one at a time, straight up the wall. Horrible it was.
> [Why did he do it?]
> He felt like it. It didn't bother my father. There was quite a lot of them like

that. It was well known, you know, each family, it was well known, you'd go home and hit your missus . . . Many an afternoon . . . when I used to go to my uncle's, which was my father's youngest brother, he used to sleep in the hearth. And he used to come in and kick the teapot . . . the teapot used to be on the hearth, you know, on those black grates you used to have, and he used to kick the teapot, and he'd be laying among the broken bits. And he'd sleep until he'd slept his drink off, and then he'd be as right as ninepence.

Her father used to go out drinking every night and Saturday and Sunday dinner-times as well, but her mother would only put on her black hat and go down to the pub for half an hour on Saturday evenings. Perhaps the most striking part of this and some other accounts is the normality of violence:

[Did you never take sides when your mother and father were fighting?]
No. Just sit there.
[You never felt that he was hard on your mother?]
If you got up to help your mother, you'd get a good hiding. Oh, he's hit us if we've gone to Mother.
[But you didn't feel at the time he was hard on your mother?]
No. I think it was just a done thing. It seemed to be a done thing – it was going on all around you, you know. A woman's place was, 'Shut up! You'll do as I say!' And if he said you weren't going out, you weren't going out, and you'd stay there. It was just a done thing, wasn't it?

Not all the daughters in this family treated it as normal, however, and one left home and would have nothing to do with her father. There had been favouritism – the speaker felt she had been the spoilt one, and recognized that her father, while favouring her, had had no time for one of his sons. If he acted with the arbitrariness of a dictator, their mother was still not cowed by him, particularly if he hit the children:

[Did your mother get black eyes and all that?]
Oh God, yes! Terrible! Smashed glasses and the lot. But I've seen my mother hit my father – she hit back, especially if he hit us. In winter we used to have a chair in front of the fire, the old kitchen, and there used to be a chair with a bowl in, and we used to have a wash. And me father used to come up, one morning, and for no reason just smack you between the eyes, you know. And I remember my mother picking the poker up, and just turning and hitting my father – and his elbow came out here. Of course my father started crying, 'She's killed, her's killed me, take me to the hospital!' . . . But me mother worshipped my father, she really worshipped him, she wouldn't have nothing said against him. Nothing at all . . . And he wouldn't let her wear make-up, no way. And our Mike was only a dot – [he] told my father she'd bought this lipstick in Blackpool – so he hit her in Blackpool, hit her on the front.

In spite of all this, the daughter whom I interviewed, a strong, capable woman, said: 'I felt all right with my dad. I never disliked him, I don't think, never . . . He's mellowed with the years.'

I have quoted this at length because it is not an isolated case; it recalls the violence that Mrs Gregory had described between her parents in the 1920s, and it finds its more modern counterparts in personal accounts of family life in the 1950s and even the 1970s. The father is always excused, the mother taken to task for being the real cause of his violence. Here is an account of a family in the 1950s:

> They used to fall out, and me dad used to fight, you know. He used to hit my mum. And if his dinner wasn't just so, he used to slap it up the wall, you know, and we all used to sit there, terrified . . . My dad was the boss, and my mum didn't dare say anything. He was in charge, so he did have the last say, no matter what. And he would never let you talk at the table – he was always very efficient on his manners: 'You're not talking in there!' . . . My mum used to work hard. Now, if my dad did five days a week at the pit, there wouldn't be any need for my mum to have to go to work, because it was a good wage, see. [He would do only two or three shifts a week.] . . . She'd got all the house to run, the shopping, and look after us, and iron, you know how you are, and all the mither of it as well . . . But . . . I used to think how rotten my dad was . . . But in actual fact I worship my father – actually it's reversed over the years . . . I've got a lot of respect for my father. I see now what it was all for, you know, why he was doing it.

This man had 'got a bit lazy' and even though his wife was 'always pregnant' she would go out to work and put the children out to nurse. The hallmark of men of this type was meanness; this is not the kind of household where the husband hands over the pay-packet:

> My dad used to keep all his wages, and he used to write it out on a Friday night – rent, say £2.50, or whatever it was, food, you know, say thirty bob '30s' or whatever it was in them days like, the milkman, the shopman, the blanketman, the catalogueman – all this lot there used to be a mile long, this list did.

This was a list of debt, so that he could get by on a minimum number of shifts and have his beer as well. The 1940s example is the same; the father would take all the children's wages and give them back 10s for cleaning materials. His money was his own, to spend in the pub, and when the children were sent out to do the shopping they had to give him accounts: 'We used to have to take a bill back and everything wrote down what we bought, and give him the change, and he'd tell you off if you spent too much.'

The question remains whether wives with husbands like this could do anything about it. Did they put up with it because they liked it (as Mayhew's informant opined in 1851: Quennele, n.d.), or because it was 'normal' and suffering of this kind was to be expected (Patient Griselda has a very long pedigree in English history), or did they really have no alternative – nowhere to go, for instance? If a woman's family lived locally, why did her father or brothers not protect her from her husband and keep him in line? Was male solidarity more important?

There are several examples in these accounts of a wife's brother either being her husband's drinking partner or accompanying him when he took other girls out secretly. A brother evidently felt no special loyalty towards his sister. Another problem was that a council or National Coal Board house was usually in the husband's name, and it would have been difficult for the wife to take all her children somewhere else. Even where no physical fighting was described to me, a woman who was at the end of her tether had the problem of leaving her children if she wanted to leave a selfish husband.

Mrs Furnivall (born in 1921) remembered that her mother and father rowed over money. He used not to work regularly – the First World War had ruined his health – but he would gamble away any money he had: 'He'd spend. If he was working, he'd spend all his money on horses and that, gambling. And me mother never knew when she was going to get any money or not.' Her mother would be exasperated: 'Me mother would say, "I'm going to leave him", you know. "If it wasn't for you children, I'd go." And I used to say, "Oh, mother, don't leave us!" ' She stayed on, working by day and washing and turning the mangle by night until she died of cancer.

This was in the 1920s, but the 1950s family described above were similarly living on a knife's edge; on one occasion, after the father had blacked his wife's eye, the children were made to draw names out of a cup to determine who was going to live with whom when they split up. When his wife left him, he threatened them all that they would be put into homes: 'Every night we used to come in from school, and I used to think, "I hope Mum's there." ' The daughter could not concentrate at school, and when her father was shouting at home 'You used to sit on the edge of your seat, dead tense.' At least two of the children were so disturbed that they wet the bed until they were in their teens.

Hard-drinking fathers with tight fists and distended bladders throng the accounts of 1930s childhoods. Mrs Caesar (born in 1927), who came from a family of three, had a father who was a miner, but her mother also went out to work because 'he spent most of the money on drink' (most of his time too, of course). He and his wife did not live happily until after he was a sick man, drink and dust having caught up with him, 'when he realized he was a sick man, of the drink and the illness, and smok[ing] was just forgotten, and it was just a casual drink'.

Mrs Barbour (born in 1931) came from a family of nine. Her father was a contractor in the mine; he too loved his drink, and his wife would sometimes have to take money from his pockets when she needed it. This seems to have worked well as far as family harmony was concerned. Mrs Kazak (born in 1931) came from a family of eight children, whose father was a buttyman in the mine and equally fond of drink. In this family the mother was obviously a very energetic person. She went out to work (putting the children out to nurse, four at a time), so that although 'we knew what it was to run with holes in our shoes, walk on bare England . . . we always had a good table'. The priority of good food before clothes or household effects is a very common one, mentioned by many of these big families.[11] Mrs Kazak's father would become the strict Victorian father when he went teetotal for a few months: 'He was as miserable as sin . . . You had to be in at half-past nine at night, you know, the strict father.'

In mitigation, perhaps I should add that all these miners flourishing in the 1930s were dead before they were old, and two of them had 100 per cent dust. The comradeship of the mine, translated into public drinking, was a safeguard in a dangerous occupation. Few are the miners who have not been injured at some time, even if their injuries have not reached official statistics. This, at any rate, is a common sociological excuse for heavy drinking; it is hardly a sufficient cause for the forms of family interaction I have described. But whether or not he was hard-drinking and mean, a miner's work was very hard, and he did not have much to look forward to. Mrs Thomas's (born in 1939) father, who was a face-worker with five children, did not conform to the stereotype, but working in the mine gave him injuries and ruined his health:

> We never went short of anything, and he never lost much time, my father didn't, you know. I remember my mother waiting up for him, and him coming home in ambulances a time or two . . . when I was little. Because then, I think it was a lot harder in the pit, wasn't it? Today I think there's more machines and press-button things, where . . . He used to tell us stories where he used to crawl for miles on his hands and knees, you know, and he used to scrape his back. Well, he used to show us the scars on his back, and they used to be blue . . . through crawling down the tunnels where they worked. Well, today it's a lot different, I believe.

He died of pneumoconiosis at 64, having stopped work through ill health at 60. He had worked in the pit from the age of 12. In the last four years at home, 'He'd only have to walk across the room and that was it, he . . . literally couldn't breathe.'

Another father was a miner in the by now more familiar pattern. Mrs Phillips (born in 1931) described him as 'a lovely, big, beautiful man that when he came through the door, the house lit up'. His wife had six children living, and 'there may have been some more as well'. She suffered from strokes and died at the age of 48. But this 'beautiful man' was also 'a mean man – nobody ever saw his money, and my mother was given housekeeping, and there was never any more'. He never bought anybody anything: 'He was perfectly fair with everybody; nobody got anything.' There were no Christmas presents and no birthday presents, and he would hide money under the floorboards. He used to go out drinking with his wife's brother (no sibling solidarity here) and come home late for his Sunday dinner, when his wife would hit him: 'She must have shoved the dinner all over him.' Here, as in the other accounts, all the criticism in the telling was for the mother, who was 'too strict'; the father was remembered lovingly, the mother without love.

Mrs Wenceslas (born in 1933) lost both her parents before she was 20 – they too had fought together, but here the mother was a heavy drinker too, and Mrs Wenceslas described her as 'aggravating'. Her father was also a miner. Another father in the 1940s was always too drunk to play Santa Claus at Christmas. He drank heavily at the weekend, and his wife used to find pound notes hidden away; she needed them, with a child almost every year and a shop-bill that was never rubbed off.

Lest one should think that the hard-drinking, tight-fisted stereotype went exclusively with working in the pit, it should be said that one of the worst examples of this type was a dipper and placer in the pottery industry, and another a steelworker on Shelton Bar. But certainly it was found among skilled workers in 'manly' jobs; it may be that, prisoners of their idea of manliness – both in taking these kinds of jobs and in fathering as many children as they could – their resentment was directed against their wives, upon whom they thrust their ideal of womanhood, as sexual object, child-bearer and servant. The idea of the husband as provider is very poorly developed at the expense of the idea of husband as 'a real man'. Mrs Kazak's father said, perhaps significantly, that there wasn't 'a real man' outside the mine. Certainly, hard drinking, meanness and induced poverty seem not to have caused daughters to reject their fathers. Where mothers were beaten, their daughters do seem to have rejected them, perhaps not wishing to identify with someone who was such a victim, or not coming to terms with their fathers' brutality.

The father who abused his power – by keeping his money to himself, in some cases using his physical strength against his wife, and also in giving her a large number of children whom he would ignore, to go out drinking instead – is a prominent stereotype among the women I talked to, particularly in the accounts of the 1930s and 1940s. But this period also produced fathers who did not abuse their power, and who were by nature loving and gentle. Joan Parsons's (born in 1934) father, who had also been a miner, is one such, in her description of him. Mrs Parsons came from a family of four:

> He works at the top of F— there, it's an engineering firm actually, and he's their little odd job man. They love him, they love him; the women in the office love him, and the men love him, because he makes the tea for them, tidies up – oh, he's a lovely tidier-up! Always been a lovely tidier-up, you know. I remember when we were little, we used to come down, and he used to work a lot of nights, and he'd have all the fire lit, and we'd have porridge, and he'd say, 'A little bit of toast for you?' and warm all your things, and off you'd go to school, you know. When I got married, there was none of that. I went into a household where it was every man for himself! So you can imagine – from a father who pampered you to . . . The first week I went home, me father says to me, 'How do you like being married?' I said, 'I don't like it, I don't like it, Dad!' . . .
>
> He'll come home from work, and then he makes pots of tea and takes some sandwiches in, just beautiful little sandwiches and all that. You'd love me father, he's a lovely little man, he is . . . 'What would you like next, duck?' and all that, you know. Me mother used to say to us, when I was reading all those [love] books, me mother used to say, 'You won't get one like your father.' And all me sisters would say, 'There's none like me dad, is there?' . . . Because that's how he is . . . He looks after everybody, and puts everybody first.

As a postscript to the hard-drinking fathers, some of whom were violent, some gamblers and most holding tight on to their purses at home, two husbands must be mentioned. Both had been husbands of pottery-workers whom I interviewed. The first wife was with her husband for over twenty years, marrying in the mid-1950s. She was, she said, beaten up in drink 'nearly every night of the week'. She divorced him in the mid-1970s. They quarrelled (as ever) over money: 'He was really nasty. He used to give me £8 a week to keep five children, and I had to work. I'd seen him bring £70-odd home from work, and he's only give me £8. A lot of the rows used to be about that.' She had her first child when she was 20, and followed him with what was a large family in the 1950s. Although she experienced violence herself, she still had the 'all-is-forgiven' attitude towards violence in men; she described her father-in-law as 'a lovely man . . . a bit violent years ago, to what Don's mother's tell me . . .

because I knew she left him about three times and went back, so I think she had her problems when the children were little'.

The second wife, growing up in the 1950s and almost a generation younger than the first, also had her first child by the time she was 20, but she was strong-minded, did not want the big family which her husband intended her to have and 'sneaked' the pill without his knowing. When she could stand life with him (which included drinking, pilfering and going out with other girls) no longer, she threw him out and lived on her own for a number of years. Determined to make a decent life for her child, she put him out to nurse and went to work on a potbank, did overtime, Saturday work, hairdressing, sewing – anything and everything to make it alone. Her determination is remarkable to listen to.

By the 1970s it was possible for these women to discard brutal or feckless husbands, to live on their own wages – even with the cost of child-minding one child at £7 to £12 per week – as long as a woman had taken contraception into her own hands, or her children were grown. Social security, of course, has meant that lone women with dependent children do not have to starve, even if they do not go out to work. Increases in women's wages and changes in divorce and benefits have thus taken away a lot of the power from the 'manly' man with his imprisoned family. But the essential change, in the Potteries and in society in general, is in the number of families in which the husband sees himself as a man not through the number of his children but through the quality of life he can provide for his family.

To see how this is happening, let us take an example of another family in which the wife is a pottery-worker, as were her mother and grandmother before her. Born in the early 1940s, once again she was married young and a mother twice over at 20, but at that point they decided together not to have any more children:

> Me husband said, 'We've got one of each, there's no other sort to have, we've finished.' So I left it entirely into his hands, and that's been it. And we had a great relationship, we always have had, you know. I'm not afraid of sex . . . I've never been on the pill, I just leave it in his hands, and he must be a good husband, that's all I can say . . . He said, 'Leave it to me. We won't have no more', and we haven't had no more.

She wished more people lived the same way they did, because 'everybody wouldn't be so hard up; people would have what they want'.

Having what they wanted meant a high standard of comfort, holidays abroad and starting to buy their council house. It also meant giving their children a good start in life with much more than they themselves had had; their married children had places of their own, and were not forced to live in lodgings or with one of their in-laws, as they had done. In order to achieve this, they both worked extremely hard, both at work and at home; they were a very close couple, able to discuss and to share, both in work and in money management, complementing one another's role, rather than duplicating it, or having interchangeable tasks. The husband's idea of manliness, well developed in sports, was modified by his concern for his wife and by their joint desire for a better standard of living. They did not work together in the same industry, but they discussed together everything to do with the home, including family planning; she did not have to 'sneak' the pill, like the younger woman described above, whose husband wanted a big family.

It may well be that the new openness about sexuality which characterized the whole country in the 1960s, coupled with the easy availability of contraception (it had never been very freely available before the war, if you simply could not afford it) and higher wages (for the average hourly earnings of both men and women doubled in the pottery industry between 1960 and 1970), began to make the 'manly' man an anachronism. As the birth rate rose in England and Wales between 1955 and 1965, the same effect was never so marked in Stoke-on-Trent, and by 1965 the birth rate stood at 16.2 per 1,000 in Stoke, while it was 18.1 in England and Wales.

An openness about sexuality also characterized, in 1981 the generation of women who were young working women during the mid-1950s and 1960s. A number of them told me that they were pregnant when they got married – and indeed, apart from bridal pregnancy, about which my informants talked, the local illegitimacy rate went up in the 1960s, just as it did nationally, and declined only after the passing of the Abortion Bill. There had, of course, been plenty of children who were granny-reared, and over whose fatherhood a veil had been decently drawn in previous generations; the important change was that these women could talk about their own sexuality in a way that older women did not.

In all the debate about domestic labour conducted in academic circles, the point has perhaps not been made forcefully enough that the great change in the amount of domestic work which women do is not just a matter of whether the husband gets out the vacuum-cleaner or not (and before the machine age, they were never very keen on brushes); rather, the point is that women today are cooking, washing and cleaning for a household of perhaps four, whereas many working-class women in the 1920s were cooking, washing and cleaning for a whole clutch of children. The great change in male mentality is in not imposing endless pregnancies on their wives; that is far more important than whether a man washes the dishes or not.

The big families of the 1930s and 1940s childhoods with which we started this chapter have much in common with the big families of the early decades of the century. There is a continuity in the culture of big families, and much of it has to do with poverty – the fact that money would not go round (whether or not it was what was left over from drink) – and with their mothers' lack of time. There was the problem of just not having enough room for all the family to sleep under one roof. Mrs Thomas and her sister slept next door with their relatives, for instance. There was the companionship (and the offloading) of large numbers of children. Mrs Fenton (born in 1941), who came from a family of nine, remembered them all being sent out with a bottle of water, jam sandwiches and money for the pictures, while her mother was giving birth to another baby. Mrs Rugeley, from a family of seven, used to take the little ones to the park in prams and pushchairs: 'We used to stick it on a swing, and it would come home with a cut head.'

Apart from the companionship which came with being a member of a large family, there were also (as in 1900, 1910 and 1920) the children's chores. Mrs Tunstall remembered shopping for the whole family from when she was 11. Mrs Rugeley had all the washing to do, and caring for her sick mother; when her mother died, she had the cooking to do as well. Mrs Thomas had the black-leading to do, like so many girls, and maidservants, since Victorian times; while Mrs Fenton's sister was still going to the pawnshop, as Mrs Powell and Mrs Madeley had done decades before. Daphne Gregory (born in 1936) used to have to go to the shop and ask for so much to be taken off the bill and more groceries to be put on tick. The same thing was going on in the 1970s; only the incidence of big families diminishes.

Not all the families were badly off. Mrs Phillips's family were not, but her mother was ill, and her daughter remembered nothing but an endless round of chores, which made it difficult to get on at school at the same time. Mrs Barbour's family were not badly off either, although there were nine children, but her mother also had a disability and needed help in housework. Mrs Barbour remembered that her workload increased as her elder sisters got married; but when they were all at home, one of them would do the lavatories, one clean the grate, one do the baking or polish the furniture or clean the floor; when it was all finished they could go out. Mrs Tunstall felt the stigma of coming from a large family, picked on at school for her thin winter dress, for looking poor. Daphne Gregory, the eldest of seven children, was ashamed of wearing other people's clothes and shoes, and tired of washing out knickers and socks so that she could wear clean underclothes the following morning. Rosie Fenton, who later became, she confessed 'clothes mad', used to have her 'posh' friend's coats; it was a case of 'If she had an apple, her core was always mine.'

Once again, among many of the women born in this period (1925 to 1941) there was a sense of missed opportunities at school, although for some people born in the early 1930s, like Mrs Barbour and Mrs Kazak, the war was responsible for their missing a lot of school. Mrs Phillips (born in 1931), Mrs Tunstall and Mrs Rugeley (born in 1939) missed school because their mothers needed them to help at home. Daphne Gregory remembered missing out on school Christmas parties; there was always so much work to do at home and so many children to mind. She and Mrs Peppard (born in 1936) loved school and had always done well at it; why did they not go on to further education? Most people still felt that they had to earn wages for their mother. Daphne Gregory said: 'There was no doubt about it, you'd got to go and get the money, and that's where the money was in those days [on the pots].' She started off in a shop earning 19s 11d (almost £1) a week, but that was not enough for her mother, so she went on a factory and got 36s (£1.80). Mrs Peppard went to a school where academic achievement would have been the norm, but she wanted to be a decorator and go into a factory. She started an apprenticeship, but when she became seriously ill her mother was able to break her apprenticeship, in order to get 10s (50p) a week; thus her prospects of work among the élite of the industry were dashed, and she had missed her opportunities academically as well.

Daphne Gregory, in particular, had a sort of longing for a world which seemed beyond what she could attain:

> I would like not to have worked on a potbank. I would like to have had a job with some sort of responsibility, some way I could express my own feelings and my own character – you know what I mean? . . . I always had aspirations about being either a writer or an opera singer or something. I'm very fond of music, and I like going to concerts and things like that. [12]

The mothers of all these women worked on potbanks, except for some of the mothers who had very large families, or who lived outside the Potteries while their children were growing up. Mrs Wood (born in 1934), for instance, came into the area as a young married woman. Mrs Flowers (born in 1927), Mrs Brookes (born in 1934), Mrs Eagle (born in 1940) and Mrs Fenton (born in 1941) did not think much of school. Mrs Brookes 'couldn't wait for grow up', and went on a factory against her mother's wishes. Her story is the opposite of Mrs Peppard's; she was the youngest of seven, and her mother was able to pay for shorthand and typing lessons for her, and to send her to an office job. But Mrs Brookes found it all too prim and proper and too much like school; she secretly went to work on a factory: 'And when I come home, she could smell this horrible smell on me clothes. She said, 'You've not been in no office!' I had a clip round the ear-hole and still went to work on a potbank.' Mrs Parsons also went against her mother's wishes, and did what she wanted to do. In other words, in this period we find a mixture of the old pattern of mothers dominating their daughters, and putting them in jobs through their connections, and just the hint of a new independence, girls knowing what they wanted to do, and going on a factory on the recommendation of a sister or friend. But still, the great imperative was the size of the wage-packet; several had tried other jobs but realized they would be getting more if they went on the pots.

Mrs Fenton (born in 1941) fits in with this pattern. Her sister put her name down on her factory when she was 13, to do some of the best-paid work as soon as she left school. But her regrets are more interesting. She, like Mrs Eagle (born in 1940), regretted having done so little at school. She concentrated only on art, needlework and cookery, because 'All I was interested in then was getting married and having a family. And that's what, to me, that's all women were there for.'

Mrs Fenton is one of an exceptionally capable and likeable group of women in an age group in which women were holding the most responsibility at work. Among the women I have mentioned so far are eight trade union representatives (Mrs Kazak, Mrs Phillips, Mrs Wood, Mrs Parsons, Mrs Peppard, Mrs Rugeley, Mrs Eagle and Mrs Fenton) and two supervisors (Mrs Wenceslas and Mrs Thomas). The other seven women were in selecting or decorating, but among the whole group of seventeen there were women in such diverse jobs as caster-sponger, figure-maker, electro-porcelain presser, aerographer, burnisher, white warehouse and first fire selector, dipper, enameller and lithographer.

Their early experience was, as I have described, remarkably traditional. One or two were granny-reared, so that their mothers could work full-time, with or without their fathers, and a few had come from outside the city – miners have migrated from other coalfields, and some families always come in from the surrounding countryside for work. Starting work was always traditional, they gave their wages to their mothers (if she were alive) and were given back pocket-money, most usually 10s, which people felt went quite a long way for such things as make-up, stockings and the cinema. The mother still bought most of the necessaries. Mrs Flowers, Mrs Wenceslas and Mrs Parsons received only 5s each. Mrs Tunstall 2s 6d.

The way that they met their husbands was also for the most part traditional, although four of them married East European immigrants. There were a number of displaced persons, Polish men in particular, who settled in the area after the war, working in factories or in the mines. One woman met her Polish husband at work on a potbank, and initially faced a certain amount of prejudice against him: 'Oh my goodness gracious! Don't bring any Polish boys here!' She looked after her parents through periods of ill health until they died, and only then, after knowing him for six years, did she marry her husband. Another woman met her Polish husband in what was also a fairly usual way: two or three of her friends and two or three of his becoming friendly at a hotel, when he had started working at the mine. Another pottery-worker met her Polish husband at tea with a friend from work; her husband was then living at a miners' hostel. Her initial reaction (but is it not traditional?) was not favourable: 'I took one look at him, and I thought, "You ugly bugger!" ' But he took her to the pictures, and they were married in six months. Again, her family were 'dead against it, all of them, you see, about this being foreign'. As a whole, this age group of women met their husbands either at work or at the fair, the pictures or out walking. There are no great surprises here.

The pattern, nevertheless, was changing. In the 1950s many of these girls were marrying younger. Jane Phillips, Pam Tunstall, Valerie Thomas and Linda Brookes were all 20 when they got married. Joan Parsons and Iris Wenceslas were 19. Jill Rugeley was 18, and Chris Peppard only 17. The long courtships that had been common in earlier decades, and the need to wait until you were 21, seem to be much rarer by the 1950s. The fact that girls sometimes 'had to get married' also suggests both a certain amount of freedom and a certain lack of sophistication. Girls at work still lacked helpful suggestions about contraception, and when one girl told her workmates about her over-amorous boyfriend, their reply was 'Well, let him, but keep your bowels well open.' No one mentioned mechanical methods of prevention, but some girls who got pregnant took quinine, had hot baths or (around 1960) were offered Beecham's pills in an effort to reverse the process. Among older married couples (parents of pottery-workers), one was certainly using condoms in the 1950s, but they had nine children!

Among the women I talked to, born between 1925 and 1940, the most common number of children to have was two, but there were three women with three children, one with four, two with five and two with only one. Among those who were born between 1941 and 1956, more women had only one child than had two, and only one family had three children. Among the women who had grown up after the war, the change seems to have occurred in the 1950s, or to those who were born after 1935. Certainly, the birth rate fell in the city between 1947 and 1955. After 1956, you may recall, it rose, but it did not keep up with the birth rate for England and Wales, which rose noticeably for a decade.

The other feature of these post-war marriages is, of course, divorce. Several of the pottery-workers had been divorced, and several were married to men who had been divorced, as one would expect among a group of more than twenty-five women between the ages of 30 and 55.[13] There were also marriages which exhibited, or had exhibited, a good deal of strain, nearly always in terms of how one or both of the partners should be allocating his or her time. Women, for instance, had in some cases to put up with their husbands saying that they had no need to work, or that they did not like them working, when the women themselves said that they could not manage without their wages. Trade union women also had problems, because their responsibilities were very demanding of their time. Intriguingly, the union women who had had problems in their marriages were also the ones who, at the time I visited them, did all the chores at home, the cooking and the cleaning, only expecting 'do-it-yourself' services from their husbands. Those who had much less volatile marriages were also the ones whose husbands shared very largely in the work at home. But when one thought of the enormous variety in the way husbands and wives acted out their roles, it was clear that shared expectations, or a willingness to discuss and compromise, were the crucially important factors.

Sheila Southwood's husband insisted that his wife did not need to work. She worked full-time on an earthenware factory, earning not very good wages, while her mother looked after her children and took them to and from school. At one time Sheila had worked part-time, but she was no longer able to do that, because part-timers were the first to be made redundant in the recession. She came from a big family, with a mother who worked on the pots when her father was out of work. She left school in the early 1960s at the age of 15 and went to the nearest potbank to her home, because it was less bus-fare: 'We got – brothers and sisters, and we believed that the money was in the pottery industry, so that's where we went, and my first wage was £3 8s a week.' She had had twelve months' training as a cup-handler, sitting with a 'lady that had been doing it for years, you know. We'd just fettle handles for so long, and then we'd learn to cut them, and then how to stick them on the cups. It took twelve months in all to learn how to do it.'

She had 10 per cent stopped out of her wages for her training. Her sister said: 'We didn't have no choosing. We didn't know anything about it, did we, really?' Sheila replied: 'No, but they always said the wages were in the clay end. It was more money in the clay end, because it was dirtier work, see, than decorating.'

Her sister, Dot, had spoken for her at the factory, and she went to the personnel for an interview. Dot was also working there, getting £5 per week.

Sheila gave all her wages to her mother and got back 10s pocket-money, while Dot used to have £1 back, so that she could save to get married. But they were restless, and in the 1960s they were able to move about easily from potbank to potbank. After eighteen months on the first, Sheila went to a 'very small and broken-down place' for twelve months. She had been bored in her job, and each time she moved she was able to learn another job in the clay end. She went to three more potteries, sometimes moving because of an argument with the manager over wages or bonus. Girls had worked together, and gone to different potbanks together, and when they had not been paid properly, 'We all put our coats on and went X—'s for a job.' She had married before she was 20, and had three children in quick succession, going back to work when the youngest was 2. Her father had loved looking after them (a not unusual situation). After he died, she had stopped work for a while, and then one of the potteries she had worked for wrote to her and asked her to work for them part-time. But since then the situation had changed.

Her sister said: 'There's no jobs now. [They] have got us where they want us now. You think yourself lucky if you've got a job today, haven't you? [They] have got us where they want us, and they think they can do anything and they'll get away with everything, they do.' They had been made redundant on one firm, and been obliged to work on another pottery owned by the same group, taking a cut in wages. But Sheila could not give up work. Her husband said: 'We'd manage, wouldn't we?' but both his wife and her sister were adamant that 'We'd be living hand to mouth.' Her husband, who always gave her the same amount of money, whether she was working or not, said: 'I never agreed her going [to] work in the first place, even though it's necessary.' Although Dot said she needed the company at work, and would be lonely at home, Sheila said she went to work definitely for the money, and not for company.

Out of the set amount her husband allotted her and all her own wages, Sheila had to pay for everything, including food, bills and clothes for all of them. She did all the work at home, including the cooking, cleaning and washing, often not stopping until half-past nine at night, and doing her major shopping at weekends. Her husband was out most of the time at weekends and in the fine weather, while Sheila's experience was that 'There isn't enough hours in a weekend . . . to do your jobs.' If it was bad weather, and there was decorating to do, her husband would do that.

It was usually fairly typical if a husband preferred to go out drinking with men, and the wife was very rarely taken out, that she also did all the work at home. Sometimes the wife blamed her husband's shift-work for the fact that he did not help, but it became clear from talking with other wives that some husbands used shift-work as an opportunity, enabling them to be more helpful to their wives, because they were off work when their wives could not get out to the shops or look after their children.

At the opposite extreme to the husbands who went out a lot on their own was the Kazak household, Mrs Kazak was a union representative, working part-time in a pottery factory, and her husband was a miner. Her children were now almost grown up but still at home, and Mrs Kazak recalled how her husband had looked after the children in the holidays when she was at work. He always worked on the night-shift: 'He'd only have a couple of hours' sleep in the morning, then he was up all day with the kids till I came home at night. Then he used to go to bed for a couple of hours. So we've always worked together, as a family, we've always worked together.' He used to bath the babies and change their nappies, and when the eldest was little he would take him for miles on the back of his bicycle. Now that they were older, they continued to share the work. She did the menus; he would fetch the meat and fresh food, she the groceries; he would cook, and she would make the gravy or a sauce when she came in, and dish up. The daughters helped with cleaning; there was, however, no mention of the son doing so. Sharing between husband and wife also extended to income management. There was none of the pattern of the husband giving as much as he thought fit and leaving the wife to pay for everything, the justification being (in some cases) that the husband was 'saving' for large items. The Kazaks pooled it all together, then decided what should go into the bank and what they were going to spend. The children paid board if they were working, and Mrs Kazak received that as well.

Jane Phillips, also a union representative, had a similar pattern of sharing. They had 'one purse' from which each took what he or she needed, although she had the responsibility for paying the bills and planning and paying for the holidays. She remembered how this had come about:

> I remember the first week we were getting married, I said to my oldest sister, 'What shall I say or do? What have I got to do with the first-week's pay-packet?' She said, 'If you get the opportunity and he asks, tell him you want the lot.' You see. And it was so funny because he did! I think he – if I can remember – [was] opening his pay-packet (I think it was about £8 then) and giving, or messing about with it . . . as if he was going to give me so much. I must have just nodded my head like that. I must have said, 'I don't want it if I can't have it all.' [Laughter.] That was it, you see, and I got it then.

They shared chores as well. She would do most of her work on a Saturday morning. Her husband would get up after about three hours' sleep, because he too was a miner on shift-work, and they would do the cleaning together, on the Saturday afternoon and the Sunday. In some households one could feel the tension or the separation between the partners, but in this one 'Years have gone by, and the love's got better.' It was not identical with the Kazak home, however, in that the husband had never bathed the babies, nor changed their nappies, but he did look after them when she worked in the mornings.

The variation is enormous in how people arrange and have arranged their marriages, but one recurring theme is the way women grow in confidence in middle life. Mrs Wenceslas described the way she had left her job when her husband left his job, after he had had a row with the manager:

> I had to leave, and yet I didn't want to, because I really did like the job. I wouldn't do it now; if I was working now with me husband and he said to me, 'You've got to leave, because I'm leaving', I'd tell him, 'On his bike!' I couldn't do it now, I mean, I'm more independent now. I do what I want to do now, but years ago you followed your man around like a little leach.

Mrs Parsons said she had never gone out with anyone but her husband, so her outlook was 'not very broad'. Mrs Fenton described herself as a young married woman: 'At one time I never used to go through the door'; as a mature woman, she was 'a very independent person'.

Another fact which emerged was that, contrary to what other researchers have found, husbands who were out of work were very helpful to their wives.[14] What emerged, crucially, was that they were very coy about this, and did not want it to be known in public. One husband, who did not want his wife to work at all ('The minute we could manage on one wage, I had to stop; he didn't like me working'), lost his job in a slump in the pottery industry. He would do the washing, but not hang it outside, so as not to be seen. There would be a blazing fire with the washing all round it. He would clean all round the house, but not a window, for the same reason. He was embarrassed to be seen doing women's work; his job was one which women never did in the pottery industry post-war. Another unemployed husband was reluctant to say that he was domesticated, but his wife said that he cleaned up for her during the day, got the tea ready for her for when she came in and did ironing. Undoubtedly these men felt a loss of status, since men still see themselves as the breadwinner, in spite of the importance of women's paid work. At the same time, marriage is seen as a partnership and even a bargain, and they had to make up for the fact that they could not carry out their side of it.

Mrs Brookes made it clear that, even as a girl, she had seen marriage as a bargain of this kind: 'Let's face it, I married him to work and keep me . . . I did. That's what I thought I was doing.' But marriage did not turn out to be what she had expected; she had had to go back to work, even though her husband would not let her do paid work when her children were small:

> I couldn't manage, could I? - on - I mean, when you're young, you think, 'Oh, I'll get married, and we're going do this, that and the other, stop home and have children. You don't realize what it involves, the amount of money it's going [to] take [to] bring children up and that. And you always think [to] yourself, 'Oh, I'm going marry someone who'll work and keep me.' You finish up working as well.

Her husband shared the cooking, went to the supermarket with her, often did the washing and helped with the cleaning: 'So you might as well say we share . . . Well, it's fair, isn't it? I mean, you're coming out to work, so let's face it, they've got to help in the home, haven't they?' In money matters, she had a lot of responsibility and kept a good deal of freedom to herself: 'I wouldn't say I come [to] work for pin-money, no. A fair amount of my money goes into the home. Then again, I keep a fair amount for myself . . . I have so much off my husband.' She paid for the bills and the shopping: 'I'd tell him if I hadn't got enough. We've got an understanding, and that's it . . . He doesn't know how much I get. I don't believe in that, that's personal. I know what he gets, but he doesn't know what I get.'

Almost all the women I interviewed said that they needed the money they earned, in spite of the wage increases of recent years and better continuity of employment than their parents had known. People talked about women they knew who had no real need to work, because their husbands were well paid, but for most people work was a necessity.

There were some wives who worked because their husbands kept them short of money. This was the old kind of poverty I described at the beginning of the chapter, closely related to the size of the husband's pocket-money. In those households, the problem continued; there were no holidays or improvements, and there was a continual struggle to keep up with chores and necessary expenditure. But in many households, husbands and wives were working together to improve their standard of living. What was normal and a decent standard of living had changed. Food had changed; it was no longer scraps from the market on a Saturday night, or a rabbit stew if you were lucky. It was steak, or chops, or other food out of the freezer. The freezer was necessary, because neither partner wanted to spend much of their free time shopping. Clothes had changed; whereas remembering the 1930s some people talked about buying from a woman who came round with a suitcase full of second-hand clothes, and always selling their own, now a mother might try to buy different clothes for her child, summer and winter. Now women ran catalogues for their friends, or went to warehouses in Manchester to buy things cheaply for their workmates. Things did not disappear between Monday and Friday, to the local pawnshops, and nobody wore clogs.

The great new expenditure was the home itself. People wanted to improve their living conditions, live in a nice area and, where possible, buy their house. Some people had done up houses, sold them, made money and gone on, trying to improve their situation. In this context, of course, the husband's do-it-yourself input had definite monetary value. The difference in living conditions between the homes of the oldest women, born in the 1900s, and the women born in the 1940s might be worth illustrating at this point. Mrs Mason (born in 1903) described how the decorating was done in the 1920s:

> When you lived in a rented house, we trusted to the landlord doing it, but he'd only do 'em every seven years. It had got [to] last seven years. And what they did, he'd paper top half, and the bottom half there'd be a picture rail all way round, and underneath that picture rail was paint . . . And of course he used to say, 'Now, that's got [to] last seven year.' And he wouldn't have it done again until, you know, it really wanted doing. Now, today they're papering, aren't they, every holiday . . . It was papered half-way, and they varnished it, didn't they, that's what they did, and made it last. And you could wash it down. And it had got [to] last seven years then.

The trade union representatives were in the main, more interested in people than they were in the 'ideal home', but this is not to say they had not struggled to buy houses or nice furniture. Mrs Eagle, who had been a child in the 1940s, described to me how her home had changed when she was a child and how, as a married woman, she had always needed to work, so that they could pay a mortgage and replace worn furnishings. Her mother had always had responsibility, since her grandmother had died when her mother's younger brother was still a child. She had brought him up, because her father (Mrs Eagle's grandfather) was a drinker and not looking after him properly. (There is no criticism in this, of course; he is described as 'one of the very, very old-fashioned men, cap and white silk scarf, and he liked to have a drink, and he liked a bet on the horses . . . he was one of them jolly people'.) But the little boy would be 'standing at the lamp-post till eleven o'clock waiting for me grandad to come home.' Mrs Eagle's parents had kept the whole family, because her father and three brothers were living with her and on the dole, 'and every time they had their dole money, she said all they thought of doing was going playing snooker with it, you know. So really, me father kept the whole family.' At the end of the 1920s, when this was going on, every penny counted, and her mother would push her baby in a pram to go and do somebody's washing 'to get a pennyworth of meat to make a meat-and-potato pie' – a huge thing, made in a tin washing-bowl for the whole family.

The services in this family look, at first sight, rather one-sided, but when the grandfather was well enough, he would look after his daughter's children, while she went out to work at a pottery factory. This, later on in the 1940s, enabled her to pay for a holiday, for instance. Mrs Eagle could remember that when she was little her mother 'had a very rough time', but when she got older their surroundings had noticeably changed. To begin with, there was coconut matting on the floor, a scrubbed-top table with a velvet tablecloth in the living-room and an old black grate. From the age of 11 to when she left school it had changed to:

> a nice carpet-square and a polished gate-leg table, and the old black grate had been taken out, and . . . a tile surround [put in]. And, I mean, we had a television, you know – I can remember when we had the television; all the family used to come and watch it. It was like going to the movies in our house, you know, because nobody else had got one, only us.

By the 1980s, of course, carpets and a television were standard. The carpet square was being replaced by fitted carpets, and people had comfortable three-piece suites. Some people had cars, but as Mrs Eagle said: 'I don't think there's anything wrong with people expecting a television and a car and a nice home.' Putting it even more precisely, why should things that are considered normal for people in white-collar jobs be considered luxuries for people who work in factories? Why should it be normal for them to be less informed (as they would be if they did not have televisions) and cold in winter (if they did not put in central heating), and for them not to have outings or holidays away from the city? Cars are, of course, a necessity for those families in which (usually) the husband's work is too far and not on a bus route. Many of the council estates, like Chell Heath, Bentilee and Abbey Hulton, are on the outskirts of the city, just as many private estates of new houses are, while work tends to be concentrated in particular areas. The Michelin factory, below Oakhill, was near at hand for people living in Stoke. Hem Heath colliery was not far from Trentham or Blurton, and not far from the large Wedgwood factory at Barlaston. Royal Doulton's Nile Street factory was a big employer in Burslem, and there were tile works and sanitary ware factories in Hanley and Tunstall.

But most of the potbanks were concentrated in Longton and the area round it at the south-eastern extremity of the city. For this reason, many of the working women I spoke to lived at this end of the city too, but husbands often had to go further afield. Essentially, for some people, their wages had to include the running of a car, as well as council house rent or mortgage. Mortgages were usually only marginally more than rent would have been, if they were buying from the council.

Mrs Eagle and her husband had bought a little terrace house and then found finances too much of a struggle, and the house too far out. So they had sold it, and shared with her mother-in-law, while they saved for the deposit on something else. She had started back to work, and they had bought their present house nearly fifteen years before. Now that house prices had risen, their mortgage seemed very small, but her wages needed to stretch to other things. The three-piece suite needed replacing, for the third time since she had got married; they lasted on average seven or eight years, before they started to split or to look grubby and go into holes. The fitted carpet, which she had bought eleven years before, was beginning 'to go in parts'; it had been a very good one, and other people who could not afford such a good-quality carpet would have had to replace them more frequently. They needed new beds: 'It's a wonder we haven't got cracked backs in the morning, when we get up, but I just can't afford them at the moment, any rate.'

In this chapter I have tried to show that the Second World War is not itself a watershed between the old penurious style of family life in this area and modernity. What has happened is that a style of manhood, which essentially looks down on the needs, desires and comforts of women, has been slowly going out of fashion. Indications from the birth rate suggest that this male stereotype had something of a revival in the 1940s, but that the 1950s saw him declining – not, unfortunately, to the level of an endangered species, but enough to allow a new style of life to emerge, based on the comfortable home, rather than on the split-site home of the threadbare but crowded house and the till-ringing pub.

In the 1950s employment was still erratic, but the vicissitudes of trade were to some extent absorbed by hiring and firing part-time women. There was no return to the large-scale unemployment of the early 1930s, when some women were getting work more easily than their husbands. But the fact that many married women did school hours helped to give the illusion that women's work was secondary, or even unnecessary. Depending on whether a woman wants to see her husband as 'the provider' or not, she will describe her own contribution as being for luxuries or necessities. Since the recession, many more women have been obliged to work full-time, or lose their jobs; their contribution to the home is thus by no means insignificant.

Women are now working for and expecting a much higher standard of living than was normal before the 1960s, including home ownership, modern kitchens and bathrooms and comfortable living-rooms. What began with televisions and carpets in the 1950s now includes deep freezers and foreign holidays. The small family has meant that women are not chained to child-minding, and the old pattern of men going out and women staying at home is seen as unsatisfactory. There are plenty of night-clubs and country pubs locally, where they would like to go with their husbands, and this can be an area of conflict, if a wife finds herself with an old-fashioned husband.

Unfortunately, it is not quite true that the 'manly' man is old-fashioned. In Chapter 8 we shall see that he exists among the youngest husbands. This is not surprising, since it has been noticeable in the last few pages that women are extremely indulgent towards violence, meanness and hard drinking in their fathers. They are also very indulgent towards their sons' lack of help in the home. As for the husbands themselves, those who came from Eastern Europe were far and away the most helpful and egalitarian in the home, whether or not they were doing 'manly' occupations like mining. The record of local men in kindness and a sense of equality with their wives is far less appealing when Polish husbands are excluded.[15] Husbands, nevertheless, are now providers of comforts rather than of hordes of children, and it is to their more pampered modern children that we now turn.

Notes

1 F. Burchill and R. Ross, *A History of the Potters' Union*, 1977, p. 203.

2 Burchill and Ross, 1977, p. 195.

3 *Pottery Gazette and Glass Trade Review*, March–December 1942, vol. 67, p. 184.

4 *Pottery Gazette*, March–December 1942, vol. 67, p. 575.

5 Burchill and Ross, 1977, p. 198.

6 City of Stoke-on-Trent, *Annual Report of the Medical Officer of Health*, 1930. In 1950 he noted that the slum clearance programme was nearing completion.

7 The birth rate did not decline in the city in the 1940s until after 1948; it was lower in the 1930s. The maternal mortality rate was high in England and Wales until the mid-1930s, but women's mortality in general was higher than men's until the Second World War. The 1939 survey of the health of 1,250 working-class wives, reported in Margery Spring Rice, *Working-Class Wives*, 1981 (first published in 1939), found that under a third were in good health; reported in J. Lewis, *Labour and Love*, 1986, p. 23.

8 City of Stoke-on-Trent, *Annual Report of the Medical Officer of Health*, 1940, 1965 and 1970.

9 Quennell, *Mayhew's London*, n. d. pp. 57, 93 and 94.

10 E. Roberts, *A Woman's Place*, 1984, pp. 118–19. See also F. Coffield, P. Robinson and J. Sarsby *A Cycle of Deprivation*, 1980, chapter 2, for a description of a family in a Midlands town whose problems related to a father of this type.

11 For Mrs Farrier (born in 1902), a 'good table' had evoked memories of ham pieces and pease pudding, or lobby (the vegetable stew of the Potteries); in the 1940s it was remembered as rabbit stews and custards; for a 1950s child, it meant chips and something – fish, or chicken, or egg – or lobby again. For Mrs Wenceslas, in the 1980s, it meant steak, or steak and kidney pie, or 'a joint at weekends with all the veges and ice-cream and fruit and salads'. Only in Mrs Gregory's childhood were there memories of really poor food, in a family where the mother, as well as the father, was out drinking during the day.

12 This rather undefined longing for another world in the arts and in the public gaze reminds me of the longings of Martha Yaxley in Mary Chamberlain's *Fenwomen*, 1977. Whenever I have discussed Martha with Workers' Educational Association students, they have always divided vehemently into those who sympathize with her

and those who think she is gutless and should snap out of it. Curiously, those with the least sympathy have tended to be ex-nurses, very intelligent and capable women whose intellectual strengths have had to take second place to responsibilities as carers at home and in the community.

13   157,000 decrees were made absolute in the United Kingdom in 1981. The Divorce Reform Act came into force in 1971, and the divorce rate in 1980 was five times what it had been in 1960, (Central Statistical Office, *Social Trends*), 1983, p. 30.

14   R. E. Pahl, in *Divisions of Labour*, 1984, p. 276, found that unemployed husbands with wives who did not go out to work were largely unlikely to share in domestic tasks. If women were in full-time employment, tasks were much more likely to be shared than if the wife was a housewife. Pahl does not, as far as I can see, show how much sharing is involved when the wife is in full-time employment and the husband unemployed, but he does say that the wife's work is always an important variable.

15   This would not fit Elizabeth Bott's (*Family and Social Network*, 1971) characterization of households with joint roles, but perhaps shows more clearly how they come about. In these households, the wives had close-knit networks in the community in which they had grown up. Their husbands, coming from Poland as adults, did not. It is the husband who decides whether or not he is going to be involved in domestic work – the wife's domestic work is almost always taken for granted – and it is his background and social orientation which make him either closer to his wife, sharing in the work at home, or seeing himself as essentially a man with other men outside the home. These husbands would go out for a drink, but they were essentially centred in their homes.

CHAPTER 8

Children Growing Up

Life in Stoke-on-Trent is not all tiled bathrooms and three-piece suites, and it would be silly to imagine that people were carried away on a tide of materialism. The other large expense for which women pottery-workers go out to work is their children. You will remember that married women work longer hours and have fewer children in Stoke than is the average for England and Wales; it might seem from these statistics that children are not a high priority in Potteries' homes, but this is not the case. Girls aim to marry and have a family even if they have no other ambitions. Many girls 'muck about' in school, and treat it as an irrelevance, because they intend to work and marry locally, where 'career jobs' are few and far between. But now that potbank jobs are becoming more difficult to come by, the options are going to be different. Marrying and having children were a course of action into which many of these post-war women hurried, but they stopped before they had large families. Their priority was to make 'a nice home' for their children, wherever possible working part-time, so that their children did not have to be put out to nurse.

The amount of time women pottery-workers took off work to look after their children varied according to their personal circumstances and was not just a matter of family tradition. A woman whose mother had put her out to nurse as an infant might do exactly the same herself, or be off work for ten years, the husband's attitude to her working, the size of his wages, the availability of someone suitable to look after the children and the break-up of a marriage were all factors which affected how long she spent at home. Let me give some examples.

Mrs Flowers, born just after the General Strike, used to spend all week with her grandparents, and go back to her parents at weekends, while her mother and father went to work. When she was married, her aunt looked after her child for her from the age of five months, until the child was old enough to have a key of her own. Her husband was in a well-paid job in the pottery industry.

A number of women started work again on the twilight shift; this might seem the most convenient way to work, as a woman would go out in the evening, when her husband came in, and she could look after her young children in the day. But it was, as Mrs Eagle explained, terribly tiring for a woman, because she had to do all the work at home during the day, look after her children, get her husband's tea and then go out to work, so that she was not in until ten o'clock. If a woman went out to work in the day, at least there was more likelihood that her husband would pull his weight in helping with cooking or cleaning, or bathing the children. But with the twilight shift, there was no need to pay for a nursewoman in the day; the wife did it all. Yvonne Chapman worked in the evenings in a night-club when her children were young, as they needed the money. She worked from 7.30 p.m. until 2.00 a.m. six nights a week, and admitted that she sometimes felt like a zombie; but doing evening work, either she or her husband was always with her children.

Women did not necessarily work only in the pottery-industry. Mrs Thomas started work when her baby was six months old – the evening shift, from 5 until 9. Her husband's work was erratic and seasonal, and she had gone on to work in the post office, in a sweet shop, collecting insurance, doing cleaning and housekeeping. Her husband looked after the children when she was on the evening shift, but she later put them out to nurse with her mother and mother-in-law. Her own mother had been a housewife. Mrs Rugeley's mother had gone out to work in between having her children, but Mrs Rugeley's husband did not want her to work, and she stayed off work for ten years after the birth of a child. In 1981 she was a union works representative, and she said: 'I love work. I love to go. I can't bear to have a day off.' She nevertheless felt that, now that they were wanting to buy a better house, she had to work, whereas formerly they had not needed a second wage.

Mrs Wenceslas's situation was the opposite. She could not work when her children were young, because she had four in quick succession, but living on one wage had been a nightmare: 'If he had a day off, I used to go to pieces. So they used to go to work half-dead, because they were frightened of having a day off.' She had gone back to work when her youngest was 5, and now that all of them were grown up and only one still living at home, she possibly had no need to work. But she loved work, like Mrs Rugeley: 'I've always gone [to] work, but I like going work, because I like people, I like the hustle-bustle all round me; I like the activity. I don't like meself – if I'm here on me own, I'm looking through that window, that window, and then I go to that window, and I just can't settle.'

Mrs Parsons's eldest child was eighteen months and her youngest three months when she went back to work in the mid-1950s. She also went back because her husband's wage was too small – or the wages he gave her:

> He took £2 out of his wages, leaving about £5 to keep us on, to clothe us. I just couldn't cope, no matter how economical I was, I just couldn't cope. I'd got people who'd got no money, I'd got nobody to buy my kiddies shoes and all that business, so the only alternative was to go out to work.

A woman whom she had been friends with since she moved to the estate looked after her children for her. She bitterly regretted having done it: 'I think it is a dreadful thing to do to your children.' But she had had no choice, even though she was earning only £7 per week on piece-work, paying the nursewoman £2 and getting only between £4 and £5 when she had paid her bus fares. She could not survive without it.

Mrs Eagle, by contrast, felt no conscience about leaving her children. She said that they were good mixers and outgoing, because they had gone to a nursery and to a nursewoman when they were small. She felt much more guilty that she came home tired from work.

Ruth Evans remembered with some distaste what it was like being put out to nurse, but she put her own son out to nurse at $3\frac{1}{2}$ with her father-in-law, paying him £7 a week. When she was a little girl, Ruth was looked after by various nursewomen:

> My mother'd . . . got to get off in the morning to be at work for eight o'clock, and she's leave me in charge of the other three, right. Therefore, my dad would be doing shifts, days, nights, noons. So on days, my father would go at half-past five, and I'd be left from half-seven . . . getting toast and tea done for the others, you know. Getting them off school, and I'd got lock up, do the fire ready for when my father come in – and it was all hectic, you know. It was hard work really. He used to leave me little note on the shelf in the morning; 'Get a loaf, get this, get that', you know, bottle of milk and different things . . . Mum used to say, 'Iron your things for school tomorrow. I haven't got time, I've got [to] cut the snappin' up . . . got to cut your dad's snap up, and I've got to cut my snappin' up.' You always used to carry out sandwiches in them days.
>
> [Did you mind being put out to nursewomen?]
>
> Yes. Because you never knew what they were going be like. I can remember one lady in particular; this shilling had gone off the shelf, you know, and we were all blamed for this shilling, 'Which one of you has had it?' you know. And I dunna know who had it, but a couple of weeks went by, and she said to my mother, 'That's it, I'm not looking after 'em no more!' My mum used to pay, I think it was £2.50 a week, £2 10s like, for the three of us. But she didn't provide any toast or a cup of tea, or a biscuit, or anything like that. It was just, 'Hello, come in, sit down. It's nine o'clock, go [to] school.' It was like that. You didn't dare do anything – crayon, or something – until it was time to go school.

School holidays were not much better:

> We used to have go to the nursewoman's, but she used to have us till like nine o'clock. And if it was sunny or whatever, we used to have [to] go out [to] play till dinner-time, come in dead on the dot for your dinner, and then go out . . . and then come in at four o'clock. And that was it.

All this made Mrs Evans 'a bit wary of who to trust' when she started back to work. Her husband worked on shifts and thought 'the woman's place was in the home, you know, old-fashioned, like . . . so therefore I was a bit restricted in getting work: 'You'd got no need go work.' She was lonely and bored at home, and she wanted to dress her son better, 'get things for the home and progress'. What was old-fashioned about her husband was that he did not share this desire to improve their standard of living or, in particular, to improve their son's material circumstances. It was up to the wife to get the money which would provide a home of their own and all the things she felt her child should have.

Mrs Tunstall and her husband had enjoyed spoiling their children with books and bicycles, dolls and prams: 'We try to make up for what we didn't have ourselves. We both do. If they ask for anything, we try and get it them, or help them to get it. They were spoilt.' But they were aware that material things were only part of what their children wanted; they had both come from big families, while their two children could share more love and attention: 'They haven't gone short in that way and they haven't gone anything short in love, because we love them both.'

In Stoke-on-Trent a larger proportion of women in their forties go out to work than any other age group. In my study, these are the women born between 1931 and 1941, upon whose experiences I initially concentrated in Chapter 7. Their reasons for working at 40 were of course different from those earlier reasons for doing part-time work or the twilight shift, when their families were younger. Then, the expense of starting up a home, often on a husband's low or insufficient wage, and without any financial help from their parents, took them back to work, in spite of the difficulties of child-minding. This was at a time when there were most demands on a woman's time, and most pressure on her to be with her children. In 1981 some of these women had grown-up children, and part of their expenditure related to the fact that they were trying to give them a good start in life, sometimes by encouraging them to go to college or by making very small financial demands on them in return for board and lodging. Some of their children were, of course, on the dole or had been made redundant. One was on a government scheme, being paid £23 a week – as his mother, Mrs Chapman (born in 1937), put it: 'doing a job, but not being paid for it'. He had been learning the building trade before he was made redundant.

The days when fathers reputedly lived off their children's earnings, 'living off the fat of the land', were now long past, and young people paid their board – usually rather a small amount – while their mothers still bought necessaries for them. Traditionally, Mrs Eagle said, boys had paid more board than girls, perhaps because girls helped their mothers more (or, surely, because their wages were so low), but her son had insisted that there should be equality in their house, and that he should therefore pay the same as a girl would. A mother whose son was on the dole took nothing from him, while the daughter knew that she would pay nothing as soon as she had the keys to the house she and her fiancé were buying, for when they were married. She knew she could count on her parents to help her financially to pay for the wedding and for the expense of starting to live in a new house.

This indulgence towards grown-up children, trying to set them up in their own homes with their own furniture when they got married, was for the most part quite different from their own experience. Women born in the 1930s and 1940s had had to struggle from lodgings or in-laws' homes, like their parents, until they had managed to get a council house or to buy a little house. Sometimes, even where parents had provided for their children, it might all seem for nothing; a house which the parents of one woman had paid for over two decades was demolished by the council, and they were given £25 compensation for it.

But people struggled on, and their children were not going to have to struggle in the same way. At least, that is what they hoped, but the recession in the pottery industry and in manufacturing industry in general was beginning to make the 1960s and 1970s, the good times, look less like progress and more like history.

Some women in their forties also worked to get out of the house, because they were used to working and found it boring at home. Some, of course, liked their jobs, both for their skills and for the 'hustle and bustle' of a potbank, but they also felt that their wages were really necessary to the home. Women in their thirties, like Margaret Birmingham and Pam Hanley, whose children were at secondary school, were even more vehement in saying that women have to go out to work nowadays. Mrs Hanley said:

> When we were first married, say about fifteen years ago, eighteen years, they were working because it brought them a car in, or they went on holiday with their wages, brought them extra material things in their home, but now it's to make up the man's wages, no doubt about it. I mean, I've got plenty of friends that have to work and feel guilty about working, because of the children, you know, and probably there's some that don't – they like to go to work. But I think the majority of them, they don't like to go to work; they wouldn't go [to] work if they didn't have to.

The younger women, like Pauline Congleton (born in 1956) and Sandra Kennedy (born in 1950), whose children were out to nurse, said that they liked to go to work, and did not want to be 'stuck in the house with kids'. But they really needed their wages as well. The golden age when women worked for luxuries is difficult to locate.

Before leaving this brief account of the home lives of pottery-women since the war, I want to return once more to the subject of mothers and daughters, and in particular to look at what the daughters of six women pottery-workers whom I talked to were becoming. Within these accounts of people's lives there has been diversity as well as common experience, and these women show the breadth of possibility that being the child of a pottery-worker can hold.

Mrs Gregory's daughter, Daphne, was mentioned in Chapter 7. She had heard about her mother's unhappy, overcrowded childhood, and her grandparents' quarrels; she had seen all the problems of another large family with no home of their own, in her own 1930s childhood, and she herself remained unmarried. She said that she had not wanted to get married because it made you poor; instead she had had romantic notions which, seemingly, could not be attained: 'Mr Right wasn't in my sphere of friends, like. My Mr Right had got to be Sir Somebody or other, very high; I didn't look at boyfriends that were near me. I didn't want anybody like that.' If she was unfulfilled, it was not so much because of a lack of home life, but because of a yearning for another sort of life, which always seemed a long way off. She wrote, but did not have the confidence to try to get published. She continued working on potbanks and did not leave home, but she put money and work into her mother's home, so that Mrs Gregory's retirement was comfortable and companionable.

Mrs Roper's daughter, Jean Kidsgrove, who was born in the late 1940s, did not become a pottery-worker. As a young girl, her mother had got her holiday jobs on potbanks, so that she could see what it was like to work on the pots. But Mr Roper, Jean's father, had come out of the pottery industry, and was determined that his daughter should not go into it. He allowed his children to play only with certain other children, and it seems that their whole childhood was geared towards cutting them off from what would have been a normal job for them to go into, like their mother, and from becoming part of that world. At school, they were encouraged to succeed academically, and Jean became a teacher and married a teacher. It seemed that she had taken on some of her father's loathing of the factories, of the women's 'mindless' conversations, but she also said that being at home all the time was 'narrow and boring, worse than a potbank'. She felt that her children were as isolated as she was, and that she was as ambitious for them as her father had been for her. She did not think she was using the full potential her education had given her, but she had felt 'idealistic' about being with her children when they were little, and did not feel she could deprive the littlest one by going out to work. She seemed, nevertheless, uncomfortable; they were glad that they had bought a house in an expensive area, but they were not on easy terms with their neighbours. It was as if they felt out of place.

Mrs Adams's daughter, Lynn Godden, also born in the late 1940s, had left the world of the potbank, but she had not rejected it. She respected the people who worked on factories, even though she had not wanted to herself. She was now a very successful woman in her own right, and had solved the problem of women of combining their work in the public world and in the private one of home, by not having children. She did not feel she could manage both jobs together, and she loved her present work and found it fulfilling. Her husband also had an absorbing and interesting job. Lynn's parents were seemingly more easy-going than Jean Kidsgrove's, and not so anxious about her getting on. They were the sort of people who knew how to enjoy themselves, who were the life and soul of the party, who liked to go on holidays and for a night out. Lynn had enjoyed playing with the children round about; she was not kept in, and she could play cricket in the 'entry' behind her house like anyone else. But she was also naturally bookish and determined, and when she finally went to a grammar school – which was considered an unusual achievement in her background – her parents were encouraging without being pushy. While she was at school, university had seemed too far outside her experience, so she left and went into a white-collar job without trying to get 'A' levels. It was only later, through her enthusiasm and determination, that she had actually got where she wanted to be; and she was growing in confidence and assurance day by day through the power and pleasure of her job. Whereas in the previous family there had been a tension between wanting to succeed and not wanting to step out of one's class (Jean's grandmother had not liked it when her mother became a supervisor, for instance), Lynn's mother was proud of her daughter's achievements but felt her daughter worked very hard; and she wanted, as soon as she retired, to come up on the bus and do her daughter's washing and ironing for her.

Turning now to the youngest women I talked to, these are the daughters of women born in the 1930s and 1940s, themselves all born in the 1960s. Mrs Wenceslas's daughter, Avril, was capable and versatile like her mother; she could turn her hand to anything on a potbank, and was useful on a little potbank, where she could take over from somebody who was ill and do another job if they were short-handed. She seemed to have turned back quite happily from all the opportunities or successes which her education offered her. She had been very musical at primary school, but pursuing music would have meant going to a different school from her friends, and she would not entertain that idea. She had also left secondary school without taking her 'O' levels, because she had been offered a job as a secretary (having done shorthand, typing, office practice and commerce at school), but she had given that up too and gone to work on the pots, because the money was better. It seemed that school was offering her choices, but that they were not really part of her world, which was the same as her mother's. Mrs Wenceslas had come from a big family, and had lost both her parents when she was in her teens (her mother when she was 12), so she had had to make her own way in the world, and that had meant going on the pots. She had eventually become a supervisor in the pottery industry, but she had a vitality, a sense of fun about whatever she was doing, that would have made her successful, in a daughter's eyes, whatever she did.

Avril had been going out with her boyfriend since she was 16 and over four years on, she was not quite sure of the future. The wedding and bridesmaids' dresses had been bought, her mother already had her suit, and the money was saved for a deposit on a house, but they were 'having a sort of think'. The way she described her fiancé is an indication that violent men were still common, but the good provider was more desirable: 'He's great, isn't he, Mum? You know, he's a real nice lad. I wouldn't find anybody better, because he's never never hit me or anything like that. And I've only had to moan about something, and he's ended up buying it me.' Her mother said: 'It's something you've got to really think about. When you get married you tie a knot your teeth don't undo.' (There was, nevertheless, hope, I felt, for him, since Avril had not liked the look of him when she first met him!)

Mrs Fenton's daughter, Maggie Cooper, was the same age as Avril, but had got married the previous year after a stormy courtship. She, like her mother, had gone to work on a potbank straight from school. Like her mother, she had not thought much of school, but she saw herself as a 'comedienne': 'We used to have such a laugh at school, taking the mick out of teachers, and scribbling on desks, you know, and I never learnt. I was always in bottom class.' The strictness of working on a big modern potbank had come as something of a shock, and she had left it after six months, when her mother told her about another job. Working on the pots had always seemed attractive, when her mother would come in and say, 'Oh, we've had such a laugh today!' And when her birthday came round, 'She used to come in with tons of cards, you know, off all the women.' She had also heard that 'at the time, the money was in the pottery industry, when I left school'.

She had been keen on her future husband when she was at school, and by the time she was 15 she was 'on nerve pills' because she was 'obsessed with him' even though he was treating her badly, hitting her and going out with other girls secretly. The doctor had said to her (she said): 'I've never known a girl of 15 having to go on Valium . . . These are for women with kids.' Her mother had been very upset about all this, but could not persuade her to finish with him, even when the young couple had had a terrible fight. In the end she had got engaged to him, against her parents' wishes. It happened, however, that they split up, and she went out with another boy, who eventually started treating her badly as well. When she began to go out with her first boyfriend again, he was a reformed character, and she was in any case much stronger; she was not going to put up with what had happened before. They had got engaged and married rather quickly, and all the relations had helped with work on the house if they were able. Both sets of parents had jointly paid for the wedding, and they themselves had not gone out at all but saved for all they were worth until they had the deposit for the house.

Now that she was married, her husband would cook, but she seemed to be doing most of the jobs which needed doing in the house, and he seemed to be out a good deal, while she was 'the busiest one in the house, right from the day we got married'. She could not imagine how they would manage if she was to stop work. She brought home about £56 for 38 hours, and her husband £67, if he worked on a Saturday morning and until 6 p.m. in the week. She had to pay out £87 a month for the mortgage, a new gas fire and a washing-machine, and she put away money each week for the electricity, the gas, telephone, rates, television licence and insurances. She spent between £10 and £20 a week on food, and gave her husband £15 for cigarettes and petrol for the car (he drove to work). She had £10 for herself 'because I smoke, you see'. The main problem was that every extra penny had to be spent on making their little house habitable, so it was a continual struggle, even with two wages.

In some ways, this seems to be a very traditional marriage, or rather it echoes one kind of tradition - volatile, with problems over money and some history of violence, the wife as manager and main worker in the home, and the husband liking to be out with his mates, or having a drink, or going to the football. At the centre of it, though, is a woman who has confidence in herself and in managing the relationship, *before* she has started to have children.

Wendy Tunstall, three years younger than Maggie and Avril, was already engaged to be married, although there seemed to be no great hurry for the wedding. It was going to be 'probably some time next year or the year after'. She had been working for a year and a half, and was taking home £45, of which £20 went into the bank to save for getting married (her boyfriend did the same), £5 went as board to her mother, £10 went on her sister's club - buying a music centre as a present for her boyfriend, and paying for it week by week - £1 went on insurance, £4 on her mother's club (or catalogue) for clothes and £5 for bus fare. If they went out anywhere, her boyfriend had to pay.

Wendy belonged to the kind of family that people liked to think of as traditional on potbanks. Her father, mother and sister all worked on the same firm. But actually, it was a sign of the times; she had tried to get a typing job, because she had typing exams, and she had tried to get other potbank jobs. Her father knew the decorating manager and she had got her job only through her father asking him for a job on her behalf. She worked with her mother, but she found that being with the same people at work and at home was difficult. If you had an argument at work, there was no one you could talk to about it at home, and vice versa. It was, in a way, rather a lonely situation.

The engagement, long and apparently traditional, in fact shows how much more important weddings – and young people – are today than they were before the war. There are new and rather lively rituals on potbanks when girls are about to get married. Wendy described how a girl's workmates would dress her up in rags, put streamers and 'L' for learner on her, or a baby's bonnet, take her to the pub for a drink and then tie her to a lamp-post, leaving her until somebody untied her. Sometimes, she said, a girl would be tied to the railings outside the police station until a policeman relieved her.

When I was visiting potbanks in Longton, I saw one such girl emerging from a pub. She was dressed in white, and carried a ball and chain. A notice, 'I Should Have Danced All Night', was pinned to her, and her face had been brightly painted. The message is not too opaque; a girl has been caught, and now she is going to be literally tied down. As this is what most girls are looking forward to, it is intriguing that they celebrate the end of adolescence and the beginning of responsibilities in this way. But when one compares it with the way they describe their schooldays – when they can do as they like – and, to a lesser extent, when they start on a potbank and are treated (in some places) with indulgence, it begins to have more meaning. Their parents subsidize them at home, and they are not bound to the house like their mothers often were, with chores and child-minding; they are enjoying, almost for their parents' sake, a freedom and luxury in adolescence which their parents never knew. With marriage, the mortgage, the HP, the quarterly bills, clothes, food and, finally, a family, they are on the treadmill of responsibility.

Wendy Tunstall and her boyfriend were expecting to buy a house for about £9,000 or £10,000 to begin with, 'and then, like, do that up'. She had already had umpteen presents to contribute to her bottom drawer: a rug, a bathroom cabinet, a washing basket and pedal bin, an ironing board, three tea-sets, a bread bin, blankets, a kettle, a food-mixer and so on. A hundred and forty guests, brothers and sisters of their parents and their families, had come to their engagement party, and they had all brought something. One corner of the front room was piled high with gifts, and there was no more room. (Maggie Cooper's wedding, incidentally, had had the same sort of numbers of relations, from her parents' large families.)

Their relationship was very orderly. On Tuesday and Thursday nights her boyfriend came to her house, 'and we stop in'; on Mondays and Wednesdays both stayed at home and did not see each other; on Friday they went to the pub for a drink; and on Saturday he would come to her house for dinner (mid-day), then they would go into town and back to his parents' house in time for tea. They stopped there until the following day, and then went to his sister's on Sunday, had dinner and tea at his place, and then she would come home. They had been on holiday together, and at his place, when his parents were on holiday: 'We didn't go short on anything. I washed, I did everything. I really enjoyed it.' She was well prepared, and so were the families involved, for this wedding, which would discomfort no one. But at the moment they were so comfortable and organized that a long engagement did not seem a hardship. Only if the situation at work became a bit oppressive – being with her parents twenty-four hours a day – would the wedding be hurried along. This was reminiscent of what Mrs Roper had said about working with her mother on a potbank; there was no suggestion that she would fail in her obligations to her as a daughter, but she wanted a bit of freedom at work.

This daughter is, of course, a very clear example of the way parents are working to subsidize their adult children, and to give them a good start in life in spite of the recession. If her mother had not been working, it would not have been possible for her daughter to pay only £5 per week for her food and lodging, and she would not have been able to put away £20 every week to save to get married. The expensive Christmas and birthday presents, setting her up in food-mixers and other household goods, would not have been possible. Her mother's situation had been very different, helping her own mother with housework, shopping for a big family when she was a child and losing her mother at the age of 17. She had turned up her wages and received 2s 6d ($12\frac{1}{2}$p) in pocket-money. She had met her husband at work, and married before she was 21. Her husband, who did very heavy work as a placer, suffered terrible headaches from carrying ware on his head, which was traditional in his job. He was worn out by heavy work, and yet under 50 years old.

Wendy's situation looked very organized and secure; she was emotionally and materially well looked after. But if her potbank were to close (and potbanks were closing with monotonous regularity) all the wages in her household would come to an end. All the care which her parents had put into her childhood and adolescence was at risk. The decisions of the multinationals which own pottery factories as well as merchant banks, newspapers, book publishers, vineyards, rubber goods and hundreds of other products, are not swayed by the desires of young operatives saving to get married. By July 1986 there were only 27,500 employees in the Staffordshire pottery industry, and since then we have had another Wall Street crash.

The last daughter I want to talk about had no intention of working on a potbank like her mother. Mrs Thomas's daughter, Valerie, was 17 and going to a sixth-form college. She wanted to be a journalist; she knew how to set about it, what qualifications and training she needed, and she was prepared to fight hard to succeed in a profession which she thought was biased against women. Like many other people I spoke to, including women pottery-workers them-selves, she believed that if you had any brains you should not be on a potbank, and she wished she could help her mother get another kind of job. Several mothers had said to me that they hoped their children would be able to do something else if they'd 'got what it takes' or 'a bit more upstairs'. The feeling that they did not want their children to work on a potbank was quite wide-spread; people felt that working on a potbank now was not what it had once been. The issue is complicated by the fact that, when grandmothers heard what working on the pots was like now, they said it was 'like Butlin's'. For Valerie, the factory treated women as machines:

> It reminds me when I work there [she had done some work on a potbank] like when you see pictures of workhouses on the television, when people – their lives are ruled by a clock. A siren goes . . . and everyone stops and they have lunch, and the siren goes again, and everyone starts back to work. I don't know, it's just . . . it's just like machines, you know they could be robots. And they are just taken for granted, they'll do that, and no one ever complains or anything . . . It's very hot in summer, and cool in the winter. It reminds me of those workhouse things . . . It's probably not so bad, and they're not forced to do it – although some of them are, because they can't do anything else.

Fanciful though this is, it is chilling to remember the words of the great Josiah Wedgwood, who, in the eighteenth century, wrote that he wished 'to make such Machines of the Men as cannot Err.' We have seen that these women are not machines, but women in a web of relationships, responsibilities and obligations, and also women with aspirations and determination to achieve their desires. In Chapter 9 we shall look at the world they go out to, behind the factory gate.

Note

1   A letter from Josiah Wedgwood to Mr Bentley, 7 October 1769, in A. Finer and G. Savage, (1965) *The Selected Letters of Josiah Wedgwood*. London, Cory, Adams & Mackay.

CHAPTER 9

Behind the Factory Gate

They've got us over a barrel (Mrs Fenton).

When the new Wedgwood factory, designed by Keith Murray, started production at Barlaston in 1940, it was a revolution.[1] First, it was in the countryside five miles to the south of the city, instead of standing in the midst of grimy
streets; secondly, it had substituted electric tunnel kilns for the coal-burning
bottle ovens, which poured out smoke and pollution whenever they were fired.
Thirdly, it was a big, open-plan factory without little workshops up and down
staircases, full of dusty nooks and crannies; and fourthly, the company had
built good-quality houses nearby for its workers (each costing £400 to build).
Even in 1940 the idea of clean workshops and fresh air was novel in the pottery
industry; there were plenty of potbanks where conditions were exactly as we
have described them pre-war. Dirt, beetles, dust and the smoke of the bottle
ovens did not disappear when the potbanks started to open again with the
post-war reconstruction of the industry.

One pottery-worker remembered coming to the city for the first time as a
little girl at the end of the war and getting off the train at Etruria (where the old
Wedgwood factory was):

> I had a camel coat and a white angora beret; and before I'd got off the station and
> half-way up the street outside, they were covered in soots, black soots . . . There
> were bottle kilns and there were black clouds of smoke going up at certain times
> when they were firing . . . and of course mines was the other big industry in this
> area. And now, where they take the top off the slag heaps, and they've covered
> them, grassed them over, like the Hanley Forest Park, they were all black tips. So
> you've got your old bottle ovens belching out smoke, and you've got your big
> black mine-tips everywhere – it really was dirty country . . . but, oh, I thought it
> was dreadful when I first came up.

It was bad enough walking about in the street, but conditions at work were
still sometimes more reminiscent of the nineteenth century. Mrs Barnes's
daughter, Mrs Greensted, became a dipper like her mother after the war, and
she recalled all the carrying and the ware still full of insects: 'Do you remember

when we used to have to fetch baskets of cups out of the warehouse? They'd be full of crickets and cockroaches and heaven knows what. Now it's all brought to you.'

I had heard tales of people standing in boxes of straw to keep warm in winter, but the dipping house where Mrs Greensted worked was no better. In wintry weather they had to break the ice on the tub of glaze before they started working in the morning, and stir it about until it warmed up. They dipped their arms in the glaze almost up to their shoulders to do this, and their arms would get very chapped; they used to put on Vaseline to try to prevent it. Now, of course, there is automatic spraying for plates and saucers; and where a tub is used, glaze can be piped instead of carried in heavy jugs.

In the 1940s the youngest worker was still the dogsbody, fetching water for her boss, the dipper, and cleaning round the tub for her. The missus might give the youngster 2s 6d ($12\frac{1}{2}$p) at the end of the week if she had been good and 'a clip round the ear' if she had not. The youngest decorator was still the 'kale girl' until another younger girl came along, to fetch the breakfasts, go to the chemist (if anyone was 'off-side') and do the errands. Even in 1981, although young girls were more independent and less likely to get a job through their mothers (less likely to get a job at all), I talked to a girl who was still getting the breakfasts for her workshop, as she was a trainee and on a set wage. She had been on the dole for eleven and a half months, and then got a job through her boyfriend, who asked the management on her behalf.

Dawn Kenton, at 17, could hardly be said to be imbued with the work ethic, but to be able to work at all was unusual among her friends:

> Most of the people I went to school with are still on the dole, and me mates from round here, like, they're all on the dole. They've had jobs – like temporary jobs, and they've got nowhere with them. All me mates, they said, 'You're dead jammy getting a job.' I hate it. I don't like working, but I'd rather be at work than sitting around at home without anything.

Her main job in the morning was to go across to the shop and fill a box full of all the orders from the forty or so women in her workshop. She seemed rather proud of the fact that she did not have to work hard:

> The shop sells bacon-and-egg sandwiches and cheese on toast, and toast and dripping, and toast and marmalade, and toast and butter and all this. And they have sandwiches and beefburgers and baps and things, cheeseburgers. There's sausage rolls and pies and things like that. I go along in the morning and I just sit there, do nothing first thing in the morning, till after breakfast. Then I slog me guts out for make up what I didn't do before breakfast, and then at dinner-time I go to sleep, and in the afternoon I just sit around talking, because if I don't do me work I get it made up anyway . . . with me only being a 17-year-old.

She said that the other women did not think much of her easy life and 'call me everything. But I say, "Shut up, else I won't fetch your breakfast." ' Whatever the habits of deference might have been between young and old in the past, they are not much in evidence now.

In the 1940s the factory owners were a people apart, even if they knew you

Figure 7. Enamelling cups in the 1950's

individually and could remember your name. One of the decorators at Susie Cooper's Crown Works told me that Miss Cooper would come down from her office and go from bench to bench, asking them, perhaps, how long they thought it would take them to do their order of work. As she moved from bench to bench, a ripple of anticipation would precede her: 'It was like the Queen coming to visit you.'

Miss Cooper was admired by her decorators partly because she was so 'quiet', and the quietness, and therefore refinement, of painting shops was something which was remembered and cherished by paintresses. Mrs Caesar showed me a photograph of the decorating shop where she worked, the women facing one another, and remembered the introduction of music and a radio for *Music While You Work*:

> At that particular time the radio rentals provided a record-player in the depart-
> ment, so they brought us lovely records to try on, also a radio, which we hadn't
> had up till then. Then it was very quiet. And they bought us a radio as well as a
> record-player for *Music While You Work*, see. We used to sit and listen to this while
> we were painting . . . It was very pleasant there. Them days were very very
> pleasant.

In the 1980s the paintresses still cherished quiet workshops. She enjoyed seeing her work coming to fruition: 'When you'd finished your work and seen it complete, and then in the glost warehouse, right at the end of all the processes, you see the ware coming out and being packed, I think it is an achievement.'

In 1981 others agreed; they preferred the factory which gave you an order of work that enabled you to recognize your own work – to decorate whole tea-sets, rather than just plates, or just cups, so that all the decorators' work was jumbled up together for packing. Factories, and presumably managers, varied very much then and now in how they organized the supply of ware to the work-people. How ware was allotted to lithographers might also make a deal of difference to their wages, because they worked on piece-work, and different items made it easier or more difficult for a woman to get her wages. Large items like tureens, for example, might be six to the dozen, while cups and saucers would be fifteen and eighteen to the dozen, and a woman would be paid so much per 'dozen' of whatever size for a particular pattern. Thus, it was often much better to be doing large items, rather than putting prints on thousands of small articles, to do the required number of dozens to get your wages. This could give rise to jealousy and cattiness, and the lithographing shops on some factories were notorious for petty squabbling. It seemed that the smaller the workshop, the easier it was for people to get on with one another.

One lithographer remembered how much she had enjoyed a factory called Co-op Bank:

> I made ever such a lot of friends, and I loved it on there. We had our own little
> canteen and that, it was great. Dead old-fashioned little place, lovely it was. And
> how they worked there . . . You used to have, like, five dozen cups in a basket,
> and your prints were on the top, and the manageress used to say, 'Go and help
> yourself what you want', to all of us. There was never ever squabbling over work.

You used to say, like, 'Do *you* want them?' or 'Do *you* fancy doing them?' There was never any arguing because you know very well that you're amongst your friends, and eventually you're all going get your fair share, you know. That was a small community, though; there was only about a dozen women.

On another factory the system was different again. You would give in your book and be given 'a hundred cups; then, when you'd done them, you'd got to have a hundred saucers, and then five inch, then she'd give you like forty teapots, or fifty sugar-boxes, something like that'.

In two big workshops which I visited on different factories, there were cliques and antagonisms among the lithographers, who were some of the highest-paid women on those particular factories. People did not discuss their wages with each other, and one woman said of her workmates: 'Cut your throat, some of them in there!' As the big Groups close down the smaller potteries they have taken over (no matter how distinguished they have been, or how fine the wares they have been renowned for producing), this problem will, no doubt, be more typical of the high-earning, piece-work workshops on big factories, where women are too numerous to be all friends. There was, however, a high degree of helpfulness in such things as clubs and catalogues, shopping for one another and doing one another's hair. If managers remarked on the level of 'bitchiness' in such workshops, the high level of helpful interaction should be mentioned as well.

The pricing of ware and setting of piece-work rates for any particular pattern are very sensitive areas. Pottery factories which impose prices without negotiating with their workforce through pricing committees create lasting resentment. A decorating manager described to me how he knew roughly how much he could sell a new pattern for, so he would have to work out what pennies would have to be paid for the lithographing, shading, firing, selecting and so on which might go into its creation. But there was no uniformity throughout the industry. Longton decorators, who worked traditionally on fine china, were paid more than decorators in Burslem, who were paid earthenware rates. One firm used this to its advantage, by making the china body in Longton and sending it to Burslem to be decorated.

It seems that often neither managers nor workers knew what people were getting for doing the same work on different factories. A lithographer, for instance, told me of the fight she had had with the management of a firm where she worked when she moved to it from another firm in the same group. Before, she had been paid 2s 6d per dozen for work for which the second factory was paying her 1s 11d. This, she was sure, was not right, but she could not get any of her new workmates to back her up, even when she produced a work-sheet from the previous factory. Finally, she was able to win her dispute and get back-wages of £14. Only the fact that she had worked on the other factory led her to discover and be able to prove that the second factory was paying a lower rate for the same job.

Contrastingly, a manager on another firm told me how he had been trying to find out what people were earning on other factories: 'We've been trying to find out other factories to see what they get, to see if we are on a par or above or below, and we seem to have got the sort of norm for a lithographer, £90 to £100 a week. You get some a lot less, of course, which you do in any job.' The problem on his factory was the discrepancy between what the decorators earned and the people in the clay end: 'Decorators shouldn't get more than clay-end people. Yes, it's something that has gone wrong on the factory, and shouldn't have gone wrong.' Casters, more highly skilled than lithographers, were getting only about £80, and others not much more than the flat rate of just over £60 for a 40 hour week. The factory had a decorating manager and a clay manager, and each decided the wages and set on people in his own end. One half of the works had 'loose' prices and high wages, and the other end 'would tend to be a bit tighter on prices, and people aren't getting excessive wages'.

The opportunities for dissatisfaction on the part of the workforce are obvious. When there were plenty of jobs in the 1960s and 1970s their solution was to move. Ruth Evans described her mother: 'She used to think, like, "I'm fed up with this now, I'll go and do that. I don't like it on this firm no more, I'm clocking on there on Monday." And they used to pay you up there and then.'

There are plenty of examples of people being sought out by managers to work in their factory and being able to pick and choose – whether it was near a bus stop, what the fare home was, what the workshop and the other women were like and so whether they would feel 'comfortable' or not. Often they would stay or go in pairs, looking for a job together so that they would never feel lonely in a new place. For perhaps twenty years – after the misery of the 1920s, the odd days and weeks of work in the 1930s, the closing of factories in the 1940s and the uneven revival of the 1950s – the boot was on the other foot, and potbanks had to dance a little to get their workers.

Changes in the last forty years have not been unequivocally for better or for worse. They can be summarized as making potbanks more healthy for people's lungs, and in many cases less healthy for people's minds. Improvements include the end of the bottle ovens; although they are as striking and nostalgic in the landscape as oast-houses are in Kent, for example, they were monsters of pollution, and pitiless task masters to the men who worked in and around them. Placers used to spend about three days filling the oven with saggars. They used to place these clay 'boxes' one on top of the other from the bottom to the top of the oven (in piles known as 'bungs' about thirty-two high and forty-two round), first an outer circle of bungs and then filling up the middle, carrying the heavy saggars on their heads, as they mounted the ladders to the top. Placers still carry ware on their heads, if they are used to it, which gives them a certain upright walk.

The biscuit firing, which was the hottest firing, used to last about 72 hours (I was told that firing earthenware teapots took 26 hours, however), the glost about 36, during which time the entrance to the oven would have been bricked up (it is called the clammin hole), and 'trials' would have been taken to see that the firing was at the right temperature. Also during this time, the ovenman would have tended the fires at the mouths of the oven. There was no leaving them for food or rest, day or night, and feeding the man who fed the ovens had been a job for many of the grown-up children I had talked to. When the firing was finished came the worst work for the placers, once the clammins had been opened: carrying out the hot saggars, in temperatures so inhuman that people remembered men fainting in the heat, gloves on their hands, rings made of old stockings in their caps, naked to the waist. A man at the top of the ladder would pass them down, to another and down again, until women, the other side of the clammin hole, would stack them 'anywhere they wanted'. Saggars were not considered too heavy for women.

In the 1950s the bottle ovens were mostly replaced by intermittent and tunnel ovens. Burchill and Ross (1977) say that there were only 483 bottle ovens in use in 1958, and 654 intermittent and tunnel ovens.[2] Tunnel ovens worked continuously; at one factory I visited, a manager explained: 'On the biscuit kiln, we do three shifts, days, noons and nights . . . but on the glost, we work a continental shift system, that's two 12 hour days, two 12 hour nights and two days off.' Women did not do this work; if a woman had come for such a job, he would not consider her, because it was shift-work, and 'I don't think that's the type of job on this particular factory is a woman's job . . . In our particular company, I don't think it would work out with a woman as placer.'[3]

As I have already mentioned, we have to wait for the 1960s before the problem of dust was dealt with. In the late 1950s most employees were in firms employing between a hundred and five hundred workers.[4] Quoting a report carried out between 1956 and 1958 by four members of the Factory Inspectorate, Burchill and Ross show that almost 50 per cent of workers were in factories which had not been rebuilt, and more than half were in factories with less than a hundred workers. Almost a third of the employed population of Stoke-on-Trent and Newcastle-under-Lyme were working in the pottery industry in 298 factories.[5] These were still the small, unhealthy, largely friendly firms of pre-war days, before the mergers and take-overs which have characterized the last quarter-century. In January 1971, in an article entitled 'Changes Ahead for Potters' in *Tableware International*, Mr (later Sir) Arthur Bryan, Chairman of Wedgwood Ltd, said that in 1959 one hundred and sixty companies were registered with the British Pottery Manufacturers' Federation. In 1969, he said, 'largely due to the incidence of mergers and take-overs', there were one hundred and nine companies within sixty-five groups of companies. The total turnover of the industry was £59.2 million in 1959, and £95.2 million in 1969, including tableware, tiles, sanitary-ware and electro-porcelains. He included in his reasons for the growing mechanization of the industry 'the declining number of people skilled in certain processes', and 'the growing competition for labour from other industries'.

The factories were by this time larger, and power was already concentrated into remarkably few hands. The average number of workers in each factory was 214 in 1969, and sixty factories employed 200 or more work-people, totalling 31,400 people in all.[6] Burchill and Ross show the concentration of power that had occurred when they add that 'Over half the labour force, some 23,000 workers, were employed in 60 establishments owned by 9 large groups.'

It is ironic that Sir Arthur Bryan also forecast that in five years there would be five large manufacturing groups, 'with a residue of small firms still performing a valuable service'. In April of the same year, 1971, *Tableware International* mentioned that, having taken over John Aynsley & Sons (Longton) Ltd in September 1970, 'the Waterford group shows signs of going for the complete table-top concept' (p. 44). At that time, no one foresaw what was to happen in December 1986: that the great giant, the Wedgwood Group, would itself be swallowed up by Waterford Glass.

If we think of some of the best-known names in pottery, it might be worth mentioning how they were grouped at the time of writing. Among Wedgwood's conquests (some of which it had taken over and closed) were Susie Cooper Ltd (merged with R. H. & S. L. Plant), New Chelsea China, W. Adams & Sons Ltd, J. & G. Meakin, Midwinter, A. J. Wilkinson, Crown Staffordshire, Mason's Ironstone, Johnson Brothers, Enoch Wedgwood, Coalport, Precision Studios, Kings Lynn Glass, Dartington Glass and Gered. The Royal Doulton Group had gathered to itself (closing some of them) Ridgway, Shelley, Shore & Coggins, Paladin, Paragon, Royal Albert, Booth's, Colclough, Minton, Crown Derby, John Beswick, Webb Corbett Glass and the parent company. Royal Worcester, Palissy, Hammersley and Spode had been linked by 1976, and later became part of the London Rubber Company, which changed its name to the London International Group. By 1987 Coloroll had bought the large group of Staffordshire Potteries including Royal Winton, and also Bilton Tableware Ltd, Dema Glass, Denby Tableware and Cartwright & Edwards.[7]

By July 1986 there were (according to trade union figures) only 27,500 employees in the Staffordshire pottery industry. In the depths of the recession, 1981–2, there were only about 20,000. In March 1981 *Tableware International* talked about the slowdown in the export of tableware products and the increase in imports of china, which were up by 19 per cent on imports in 1979. It attributed this to the high level of the pound against other currencies, especially the dollar. Monetarism did not favour the potters.

Against this background, women described to me in 1981 what it was like on their potbanks. Some worked on large factories (with well over a thousand workers) in the big groups I have mentioned above; others were in smaller ones (with a few hundred workers) taken over by the big groups; some were with family firms of the old type, and yet others were in very small independent firms only a few years old. The experience of working at the two ends of the scale of size and of management – on the one hand answerable in the end to the bosses of multinationals, and on the other to the boss there in the office – was vastly different, and people had strong feelings about it. Two aspects, the physical and the social, should perhaps be taken separately.

Chris Peppard, union representative at a middle-sized firm of a few hundred people, did not think that modern factories like hers were necessarily comfortable to work on. In the new factory there was so much noise that people could not talk to one another:

> The difference must be that, instead of having a load of smaller [work]shops that one went through – a shop would be like three times this room, and then you'd go through another way or up some stairs, or round a corner, and you'd find another

one – now everything's under one roof, so you've got the gilders there, the litho there, the kiln there, the selectors here, the ware stood there. Everything is under one roof like a supermarket is, and of course every noise that everybody makes is all under one roof. And then the bell for the kiln-trucks to be pulled out or pushed in, a bell goes for that. And when – even where the sound of the blower, the motor that is the air-conditioning . . . heating thing, that's going, when that's switched off, it's absolute heaven, just for a second until all the other noises come crowding back at you.

A union representative on another firm which had been taken over said that the women in her workshop had stopped work because they could not stand the noise from a neighbouring machine. 'It's like having your teeth ground all day,' she said. 'It's very rare if I'm in on my own I have any noise on, because I can't stand it, because you've been in this noise all day. You don't want it when you come home.' Modernization in her factory also meant putting them under artificial light:

Years ago our job was always put by the window, but now they put you in the middle of rooms, all in little work areas, where you've got to have electric light all the time, so it doesn't do you any good, does it? But what do they think you're going to do if you're working by a window – looking through the window? If you're busy getting your wages, you haven't got time to look through a window!

The factory was not modern in every sense. She used to go in early in the mornings to make sure that the sweeping-up was done properly – an absolutely crucial part of the running of a factory, if they are concerned about the health of the workforce – and said that 'They never wipe window-ledges', where, of course, dust will collect like anywhere else. She, and other people, said that dusty workshops were not just a thing of the past: 'There's still filthy places you can go on to. I mean, they've just closed one, X— Pottery. And if you went past there, the people worked in like little dungeons, lights on all day, like little dungeons.'

I visited some of the largest factories in various groups, and as one would expect, the physical conditions were on the whole better, and especially light and airy in departments where people were decorating or figure-making. Where factories are on several floors, the potting shops tend to be downstairs, and the people doing hand-work, sticking up figures, lithographing, flower-making, enamelling and gilding, tend to get the benefit of natural light. I also visited a small factory belonging to a young firm which had received considerable praise on the business pages of a newspaper. It was built with all the processes under one roof, close together. There were no windows; but when the heat was intolerable, large loading doors were left open. The machines were kept on without interruption from morning till night. If a woman wanted to go to the lavatory, she had to ask her supervisor to take over for her for a minute, and at lunchtimes the managers took a hand to keep them going. The pace of work was unbelievable, and I have rarely seen women look more exhausted, white-faced, listlessly responding to their relentless machines.

One of the workers described it as a 'dirty potbank'. Another said:

> Even . . . the young manager on there – even he admitted himself that they really are slave-driving them. Normally a girl can go, perhaps go and sit in the toilet for five minutes, have a cup of coffee or, you know, a smoke. Now they can't. They can't go off their benches now unless somebody takes them off.

She, like the other potters, had been having a week's holiday when I went to see her, and she had spent several days recovering from work:

> I got myself so stewed up last week, because the job was that hectic. And every-body was – I felt, I always feel ill for other people who feel ill, you know. And we'd all tied ourselves up in such knots by the end of the week, that you just couldn't relax, and I ended up having a Valium – which I've always got in. And I've had them three days this week, and I feel champion now, so I shan't touch them again.

Another worker stressed the same point, that it was really hard work from when they clocked on until when they clocked off. The work was made harder because the factory used second-hand tools and old machinery. A job like foot-wiping (taking the glaze off the bottom of ware when it has been dipped) could normally be done in one action; here, it had to be done twice or three times to get the glaze off, because 'They're that old, you know, and the rubbers are no good.' The mangles were second-hand, she said: 'It's what other firms probably throw away . . . All the cog-wheels and everything are that rusty on them . . . you can see it's been patched up. But, like I said, it's doing the job, so they aren't bothered.' The materials were not much better, the quality of the clay such that the handles kept falling off: 'We say, "Are you using bloody chewing-gum again?" because you've only got to pick them up some days and they fall off.'

There was noise, heat, inadequate ventilation or natural light, but there were other advantages. The pay was above union rates, 'the wages aren't too bad at all'. But at the end of the day they felt 'shattered, absolutely shattered, really and truly shattered, we are'. One of the owners would go through the factory turning off fans to cut down cost, and the heat would be terrible. The union representative mentioned that they had introduced machines in the clay end which they had since speeded up, 'and they're working faster and quicker. But because there's four people at it, they've cut the wages down. And one particular fellow that I'm dealing with now, this week, they've cut his wages down £30 because they said they can't afford to pay him!'

Nevertheless, they were producing more with the new machines, which meant unceasing work: 'They're at it all the time, you know . . . They're never still, never.' She was taking it up with the full-time officials of the union.

It would be simple if one could say that the social side of work in a small factory (with less than a hundred workers) made up for the physical disadvant-ages, but this was not always the case. The manager of a little factory could take against someone under his supervision, as might have happened in a larger one. The union representative felt that she was victimized for her union work even though she was a hard worker and always did of her best.

At many factories there were constant references to the meanness of management, the cost-cutting which sours the relationship between workers and the people for whom they work. Keeping people away from windows lest they should waste time, turning off ventilation fans to save money, providing seating arrangements so that people do not face one another, preventing them from talking quietly and comfortably together, locking the factory gates just before dinner-time so that women do not go off before they are allowed to: it was as though management was trying to squeeze the last ounce of effort from the workforce on these potbanks, even though it was obvious that women were working very hard to get their money on piece-work, and that most of them believed in an honest day's work for an honest day's pay.

People who liked working on small factories did so because of the informality and because of the variety in their work. A woman working in the clay end was more likely to be asked to do a whole range of jobs, if they were short-handed, than a woman on a big factory, although women had to swop around on big factories as well. This prevented the boredom of working on what have become, in many cases, machine-minding jobs (making, turning, handling, printing and spraying), especially at the cheap end of the market – for instance, making mugs for supermarkets or chain stores. On the other hand, the work would often be much harder; a girl in another small firm had to do all her own labouring, that is carrying 162 boards a day, each with three and a half dozen mugs on it. She was given no time for washing, and used to come home covered in clay. She was obliged to work on Saturdays, whether she wanted to or not, from 6 to 10 a.m., and if anything went wrong with her machine she had to try to mend it herself. None of this was very satisfactory, but she could cup-handle, dip, print, select, cast and pack, so she was kept on at the factory when others were laid off, and she was in a good position to get another job if she ever had to leave. More important still, she was bringing home upwards of £60 a week, whichever work she was put on to, whereas other girls on full pay were still getting only about £45 after deductions on some other factories. Everybody was paid the same on her potbank, so they could swap around. On the first small potbank I mentioned, people were all paid differently, and this gave rise to jealousies and accusations of favouritism against the managers.

The other advantage of smaller factories was the informality and the closer relationship between staff and workers (although this may have contributed to the jealousies mentioned above). People enjoyed knowing the managers by their first names (which was not usual on big factories) and going out with them at Christmas. The close relationship on a small firm was traditional. Women helped by working part-time when factories were too busy to get their orders out. Mrs Kazak's mother used to do work on several different potbanks, doing a couple of hours a day for them: 'P—'s Manufactury was a family concern, and they used to come and fetch me mother in a car, you know, the owner. He'll say, "Kath, c'mon, I want you do me so many boards, cup-handling." And he used to fetch her and bring her back.'

Mrs Kazak herself had worked for a small firm where the conditions and wages were terrible, but they had had good industrial relations and flexible hours, so that a woman could be at home when her children needed her, after school and whenever they were poorly. This was so important that she had worked there for five years, even though she had no doubt about what she thought of the work: 'Oh, it's terrible how we used to have to work on there, absolutely terrible. I used to say to the manager: ''All you want is a nosebag on your face.'' They wanted horses there, they didn't want women. Oh it was murder, absolute murder.'

The relationship between management and workforce was the single most important factor which people mentioned determining whether they were happy or not at work. One of the big factories had a very poor reputation for industrial relations, and several people who had worked there in the past described it independently as 'like a concentration camp'. Here and in other factories where managements' time-and-motion studies prevailed, the physical and mental aspects of work could not be separated out; the organization of work was meticulous, the work itself repetitive, tedious and stressful. Daphne Gregory had been able to stand the atmosphere for only six weeks: 'I hated it. It was like being at school again, because the bosses were real awful. They looked on you as a worker, not as a human being. You were part of the huge machine, and if you were told to do something, then you had to do it, regardless of how you felt about it.' Ruth Evans had also hated it; she had been made to sit in a room on her own if she had not got enough work done. She too had left.

Time-and-motion studies were designed by managements to use the work-force to the full, but not to allow them a moment of rest. The union representative at another factory explained that it mattered to have moments unaccounted for:

> They've had time-and-motion studies . . . but one tends to forget that if you've got a job that perhaps wasted a minute or two, one had a breather before you got back on to the next job, and now you've had your work done to the nth degree so that there are no wasted efforts, and it's like a lot of battery hens. I mean, you're like a zombie.

The words 'zombie' and 'robot' recur in people's descriptions of their situation. Work is organized to reduce their humanity, not to give expression or value to their skills. An enameller described to me how her work was divided up into minute values, so that she had nineteen minutes to do the eight colours on a plate, but had to do it in much less time in order to achieve a good performance:

> It's the stress – it's so tedious, so you get keyed up . . . I mean, they joke about it now, don't they? 'I'll have a Valium sandwich', you know, they joke about it all the time. And it's so quiet and so tedious. And you're sitting there. Well, if they aren't getting the values and getting the minutes, they're getting all keyed up, you know, and you can't get on, you can't get on if you can't relax.

At one factory, down to less than three hundred workers, the union representative said: 'We've been saying for a long time throughout the industry that there's far too many chiefs and not enough Indians . . . There seems to be so many people on our factory, running round with pieces of paper, so that somebody else can look and check.' She was not alone; the feeling that there were people 'at you all the time' was an expression of the distress of these women who could not just work but had to put up with being organized and 'bossed' in the worst sense of the word.

The individual character of managers and supervisors made a great difference to the enjoyment or discomfort of work. A supervisor told me that she thought women preferred a woman as supervisor. Indeed, supervisors were mostly women, managers mostly men:

> I think we get on better with a woman, because in my position you have to listen to all their little tales and the little woes, and if they fall out with their husbands, you know, where they won't tell somebody else, they'll tell you . . . And women have little problems where they can't talk to a man, they talk to a woman, you see.

The women came to her rather than to the manager who was over her, so her duties were importantly social, but she explained that the manager, who was paid more than she was, had the responsibility for the work:

> He takes the can . . . We're in glazes . . . they have to be checked practically every half-hour, because the glaze settles out. That's his job, you know; I could do it, but that's his job. They don't pay me his wages, so I don't do it, you know. A manager gets a lot more money than a supervisor as well.

She tried to be fair rather than vindictive: 'My job is to stop faults going through. Now, I'm not there to fall out with the person who's doing it wrong. My job, and I firmly believe this, is to find a cure for the fault, not to fall out with the person.' She did the wages for her section, and had to cope with attempts at bribery, cigarettes and chocolates, and requests to 'put us a bit extra in'. It was no wonder another supervisor told me that becoming a supervisor made you unpopular; you were there between managers and workers, in a world of antagonistic interests.

On another factory there was no doubt that a supervisor treated the women under her like a class of school children. If the women went too early to make toast for their breakfasts, she would order them peremptorily into her office to be reprimanded, like the old-fashioned headmistress of a preparatory school. In her department, where there was no machinery to make any noise, people could no longer discuss anything to ease the monotony of their work. Pam Hanley blamed the atmosphere on the fact that the supervisor was a woman. She had been happier on another (bigger) factory:

> Then we didn't have a woman over us. It's much better working just for men . . . we always talked about everything, from religion to hanging and everything, you know, otherwise your mind goes stale, doesn't it? On there, you feel as if you're just keeping ideas in all the time, you know. Nobody talks, only about small talk: 'Have you had your electric bill in?' and, you know, 'Is it gonna rain tomorrow?' That's the only thing they talk about. It bores me to death, bores me to tears.

The supervisor was responsible: 'She comes out and says, "Who's making the noise? Who's talking?" ' As a result, Pam Hanley had no love of her job at all: 'It's not nice, it's just a job, it's just somewhere to go from 8 till 5 to get your money on a Friday and come off quick.'

On several of the factories which were part of larger groups, the problem of management was complicated; it lay partly in the number of managers, some-times in the personality of a manager, which put him on a collision course by imposing prices on people, rather than negotiating them, and often in a feeling that managers were no longer competent, since nowadays certificates and education counted for more than knowing the job. Formerly, managers worked their way up from the shop-floor, I was told, but now they were work study engineers, who knew nothing about handling people or about pottery. A former warehouseman, Arthur Meeke, said: 'Everyone mistrusts the young chap with the white coat on.'

It was also felt that some of lower management cared more about quantity – about getting the work through – than about quality. Women who worked under them resented having to produce ware that was useless or poor quality, because machines were not set properly, or because of some other fault. Some-times they would tell their manager and be ignored:

> I've been a presser from when I was 15; I am 40 this year. Now, I reckon that if there is something wrong with my job, I know that. And when I tell my manager, 'I don't like this, either the dust is wrong I'm using, or the dye is at fault', I would expect him to take my word for it, which years ago they would do. Now they don't, they just think you're skiving.

From examples like this, it is clear that one of the main problems in industrial relations with the new management is their lack of respect for the experience and integrity of their workers. It is also clear that some junior managers cost rather than save their firms money by allowing work to continue to go through that they know to be faulty, by sending out orders which they know to be incorrect, by keeping whole production lines going when they should be stopped – because the appearance of work going on and of production going smoothly is what counts. A very small potbank I visited, with under a dozen full-time workers, had no need for a manager, and the owner found that, without one, people themselves dealt with any problems which came up. When he had tried a manager, people had been far less self-reliant.

Mrs Roper, who was a woman manager, felt that women had come on much more in management in recent years, through their own efforts; but even she noted that when at her firm a large order had come through, only the male managers were invited to go and celebrate it with whisky and sherry; women managers were only tolerated. One of the women who worked for her said: 'It'll be a hell of a lot better if it were all women bosses.' There was still prejudice against women managers, both from men and occasionally from women, but they were in any case a rare occurrence at this time; it was much more common for the person in charge to be a man in a white coat, and for the person who saw to the welfare of the workforce and the faults they were produc-ing to be a woman.

Very often the fact that women had first-hand experience of doing the work themselves was invaluable when it came to identifying what was wrong with the ware which was coming through. A woman supervisor doing a 'dissection' could tell where the faults had occurred in all the various processes which the ware had gone through before it reached her; she had the accumulated skill of long experience. But when it came to power, women were thought unsuited to the task – or that is what Jo Tennant and Arthur Meeke believed – because 'women and men do not like working under women. Women don't like another woman telling them what to do, or telling them off if they've done wrong. They'd accept it from a man, but not a woman.' Although only a few women gave an opinion on this, my impression was that women who were singled out, either as supervisors or as union representatives, could expect a good deal of criticism from their fellows, merely because they have stepped out of the ordinary. This was the same kind of reaction to success which made people who were very quick on piece-work feel they were disliked by the women who could not keep up with them.

Many women, but by no means all, were very lukewarm about the trade union, feeling either that it had never done anything for them or that it was weak. Sometimes the crucial factor was whether the union had helped them in a dispute with management; if it had not helped them when they needed help, it was a waste of time. Several union representatives felt that women would not stand up for themselves, that they did not take the union seriously and that a lot would rather go to Bingo than go to their lodge to vote someone on to the national executive. There was certainly a noticeable difference between the commitment of the women union representatives and the home-centredness of other women. But it was not true that women would not stick up for themselves; on at least one factory in recent years they had done precisely that, fighting for equal pay.

On the whole, the women with responsibilities as union representatives or as supervisors enjoyed their work much more than other people. What they enjoyed was the social side of work, being involved with other people, which was very different from their ordinary work, being married to a machine in the clay end, or counting minutes in the decorating shop. They were caring, almost maternal, enjoying being involved in other people's lives. Jane Phillips is typical: 'I love to meddle, you see, and get concerned about people.' Joan Parsons did not love the work itself:

> I think there's more interesting things to do than going to work . . . I like going and helping people, I like going and sorting people out . . . Because I think work's boring, I think to be locked up all day . . . Those are dreadful days, really, aren't they? They are long days, I mean, I'm talking about eight hours.

To begin with, they found all the responsibility and the disputes very strainful, and once again people talked about being on tranquillizers. But, having got used to it, there is no doubt that responsibility gave them a vigour and a vitality, and a sense of fairness, which can only have made them an asset in their workshops to management and workers alike. It was rare to hear from a woman without responsibility as a union representative or a supervisor the enthusiasm of 'I've always loved my job' (Mrs Kazak) or 'I like the beginning of the potbank, I like all the way through, whatever job there was going, I really enjoy it. I like packing cups, I like making 'em, or handling them or, you know, whatever it entails' (Mrs Wenceslas). The important factor was to be a person, not just a battery-hen.

It is difficult not to be pessimistic about the changes which have happened in the last thirty years. There is a diminution in skills, not only through automation in making, turning, handling and dipping, but also through water-slide lithographs taking over from dry lithographs, painting and aerographing. Even gilding has been automated for plates, and has turned a pleasant job into a noisy, jarring form of machine-minding in which the only skill is an almost robotic, mechanical speed. When a particular skill is not needed any more, the skilled person is very vulnerable, as this aerographer found:

> Aerographing, you see, at that time, went out, so they hadn't any work to give us. We were put on all sorts of jobs, sweeping kilns, emptying boxes – you name it, I think we did it – but they wouldn't make us redundant, because they didn't want to pay me nineteen years' redundancy money, you see. So in the end, there was nothing left. We just gave our notices in.

We cannot compare this situation with the girl mentioned earlier, who enjoyed moving from job to job on her factory. The young girl was not a highly skilled worker, identified over two decades with her skill and, of course, used to a wage in accordance with it.

Being taken over three times, each company swallowed up by the next, could also be something of a sad experience, especially when it got to the final, fourth transformation:

> When it was the other three, we've had some fun down there. We've gone to Hanley and come back, started to work, you know, not clocked off or on. Gone anywhere, done anything, you know, we've had that much fun on there. It was hilarious. We've had the old ladies – of course, they used to work till they were in their seventies. When X—'s took over, they made everybody redundant that was over retiring age. And we used to have old Alice, and she used to have her skirt up, and she used to wear those big long knickers that were elastic round her knees, you know, and . . . she'd do 'Knees Up Mother Brown' with the executive of the place – and he'd do it with her. It was great, you know! That stopped when X—'s took over. It slowly turned round as now you work for eight hours, and there's a rule and a rule, and you have verbal warnings if you don't . . . Spoilt a lot of it actually, because I think if you can have that laugh, I think . . . it is better. I can't see as it improved the work being restricted. I don't think it has, because we've turned more work out when it was the others [the other firms] than we do because it's X—, just as good, like. But we don't get the characters. It's a very young place, this is.

It is important to insist on this. Fun did not mean poor work or less work. The regimented, organized modern factory can be inefficient because it is boring, sending the mind and the hands to sleep. Skills are also difficult to acquire because training is so short; a caster-sponger now had only six weeks to learn her job before she started on piece-work. Enamellers had under three months' training before they too were on piece-work. One could argue that formerly people were kept as trainees for far too long, and in the case of women this was certainly the case; but if a woman went on piece-work before she was experienced she could not keep up her wages painting on unfamiliar patterns.

One cannot say either that work has no deleterious physical effects any more. Apart from the continued claims for dust, particularly from spongers, fettlers and sanitary casters, the trade union is helping with thousands of claims for tenosynovitis. When I was doing my research, some figure-makers suffered from this painful condition to their arms: 'From there to there it's all swollen, or it's all raw, red raw, and in winter, you know, when it's damp and cold, they've got 'em all cracked. They've always got bandages up their arms.' The problem in 1981 was that the factory could solve the problem – by bringing in machines and dispensing with the workers, but then the figure-makers would have been out of work.

A burnisher noticed deformities among her companions:

> Some of the girls that have been burnishers over the years have got all crooked fingers, because they use the fingers with pieces of material to rub . . . What happens with your burnishing finger [is] it begins to go thin there, and then it broadens out at the end, and it goes all a funny shape, you know. Some of them have got fingers that turn the corner, sort of go round the side, like arthritis. It isn't arthritis, it's been caused through the work. But there's nobody to prove that; there's nobody ever made a claim.

The conditions in some factories did not run to a sick-room: 'If you fainted over, I don't know where they'd take you . . . They'd stick you back on your chair, shove a bottle under your nose', was one laughing comment. But that speaker's factory, an old-fashioned family firm, had kept her job for her for almost six months when she was off sick, nervously exhausted after looking after a dying relative.

The most worrying changes in the recession have been the way people have been presented with unacceptable demands from management, and sometimes been unable to refuse. There were, of course, redundancies, closures and short-time – several people whom I interviewed were on a three-day week when I visited them – but there were other more sinister stories. A woman told the (Women's) Advisory Committee of the union that the managers at her factory had asked them to work for an hour for nothing. They had refused when they saw the new company cars arriving! Another group of workers were told that their unit costs were too high, and that they must take a cut in wages. The women took a vote on it, and would not agree; then they were shown a redundancy list with all their names on it and, frightened by this, they took another vote, so that they would either all stay, and agree to the cut, or all go. The majority decided to stay. The manager seemingly gloated in his power, saying to them: 'Well, the ones that voted against it, tell them by all means they can still go.' A year later, after the usual pay rise across the industry, negotiated by the union in March, they were still below their previous wages.

These examples show the present weakness of workers in the pottery industry and remind me of the way their mothers and grandmothers described the 1920s. Because there are fewer and fewer jobs, workers can be exploited more easily. It is tragic, nevertheless, that in the examples I have described the managers have tried to exploit their workers' weakness, rather than trying to gain their support in working to surmount difficulties in the industry. Even in an industry full of verbal and written warnings, rules and regulations, surmounted by higher, middle and lower management, firms rely on the goodwill of their workers. Women may be needed to come in and do overtime when it is not necessarily convenient for them, or to work during their lunchtimes when there are special orders to get out. Antagonized by managers who abuse their power, women are not going to do any favours. Nor, of course, are they likely to sympathize with a management that does not tighten its belt before asking them to tighten theirs, as the first example showed.

It is not surprising that so few women whom I spoke to wanted their children to go into the pottery industry. It is not just a matter of wages, because people feel there have been great improvements in this area; it is because the organization of work has reduced their pride and their freedom. Nobody wants to be a battery-hen. That many women still enjoy their work is partly attributable to the fact that the whole industry has not been as streamlined and rationalized as many people told me it had. I could still visit workshops where old ladies of 70 years sat at their benches, telling me they enjoyed work now as much as ever they had in the past. I could talk to women handle-casters, and be told solemnly elsewhere that it was always a man's job. I could see casters with big jugs of slip, and be told that the slip was always piped to casters nowadays. I could sit in a cosy little studio full of men painting, and be told elsewhere that women were more suited to decorating. I could be told that firms were not taking on any young people at all, and meet a kale-girl getting the breakfasts in the chilly morning air.

The Potteries is a region full of history and full of myths, and in writing about the women in the industry this century – through their own words – I have tried to give back to women something of their lost history. In particular, the women potters in the clay end have never been remembered, never publicly celebrated, never pictured except as those scruffy women in pinnies and curlers, walking about in trashers, cigarettes in their mouths, covered in clay. These women, who also kept the factories – and their families – going, in boom and slump, in every decade this century, do not fit in with the image of femininity which women locally must have if they are not to be considered 'common'. The little paintress sits as the only woman in the relief surmounting the entrance to the City Museum and Art Gallery in Hanley, celebrating the work of the area. She is one of the women of whom the industry is proud, ladylike, fit for fine china, one of 'all those women who, in their own right, contribute to the life of this country by working in their feminine sphere, not in opposition to but side by side in harmony with their male colleagues', as *Pottery and Glass* put it (vol. XXX, 11, July–December 1954, p. 351). The rest are forgotten – but not, I hope, from now on.

Notes

1 Murray was architect-in-chief of the factory.
2 F. Burchill and R. Ross, *A History of the Potters' Union*, 1977, p. 232.
3 Of course, he was too young to remember. 'During the war they were placing, women were,' as Mr Hilditch remembered.

4 Burchill and Ross, 1977, p. 232.
5 Ibid.
6 Burchill and Ross, 1977, p. 256.
7 I am grateful to Kathy Niblett of the City Museum and Art Gallery, Stoke-on-Trent for discussing with me the take-overs and mergers of the last twenty years, which have resulted in these few giants and these few workers.

Women Pottery-Workers Working Between the Wars

This is a list of women from whose interviews I quote in the book. There is no similar list for women below retiring age, since it is important that the factories for which they work should be totally unrecognizable. Dates of birth are correct within one year; informants are not always clear about numbers of children.

Abbreviations: mo.: mother, fa.: father, b.: born, m.: married, d.: died.

Mrs Powell: b. 1894, transferrer's cutter, sorter in glost warehouse; mo. d. when she was 12, aged 43; fa. d. aged 70; husband placer, d. aged 80; 2 children.

Mrs Madeley: b. 1898, handle-maker, wheel-turner, baller, lathe-treader, cup-maker; mo. took in washing, 10 children; fa. 'never worked', d. aged 53; husband miner, pneumoconiosis, d. aged 80; 1 child.

Mrs Farrier: b. 1902, mouldrunner, bowl-jollier; mo. bowl-jollier, lathe-treader, 11 children; fa. mouldmaker; husband sliphouse, war wounded, collier, d. aged 83; 5 children.

Mrs Dove: b. 1902, clerk, office in factory; mo. handle-maker before marriage, d. 1936; 2 children; fa. baker, d. 1938; husband motor-coach bodywork-builder, odd job man; no children.

Mrs Mason: b. 1903, biscuit warehouse; mo. spout hole-borer, 2 children; fa. worked in marl-hole; lst husband killed in pit aged 35; 2nd husband bill-poster with children from previous marriage; d. aged 72; 2 children.

Mrs Van Hallen: b. 1902, modeller; mo. at home, 3 children; fa. sold engravings for family firm; husband in insurance; 3 children.

Mrs Box: b. 1904, spout-maker, caster; mo. spout-maker, d. aged 88, 5 children, lost 4; fa. placer, d. 1931; husband collier, window-cleaner, d.; no children.

Mrs Bede: b. 1908, freehand paintress; mo. at home, 10 children, reared 4; fa. boilerman, d. aged 86; husband salesman, many jobs, d. 1973; 2 children.

Mrs Bloore: b. 1909, white warehouse, gold-bander; mo. brick-trimmer before marriage, than at home; 6 children, d. aged 84; fa. collier, d. aged 70; husband thrower, d. *c.* 1931; 1 child.

Mrs Neale: b. 1911, transferrer, then warehouse; mo. at home, 18 children, 5 lived, d. aged 82; fa. placer and oddman, d. 59; husband made engines, unemployed then pit blacksmith shop, d. aged 39 in pit; 4 children.

Mrs Barnes: b. 1911, handle-maker, dipper; mo. ware-cleaner, at home, took washing in, 13 children; fa. killed First World War aged 28; step-fa. labourer; husband railway worker, d. aged 68; 3 children.

Mrs Gregory: b. 1915, looker-over, biscuit-warehouse, mouldrunner; mo. cup-handler, odd jobs, took washing in, numerous children, reared 6, d. aged 85; fa. scene-shifter, labourer, d. aged 39; husband railway-worker, coal-deliveryman; 7 children.

Mrs Champion: b. 1916, freehand paintress; mo. gilder till stroke, then cook, 2 children; d. aged 79; fa. farrier, labourer in iron foundry, d. aged 67; husband electrician then sales rep. for potters' materials; 2 children.

Mrs Bentley: b. 1916, transferrer's cutter, caster, market-worker; mo. died young, 3 children; step-mo. 'sickly woman', 2 children, d. aged 50; fa. oddman; husband mouldrunner, saggar-maker, dust; 1 child.

Mrs Hewell: b. 1917, freehand paintress, ground-layer; mo. dairy maid, reared 12 children out of 16, d. aged 82; fa. baker, collier, roadwork, military policeman, d. aged 82; husband painter and decorator, electrical firm, retired; 2 children.

Mrs Goodrich: b. 1918, decorator, then on munitions; mo. tilemaker, 4 children, d. aged 72; fa. miner, d. aged 72; husband placer, steelworker; 1 child.

Mrs Parker: b. 1919, gilder, mo. hospital cleaner, died with milk-fever, 5 children; fa. gassed in First World War, miner, d. aged 42; husband in brickworks, d.

Mrs Furnivall: b. 1920, gilder; mo. hospital cleaner, 4 children, d. aged 55; fa. invalid from First World War, unemployed, d. aged 78; husband plasterer, several jobs, now made redundant; 2 children.

Mrs Roper: b. 1923, dipper, aerographer, glost warehouse, manager; mo. supervisor in dipping house, 1 child; fa. many jobs, jugmaker, placer, teapot-maker, husband dipper, telephonist; 2 children.

Mrs Adams: b. 1923, caster, caster-sponger; mo. cup-maker, 3 children, d. aged 77; fa. sanitary-caster, d. aged 64 of pneumoconiosis; husband painter and decorator; 2 children.

Mrs Atkins: b. 1923, shopworker, printing works, fire service, at home, print room of potbank; mo. did cleaning, 3 children, fa. joiner; 1st husband mine engineer; 2nd husband retired; 1 child.

Mrs Havelock: b. 1924, thimble-picker; caster-sponger, cup-bander, overlooker, machine and hand cup-handler; mo. twice married, at home until Second World War, 6 children, d. aged 82; fa. railway worker, d. aged 67; husband accountant; 1 child.

Glossary

baller: person who prepares the clay in balls of a convenient size for the thrower.

bank: hill, so *potbank*: where the clay was piled up outside a pottery factory.

bedding: to put the ware in powdered flint inside the saggars, ready for firing.

biscuit: ware when it has been fired once in the kiln to harden it.

boards: wooden planks, usually six feet long, on which the ware is placed to carry it from one process to another in a pottery factory.

bottle oven: the old kilns made of brick and fired by coal.

bung: pile of (saggars) in a bottle oven.

burnish: to rub (best gold) after it has been fired, to bring up the colour.

cast: to pour liquid clay (slip) into moulds, leave it for a few minutes until a layer of clay has hardened on the inside of the moulds, then pour out the remainder of the liquid clay, to be left with, for instance, the shape of a jug or teapot; so *caster*, and *caster-sponger*, who sponged the casted ware, to smooth it.

china: pots you can see through, like bone china or porcelain.

clay end: the potting shop where the clay is made into cups, bowls, plates, etc.

dip: to immerse the ware in a tub of liquid glaze; *dipper*, the person who did this.

draw the ovens: to empty the ovens of saggars full of ware.

enamel: to paint on-glaze colours on to pots, usually within a printed design.

fettle: to smooth ware with a little piece of tin.

flatware: plates, dishes; *flat-presser*, plate-maker.

gild: to apply a layer of gold to glazed ware, before it is fired again.

glaze: to cover the hardened biscuit ware with a liquid layer to give it its non-porous, shiny surface.

glost kiln: the furnace in which glazed ware is fired.

green: ware before it has dried or been fired; so, *greenhouse*, where it is put to dry.

handle: to stick handles on to cups, mugs, etc.

hollow-ware: cups, bowls, etc.

jigger: a profile, or tool, which makes the outside shape of a piece of ware.

jolley or *jolly*: a profile or tool that makes the inside of a piece of ware; so, *bowl-jollier*, person who made bowls with a joll(e)y.

kale-girl: young girl who runs errands and fetches the breakfasts for journeywomen, as her first job on a potbank.

kiln: a furnace in which ware is placed, to submit to very high temperatures, which is called *firing*.

labourer: person who carries the ware from department to department.

ladding: going after boys.

lathe-treader: person who drives the lathe for a turner, by working a treadle with the foot.

lithographer: person who applies water-slide transfers as decoration to glazed ware.

make: to shape or form ware from clay.

missus: woman in charge of a process in a pottery factory.

mouldrunner: girl or boy who helped a maker, by bringing him or her moulds and clay, and by taking away the cups or bowls (s)he had made, to put in the greenhouse to dry.

oddman: person who works round the ovens, getting coal, sweeping, etc.

on-glaze decoration: decoration which is applied to the ware after it has been glazed and fired.

ovenman: man who tends the oven, or furnace, when it is being fired or brought up to high temperatures.

pencil: brush.

placer: person who carries the ware to the oven; nowadays there are trolleys; formerly, placers carried saggars into the bottle ovens in their arms or on their heads.

polish: to smooth off faults, stilt marks, etc. with a machine with different wheels.

potbank: pottery factory; *pot* is any kind of ware, earthenware, china or stoneware.

saggar: earthenware box of varying shape, in which pots were placed for firing.

sanitary ware: basins, lavatories, etc.

scour: formerly, to remove the flint from biscuit ware after firing.

slip: liquid clay; so, *sliphouse*, place where the clay bodies are mixed and purified.

tata: character, difficult person.

throw: to make a piece of ware on a potter's wheel.

tower: person who smooths ware with a piece of horse-hair as it whirls around.

transferrer: person who rubs a dry print on to the surface of a piece of ware.

ware: any pot or piece of china or earthenware.

wedging: lifting and dropping large slabs of clay to remove air bubbles.

References and
Select Bibliography

John Baddeley's Day-Book, manuscript, Stafford, Staffordshire County Record Office, D1788, v. 96.

Beechey, V. (1983) 'What's so special about women's employment?', *Feminist Review* no. 15 Winter, pp. 23-45.

Bell, Lady, (1985) *At the Works*, London, Virago; first published in 1907 by Edward Arnold.

Bott, E. (1971) *Family and Social Network*, London, Tavistock.

Briggs, J. (1982) *A History of Longton*, Dept. of Adult Education Univ. of Keele, Keele, Staffordshire.

Burchill, F. and Ross, R. (1977) *A History of the Potters' Union*, Hanley, Ceramic and Allied Trades' Union.

Celoria, F. (1983) 'Working and living conditions of nineteenth-century potters in Staffordshire', in G. Godden (ed.), *Staffordshire Porcelain*, London, Granada.

Central Statistical Office (1983) *Social Trends*, London, HMSO.

Chamberlain, M. (1977) *Fenwomen*, London, Virago.

City of Stoke-on-Trent (various years) *Annual Report of the Medical Officer of Health*.

Coffield, F., Robinson, P. and Sarsby, J. (1980) *A Cycle of Deprivation?* London, Heinemann Educational.

Coote, A. and Kellner, P. (1980) *Hear This, Brother: Women Workers and Union Power*, London, New Statesman Report 1.

Department of Employment (1976) *New Earnings Survey*, London, HMSO.

Dupree, M. (1981) 'Family structure in the Staffordshire potteries 1840-1900'. Unpublished D. Phil. thesis, Oxford University.

Finer, A. and Savage, G. (1965) *The Selected Letters of Josiah Wedgwood*, London, Cory, Adams & Mackay.

Forman, C. (1979) *Industrial Town Self Portrait of St. Helens in the 1920s*, London, Granada.

Gittins, D. (1982) *Fair Sex, Family Size and Structure, 1900-39*, London, Hutchinson.

Glasson, M. (1985) *City Children: Birmingham Children at Work and Play, 1900-1930*, Birmingham, Museum and Art Gallery.

John, A. (ed.) (1986) *Unequal Opportunities: Women's employment in England, 1900-1918*, Oxford, Blackwell.

Land, H. (1982) 'The family wage', in M. Evans (ed.), *The Woman Question*, London, Fontana.

Lewis, J, (ed.) (1986) *Labour and Love: Women's Experience of Home and Family*, 1850-1940, Oxford, Blackwell.

Llewelyn Davies, M. (1977) *Life as We Have Known It*, London, Virago; first published in 1931 by Hogarth Press.

Llewelyn Davies, M. (ed.) (1978) *Maternity: Letters from Working Women*, London, Virago; first published in 1915 by G. Bell & Sons.

Martin, J, and Roberts, C. (1984) *Women and Employment: A Lifetime Perspective*, report of the 1980, Department of Employment Office of Population Censuses and Surveys women and employment survey, London, HMSO.

Office of Population Censuses and Surveys *Census of England and Wales* 1971 and 1981, London, HMSO.

Pahl, R. E. (1984) *Divisions of Labour*, Oxford, Blackwell.

Pember Reeves, M. (1979) *Round about a Pound a Week*, London, Virago; first published in 1913 by G. Bell & Sons.

Pollert, A. (1981) *Girls, Wives, Factory Lives*, London, Macmillan.

Pottery and Glass, started in August 1909.

Pottery Gazette and Glass Trade Review, name later changed to *Tableware International*.

Quennell, P. (ed.) (n.d.) *Mayhew's London*, London, Spring Books; first published in 1851.

Rhead, G. W. and Rhead, F. A. (1977) *Staffordshire Pots and Potters*, London, Hutchinson; first published in 1906.

Roberts, E. (1984) *A Woman's Place: An Oral History of Working-Class Women, 1890–1940*, Oxford, Blackwell.

Sarsby, J. (1985) 'Sexual segregation in the pottery industry', *Feminist Review*, no. 21, Winter, pp. 67–93.

Scriven, S. (1843) *Report on the Employment of Children and Young Persons in the District of the Staffordshire Potteries* (written in 1841), reprinted in *Children in the Potteries, Parts 1 and 2*, Staffordshire Study Book, Stafford, Staffordshire County Council, 1975.

Shaw, C. (1980) *When I Was a Child*, Firle, Caliban Books; first published in 1903.

Shaw, S. (1970) *History of the Staffordshire Potteries*, Newton Abbot, David & Charles; first published in 1829.

Spring Rice, M. (1981) *Working-Class Wives*, London, Virago; first published in 1939 by Penguin.

Tebbutt, M. (1983) *Making Ends Meet: Pawnbroking and Working-Class Credit*, London, Methuen.

Weatherill, L. (1971) *The Pottery Trade and North Staffordshire, 1660–1760*, Manchester University Press.

Thomas Whieldon's Notebook, manuscript, Stoke-on-Trent City Museum and Art Gallery.

Whipp, R. (1979) 'The women pottery workers of Staffordshire and trade unionism, 1890–1905', unpublished MA thesis, Warwick University.

Willmott, P. (1979) *Growing Up in a London Village*, London, Peter Owen.

York Oral History Project (1984) *York Memories: Nine First-Hand Accounts of Life in York*, 1900–1930.

INDEX